"Deserves the widest circulation." —Isaac Asimov

"An admirable work." —Sunday *New York Times*

"A clear, informative account of the clash in the dark heart of the rain forest." —*The New York Times*

"The definitive Mendes biography. . . . Revkin flies above the forest providing a hawk's-eye view of the whole panorama, from the intricate fertility dance of bees and Brazil nut trees, to the powerful international forces that play a hand in the fate of the forest." —*Bloomsbury Review*

"Excellent. . . . Reads like a true-crime mystery." —*Entertainment Weekly*

"A powerful work that reveals a great deal, not only about the rain forest, but about how it affects the environment in which we live." —Studs Terkel

"*The Burning Season* contains authentic voices of the Amazon's inhabitants, villains as well as heroes, and sensible judgments about their actions." —*The Wall Street Journal*

"Told with a lively narrative that reads like a murder mystery, *The Burning Season* is rich with natural history and a broad view of the politics of Brazil that put the story in its full context." —*Miami Herald*

"An eloquent and expert account of the Amazon rainforest. . . . with a harrowing compendium of the forces that are destroying it." —*The Sunday Telegraph*

"Transforms the drama of the forest into a reality both horrifying and hopeful. . . . Because of works like Revkin's, there is hope for the rain forest." —*St. Louis Post-Dispatch*

"Andrew Revkin's account of the killing of Chico Mendes is much more than a tale of murder in the rain forest. . . . It is a parable for all the world." —Morley Safer, CBS *Sixty Minutes*

"A compelling story of global connections, the environmental imperative, and how one man made a difference." —Thomas Lovejoy, president, The Heinz Center

THE BURNING SEASON

THE
BURNING
SEASON

The Murder
of Chico Mendes
and the
Fight for the
Amazon Rain Forest

Andrew Revkin

Island Press / Shearwater Books WASHINGTON · COVELO · LONDON

A Shearwater Book
Published by Island Press

Copyright © 1990 Andrew Revkin
Map on page 315 copyright © 1990 Linda Lieff and Joyce Weiner

Previously published in hardcover by Houghton Mifflin in 1990
Previously published in paperback by Penguin Plume in 1994

First Island Press/Shearwater Books printing, October 2004

SHEARWATER BOOKS is a trademark of The Center for Resource Economics.

Library of Congress Cataloging-in-Publication data.

Revkin, Andrew.
    The burning season : the murder of Chico Mendes and the fight for the Amazon rain forest
/ Andrew Revkin.
            p. cm.
    Previously published: New York : Plume Book, 1994.
    Includes bibliographical references.
    ISBN 1-55963-089-2 (pbk. : alk. paper)
1. Mendes, Chico, d. 1988.   2. Conservationists--Brazil--Biography.   3. Rain forest
conservation--Brazil.   4. Rain forest conservation--Amazon River Region.   5.
Deforestation--Brazil.   6. Deforestation--Amazon River Region.   7. Rain forests--Brazil.
8. Rain forests--Amazon River Region.   I. Title.
    SD411.52.M46R48 2004
    333.75'16'092--dc22

                                                            2004020449

British Cataloguing-in-Publication data available.

Printed on recycled, acid-free paper

Manufactured in the United States of America

10   9   8   7   6   5   4   3   2   1

This edition is dedicated to my parents and my grandmother, in her 99th year, who inspire me daily.

"If a messenger came down from heaven and guaranteed that my death would strengthen our struggle, it would even be worth it. But experience teaches us the opposite. Public rallies and lots of funerals won't save the Amazon. I want to live."

— CHICO MENDES, December 9, 1988

"At first, the people talking about ecology were only defending the fishes, the animals, the forest, and the river. They didn't realize that human beings were in the forest—and that these humans were the real ecologists, because they couldn't live without the forest and the forest couldn't be saved without them."

— OSMARINO AMÂNCIO RODRIGUES, Secretary, the National Council of Rubber Tappers

Contents

Foreword

FIFTEEN YEARS AGO, I crisscrossed the western reaches of the Amazon River basin to chronicle the life and death of Francisco Alves Mendes Filho, better known as Chico Mendes. His murder a few months earlier, in December 1988, was a major international story, and I was hunting for any scrap of paper in a police file, any fading recollection of Mendes's friends or enemies, any detail revealing how an all-but-invisible man extracting latex from rubber trees and organizing a union deep in the world's biggest rain forest could wind up influencing global environmental policy and making headlines around the world after he was gunned down.

The Amazon region itself was in the news. In the scorching summer that year, climatologists testifying before Senate committees said the unbridled burning of fossil fuels and forests was releasing an unprecedented torrent of greenhouse gases, mainly carbon dioxide, that were trapping heat in the air and apparently turning up the global thermostat. Much attention focused on the Amazon. Although it held the world's largest rain forest, cloaking an area as big as the United States east of the Rockies, it was largely unknown to the public, both in the North and in Brazil itself. It was one of the world's few remaining frontiers, where developers, dreamers, con artists, fugitives, and peasants pushed into largely virgin wilderness.

But the frontier was retreating, in a twentieth-century hurry. During the September burning season, satellites recorded more than eight thousand places across Amazonia where fires glowed, marking the progress of this fast-moving invasion. On September 29, 1988, George "Pinky" Nelson, an astronaut on the first space shuttle flight following the explosion of Challenger, photographed a smoke cloud the size of India stretching unbroken from the Andes to the Atlantic. With the Amazon burning, with record-setting heat year after year, the notion was finally beginning to emerge that humans around the world, from those driving cars in Detroit to those burning trees in Brazil, were wedded through their shared ability to alter the dynamics of the atmosphere and climate.

The global issues were riveting but lacked a human face until the world learned the story of Mendes, with his sad owlish eyes, wide moustache, and plain-thinking ability to cut to the root of a problem and do whatever needed to be done to solve it. He had been to the United States several times to press international development banks and lawmakers to halt loans for road-building projects in the Amazon until they incorporated the goals of the people living in the forests in front of the bulldozers. His demands were for schools and jobs and health care, hardly a green agenda. But his goal was to sustain communities of rubber tappers and indigenous peoples who knew how to live in a living forest without wrecking it.

This overlap with environmental preservation brought the union man to the attention of conservationists who shared his goal of preserving the rain forest, but for far different reasons. He would chuckle sometimes about these head-in-the-clouds types, with their talk of biodiversity and atmospheric circulation. But he knew an ally when he saw one.

He remained an obscure figure outside a small circle of human-rights and conservation campaigners, but his work had been chronicled by a sufficient number of American and European journalists that, when he was gunned down one week after his forty-fourth birthday, everything crystallized: the burning of the forests, the global link created by those rising plumes of greenhouse gases, and the compelling story of a man who had a rare, and crucial, skill set with which to confront ungoverned violence against man and nature.

Mendes's life is studied now in some business schools, which might seem odd at first, until one examines his character and tactics more carefully. He was the consummate achiever, starting with a clear goal but never getting locked into one strategy to achieve it. As a youth, he embraced Communism, learning of its power from a fugitive revolutionary who settled in the jungle near his family's home. He followed that route as a labor organizer, but moderated politically when he saw the limits of a rigid worldview. He tried politics but shifted again when corruption and his own limits as a speaker led to a string of defeats. As he switched tracks, one thing he never abandoned was a core focus on nonviolence. He put a tropical spin on the tactics of Gandhi and King, organizing downtrodden rubber tappers into a determined but peaceful resistance force that stood between the forest and the chainsaws of land-grabbing cattle ranchers. Like his predecessors, Mendes chose peace in part out of pragmatism, knowing that any other stance would be brutally crushed.

The tappers' goal in this resistance was twofold: to protect their rights to the land they had utilized for generations without title and to protect the rubber and Brazil nut trees that, while an impediment to a rancher, represented a renewable source of income to people willing to live within the standing forest.

The tools and tactics Mendes devised to deal with road builders, ranchers, and the government still influence efforts to both develop and preserve the Amazon—and the planet itself. Particularly enduring is the concept of the extractive reserve, an area of land held in trust and exploited in a way that does not diminish its bounty. While the number of reserves remains small, they stand as microcosm of the bigger models for sustainable development now being promoted to help enable the growing human population to prosper without diminishing Earth's gifts.

Mendes's insistence on nonviolence also helped bring some

semblance of justice to the frontier. Indeed, after a string of 982 killings of union and land-rights organizers from 1964 to 1988, pressure for change was so intensified by his murder that prosecutors for the first time were not only able to convict the gunman, but also the person who ordered the trigger pulled.

Mendes's saga has moved from news to history, but instead of fading, his legacy has broadened. He is increasingly recognized for his pursuit of a pragmatic strain of environmentalism in which the goal is reasoned exploitation of a living resource. While forging partnerships with green groups, he insisted that humans should not be held separate from nature but instead considered as an integral component of the natural landscape. He was a pioneer in what is now called environmental and social justice, as well, promoting the rights of communities to help shape their destinies from the ground up.

More significant, perhaps, with allies from the North he invented a reverse form of globalization a decade before the word became part of the buzz of international development debates. This labor organizer in Brazil's least-developed state realized that the most likely way to accomplish what mattered most to him—giving forest residents control over the forests around them—was not just to stand in front of cutting crews, but to touch pressure points thousands of miles away. To do so, he up-linked his home-grown land-rights movement with international forces like environmental groups, development banks, and the media.

Environmentalists had often sought local allies to help make their global points, but such partners frequently ended up employed more as props than vital players. The pitch would go something like this: "Save the Amazon—home to exotic birds, photogenic Indian tribes and rubber tappers, and a vine that can cure what ails you." In the arena of politics and public opinion, every campaign needed a symbol, and there was not much to distinguish an Amazonian Indian from a wolf or spouting whale. They were all, in the end, charismatic megafauna, useful tools for capturing public opinion.

But Mendes was not satisfied with being a sentimental icon.

He demanded a true partnership with the Northern Hemisphere activists who met him and saw mutual interests. He was radical in the word's purest sense, with the ability to cut to the deep root of an issue and the source of solutions. When he saw a road advancing into the forests, he insisted on finding out where the money was coming from to pay for the saws and bulldozers. He pushed out along those connecting lines of support and followed them back to their source—the halls of Congress and the purses of bankers.

That was his triumph. His tragedy was that he was not just a human being, but a Brazilian man. As he moved ahead in his effort to reverse illegal takings of rain forest lands and curtail funding for destructive road projects, he was confronted not only with the threat of violence, but the pronouncement of his certain death. Everyone he knew, from his closest friends and neighbors to his environmentalist allies 4,000 miles to the north, urged him to leave his home for awhile in December 1988—to head south to São Paulo or north to the United States, anywhere just to get away from the venomous men who were taking pot shots at the union headquarters.

Yet he stood his ground, refusing to leave the Amazon for safer terrain. And so his life was cut short by a single shotgun blast as he opened the back door of his shanty to take a shower in the outhouse before a fish dinner with his wife, two children, and a couple of police bodyguards.

His killers were caught and then escaped after serving a short span in an Acre prison without window screens, let alone bars. Darly Alves da Silva, the man who ordered the shooting, and his son Darci, who pulled the trigger, were later recaptured and sit in federal prison today.

Mendes's compatriots have risen to prominence throughout Brazil. As the new millennium began, the daughter of a rubber tapper from Acre, Marina Silva, became the federal minister of the environment. A forest engineer and former political advisor of Mendes's, Jorge Viana, was elected Acre's governor. The mayor of Xapuri, Mendes's home town, was Julio Barbosa de Aquino, a rubber tapper who stood shoulder to shoulder with Mendes in the confrontations with ranchers. And although Brazil's first working-class president, Luis Inacio "Lula" da Silva, was criticized early in his administration by environmental groups inside and outside of Brazil for allowing deforestation rates to climb, his presidency clearly signaled a great transition. Lula once stood trial in military court alongside Chico Mendes for their union activities.

Stephan Schwartzman, an anthropologist for the American nonprofit Environmental Defense and one of Mendes's early contacts outside Brazil, says the friction points leading to violence have shifted to where the conflict over land use and development is most intense, the sprawling state of Para, which spreads south of the mouth of the vast Amazon river system. In that region, Mendes's philosophy has been adopted by rural Amazonian communities of small farmers and settlers, including those lured up the spreading road system in the 1960s by offers of free land dangled by the military dictatorship. Some of these farmers, seeing the limits of the old methods of cut, burn, plant, and move on, have embraced new forms of agriculture that can be sustained on fragile Amazonian soils.

More than one hundred grassroots groups and unions have formed a coalition—the Movement for the Development of the Transamazon and the Xingu—devoted to advancing education, nondestructive agriculture techniques revolving around tree-grown crops, and small-scale development projects, Schwartzman told me recently. The groups have proposed a conservation strategy for the region that could create an intact corridor of different kinds of reserves spanning 62 million acres, he said. Together with existing reserves and Indian lands, this could preserve a swath of ecosystems ranging from the drier savanna to the depths of the still-undisturbed rain forests of the deepest Amazon. The corridor could serve as a shield against development that still spreads apace along the Transamazon Highway, the original spearhead for destruction.

The effort has the support of the federal and state governments but has run up against the same barriers Mendes faced: corruption and fraud in land transactions, illegal logging, real-estate speculation, and the threat of violence. Overall, following Mendes's death the pace of killings on the Amazon frontier dropped sharply, but important leaders are still targeted and picked off, as needed. In August 2001, for example, the leader of this new-style land reform movement, Ademir "Dema" Federicci, was assassinated. Another organizer in the movement, Bartolomeu Morais da Silva, was killed in July 2002.

And the pace of deforestation, which had also dropped for a few years after Brazil became the focus of international attention, has sharply accelerated. Brazil is promoting road-building projects, including one, Avança Brasil, that biologists say could open the long-shielded heart of the rain forest to development. If development happens as planned, 40 percent of the Brazilian portion of the Amazon forest could be gone in two decades, with only 5 percent left that can be said to be pristine. In November 2003, the government seemed to recognize how untenable this was, concluding in one report that projects in the region generally still "reproduce the model of development which has predominated in Amazonia over the last twenty years, based on the expansion of new frontiers."

Globalization may have allowed Mendes to link with distant allies he never knew existed, but it also clearly is adding to pressures on the world's remaining forests. Indeed, the influence of the outside world is apparently being felt even in places far from any road or settlement. Scientists monitoring still-undisturbed portions of the rain forest already see ecological changes that are apparently being driven by the buildup of carbon dioxide in the atmosphere, which is headed toward at least a doubling in concentration from its pre-industrial levels later this century. Some researchers have noted accelerating growth of weedy species; others have reported that the tallest tree species are growing faster while those in their shade are more often struggling. The shifts are subtle, but significant, with biologists saying that the rise in carbon dioxide—even outside of its influence on climate—is likely to substantially alter the composition and dynamics of the rain forest.

It is evident from the Amazon outward to the rest of the world that humanity is entering a new stage in its relationship with its environment. No longer can we push ahead blindly with no awareness of the broader impact of our actions. A company or community or country can no longer despoil a global resource without the assault being noticed via satellite or other means. A tree henceforth will always make a sound when it falls. The question is whether awareness of environmental impacts will foster concrete change in the way the human adventure unfolds.

There is reason for hope, tempered by concern. One of Mendes's earliest allies from the other Brazil—the developed, industrialized south—was Jose Lutzenberger, an agronomist who became the country's leading ecologist and then briefly its environment minister shortly after Mendes's death. He helped raise money for Mendes's union, recognizing its extractive reserves as a vital experiment in sustainable economics. He saw the Amazon as a smaller mirror of the global environment, something that could be pressed continually for a long time without outward signs of trouble—until a tipping point was reached. "A complicated system can take a lot of abuse, but you get to a point where suddenly things fall apart," Lutzenberger once told me. "It's like pushing a long ruler toward the edge of a table. Nothing happens, nothing happens, nothing happens—then suddenly the ruler falls to the floor."

The challenge, he said, is to act before the point of no return is reached. Lutzenberger pursued the protection of the Amazon and global ecology with the fervor and fire of a missionary facing a looming deadline, until his death several years ago from an asthma attack. Back in 1992, just before the much-heralded Earth Summit in Rio de Janeiro, at a point when the rate of Amazon forest destruction had slowed, I asked Lutzenberger if he was optimistic about the future.

"In the environmental movement, our defeats are always final, our victories always provisional," he said. "What you save today can still be destroyed tomorrow, you see—and so often is."

With all of Mendes's successes, the central lesson of his life may well be that the vigilance and resolve of the individual must be passed to the community, and then down from one generation protecting an environmental legacy to the next. As long as the ideas Mendes nurtured are propagated and acted upon, the Amazon and other places like it have a chance of remaining rich, functioning—and inhabited—ecosystems even as they are inevitably and increasingly utilized and affected by people.

Andrew Revkin
Garrison, New York (July 2004)

Chapter 1

The Burning Season

AT SIX-THIRTY ON A THURSDAY EVENING in the Amazon town of Xapuri, the bell in the spire of the yellow stucco church on the town square began to ring. It was three days before Christmas, 1988, and the bell was the first call to a special mass for the children who were graduating from elementary school. The cicadas began their nightly drone, enfolding the town and the surrounding rain forest in a blanket of sound that resembled an orchestra of sitar players tuning their instruments. Although it was well into the rainy season, the regular torrential downpours had held off for a day. Bicycles and pickup trucks rattled along the uneven, cobbled brick lanes. In the darkness, bats began to feast around the streetlights, swooping in time and again, sending out shrill, curt chirps of sonar and snatching moths and winged ants from the whirling clouds drawn to the bulbs. An occasional dugout canoe passed the shabby bars and shops that overhung the muddy, crumbling embankment of the Acre River. The staccato popping of the boats' single-cylinder diesel motors echoed against the steep sandstone cliff on the opposite shore.

Until the night of December 22, there was little to distinguish Xapuri from many of the other river towns of the Amazon. Xapuri (pronounced shah-poo-*ree*) is a sleepy rubber trading outpost of five thousand people in the state of Acre (*ah*-cray), the westernmost part of Brazil, deep in the tropical belly of the South American continent. The town perches at the spot where the Xapuri River makes its small contribution to the Acre River, which pours into the Purus, which in turn empties into the milky Solimões, one of the two great arms of the Amazon River. Some 2,000 miles downstream, the effluent from the Xapuri, combined with that of the rest of the ten thousand tributaries that lace the Amazon basin, flows into the Atlantic Ocean.

The town is quiet and orderly, the kind of place where the elderly streetsweepers come out every morning at dawn to clear leaves and litter from the shady lanes, where no one cares that the newspaper does not arrive until the noon bus pulls in from the state capital, raising a cloud of orange dust. The town is much quieter now than it was when the brick paving was laid at the turn of the century. (A curious geological fact about the Amazon is that there is no usable stone in most of the region—thus the bricks.) Back then, Acre was the center of a rich rubber boom that flourished as the industrial world's appetite for rubber exploded and thousands of men were lured into the jungle to tap latex from the rubber trees. Seven decades have passed since the rubber boom went bust, but the market for natural rubber persists—albeit subsidized by the government—so hunched laborers still haul hundred-pound slabs and balls of cured latex up the steep riverbank to the dark warehouses of the wealthy merchants who control the rubber trade.

On this night, in the fifteen minutes after the call to mass, Xapuri would forever change, all because of a man who now sat in the kitchen of his four-room cottage, playing dominoes. The small house was nestled in a row of similar shacks along Dr. Batista de Moraes Street, a five-minute walk from the bars and warehouses along the waterfront, across the treeless square that was always 10 degrees hotter in the daytime than the surrounding forest. The cottage was little bigger than a single-car garage, raised on stilts 2 feet off the tamped, grassless soil. It had a steeply pitched roof covered in terra cotta tile, baked of the same red earth as the bricks of the streets. The siding was painted pale blue with pink trim. As with most of the houses in town, the only running water was in the outhouse in the back yard.

The man sitting on one of the five small stools around the kitchen table was Francisco Alves Mendes Filho, known to everyone as Chico Mendes. He was a rubber tapper and the president of the local rural workers' union, which was fighting to save the rain forest for the thousands of rubber tappers and Indians who lived and worked in it. Mendes had just returned home after a busy month that included visits to Rio de Janeiro and São Paulo, two of the great cities in the south of Brazil—rich, industrial cities that are separated from the impoverished Amazon by much more than distance. There he had stayed in the plush apartments of environmental activists who were helping the rubber tappers with their struggle. In recent years, he had traveled increasingly between these two different Brazils. But now, with Christmas approaching, Mendes planned to stop and relax at home with his family for a few days.

Relaxing did not come easy to him. That was clear from Mendes's face, a round face dominated by puffy, owlish eyes. It was a face that usually smiled but had recently begun to show signs of stress. He had turned forty-four one week earlier, but only this year had he started to look his age. A graying mustache broadened his grin and a deep dimple appeared in his right cheek every time he smiled. His perpetually tousled black and silver curls gave him a distracted look. His thin legs sprouted beneath a firm potbelly that he displayed with a certain sense of pride. Mendes was playing dominoes with two bodyguards provided by the Military Police. Although they were not in uniform and both were neighbors—one had done typing for the union when he was a teenager—they were nonetheless an unnerving presence. Mendes had resolved to ask the police to withdraw the security.

Now that it was dark, one of the guards got up from the game and, despite the muggy heat, closed the wooden shutters over the glassless windows and slid home the bolts. The guards had been assigned to Mendes because persistent death threats had been made against him. Xapuri was peaceful on the surface, but the underlying tension was palpable and had been rising steadily all year. Mendes's union, consisting of rubber tappers and small farmers, had scored a series of victories in its war against encroaching cattle ranchers, who were incinerating the rain forest to create pasture and to profit from tax breaks and booming real estate prices.

Starting in March, the tappers had staged a series of *empates* (em-*pah*-tays), forceful demonstrations in which chain saw crews were confronted and driven from the forest. And, in October, they had convinced the government to declare a 61,000-acre tract of traditional rubber tapper territory near Xapuri, called Seringal Cachoeira, an "extractive reserve." Cachoeira was where Mendes had grown up and first worked as a tapper; the forest there had been his only school. The new designation meant that the forest could not be cut and must be used only in sustainable ways—for the harvest of rubber, Brazil nuts, and the like. The concept of the extractive reserve had been invented by Mendes and the tappers, then refined with some help from environmentalists and anthropologists. With the establishment of this and three other extractive reserves, Mendes had pulled off one of the most significant feats in the history of grass-roots environmental activism—and he had only known the word "environment" for three years.

His wife, Ilzamar, told the domino players to stop so that she could set the table for dinner. There was fresh fish waiting to be fried. Ilzamar, twenty years younger than Mendes, had a classic Amazonian beauty that hinted at both Indian and European features. The overall effect was remarkably Polynesian: full lips and huge black eyes framed by a long, thick mane of black hair.

"In a few minutes," Mendes said. "Let us finish this game." He was competitive and very good, and he liked to play the game to the end. Mendes and the guards were playing a difficult version, called *domino pontó,* which involved some mental arithmetic. He liked to make a point of triumphantly slapping his tile down when he had finished contemplating a move. The clacking of the bone tiles on the Formica tabletop carried through the thin walls of the house and into the darkness.

Mendes's five-year marriage to Ilzamar had faltered recently, as he traveled more and more and earned less and less. (A previous brief marriage had failed as well.) In 1986, he had crisscrossed Acre in a futile campaign for the state legislature. He had been a candidate of the leftist Workers party, PT, in a state that never swayed from center-right. In 1987 and 1988, he continued to hike through the forest, seeking rubber tappers for his union, and traveled to the south, recruiting allies from Brazil's burgeoning environmental movement. In 1986, Ilzamar almost died giving birth to twins, one of whom was stillborn. Mendes could not pay the hospital bill. Ilzamar was never allowed to go with her husband on his trips. "My work is not play," he would say, as their arguments echoed through the neighbors' yards. "This is business and you can't keep a secret." It was only in March that they had moved into a house of their own—and only because Mendes's environmentalist friends had chipped in to buy it for him. Ilzamar once said that she had not spent more than eight days with Mendes from 1986 to 1988.

His work so dominated his life that it was even reflected in the names he chose for his children. As the men finished their game, the two children played on the floor in the front room of the house, where Ilzamar had returned to watch the soap opera *Anything Goes,* which both lampooned and glorified the lives of Brazil's rich. The surviving twin, now a beautiful two-year-old boy, was named Sandino, after Augusto Cesar Sandino, the leader of the 1927 guerrilla war against American marines in the mountains of Nicaragua (and the man for whom the Sandinistas were named). Mendes had named his four-year-old daughter Elenira, after a legendary female guerrilla who stalked both police and soldiers in the Amazon state of Pará in the early 1970s, at the height of the military dictatorship. Elenira was famous for her marksmanship; she invariably killed her target with a rifle shot between the eyes. Mendes had always been attracted to radical social history, although his own activism was generally less extreme than that of his idols. As one of Brazil's leaders in the fight to save the rain forest, he insisted on a nonviolent approach.

But his opponents were not so civil. In May of 1988, two teenage rubber tappers participating in a peaceful demonstration were shot by a pair of hired gunmen. In June, Ivair Higino de Almeida, a member of Mendes's union and fellow PT politician, was shot dead. In September, another tapper fell. And now, as Mendes sat slapping dominoes on the table with his guards—he was winning, as usual—two men were slowly creeping into the flimsily fenced back yard. They had slipped through the thick underbrush behind the house, following an eroded gully cut by a small stream. They wore dark jeans and, because of the sticky heat, had tied their shirts at their waists. One had a white handkerchief covering his mouth and nose; the cloth fluttered in and out with his breathing. They had heard the church bell; now they heard the laughter and the domino game and the sound of the soap opera, which echoed eerily from television sets up and down the street. It was one of Brazil's most popular shows, and everyone was watching to find out who had murdered a key character.

This was not their first visit to that yard. Hidden in the bushes near where the river curled around this side of town, two small areas of grass had been crushed where they had been camping on and off for days, patiently watching. Cigarette butts and spilled *farinha*— a baked flour of ground manioc root that is a staple starch in the Amazon—littered the *tocaia*, ambush. Five moldy tins of Bordon sausage lay in the grass, swamped with ants, and two wine bottles with water in them lay nearby. Now the men settled down to wait once more, crouching on a pile of bricks behind a palm tree 30 feet from Mendes's back door. They were adept at being quiet, perhaps from their experience stalking game in the forest. No chickens clucked, and the many dogs in the neighborhood did not so much as growl.

In the rain forests of the western Amazon, the threat of violent death hangs in the air like mist after a tropical rain. It is simply a part of the ecosystem, just like the scorpions and snakes cached in the leafy canopy that floats over the forest floor like a seamless green circus tent. People from the Amazon say that the trouble always starts during the burning season, a period of two months or so between the two natural climatic seasons of the region—the dry and the wet. By then, the equatorial sun has baked the last moisture out of the brush, grass, and felled trees, and the people of the Amazon— sometimes Indians and rubber tappers, but most often wealthy ranchers and small farmers—set their world on fire. The fires clear the clogged fields or freshly deforested land and, in disintegrating vegetation, put a few of the nutrients essential for plant growth back into the impoverished soil. The burning season is the time before the return of the daily downpours that give the rain forest its name.

The trouble arises when one man's fires threaten another man's livelihood. Most often, that happens when one of the hundreds of ranchers or speculators who have been drawn to the region's cheap land acquires the title to property that already is the home of people who have squatted there legally—sometimes for decades. Often the new titles are acquired through fraud or coercion. And because the most efficient way to reinforce a claim to land in the Amazon is to cut down the forest and burn it, the new landlords do just that. Or they loose their cattle, which make quick work of the settlers' crops. If that does not work, they send out their *pistoleiros* to burn the families out of their shacks or, if they resist, to shoot them down.

The only thing that has prevented the Amazon River basin and its peoples from being totally overrun is its sheer size and daunting character. It is a shallow bowl covering 3.6 million square miles, twice the expanse of India. An average of 8 feet of rain falls here each year, inundating great stretches of forest, turning roads into bogs, and providing vast breeding grounds for malarial mosquitoes. The water drains eastward through a fanlike network of streams and rivers that together disgorge 170 billion gallons of water each hour into the Atlantic—eleven times the flow of the Mississippi. Besides producing this riverine sea, the deluge also nourishes the largest stretch of rain forest left on Earth. Rising from a dank forest floor —a seething mat of decomposition and decay—dense stands of trees support a verdant canopy of foliage, fruits, and flowers. Innumerable species of animal and microbial life have found niches in which to flourish, all intricately interdependent.

One of the tens of thousands of plant species in the forest is a tree with a smooth trunk that produces a white fluid in a reticulation of tubules beneath its bark. Its local name is *seringueira;* botanists call it *Hevea brasiliensis.* Its common name is the rubber tree. The fluid is thought to protect the tree from invasions of boring pests by gumming up the insects' mouth parts. This same fluid, congealed and properly processed, has remarkable qualities of resilience, water resistance, and insulation to the flow of electricity— all of which made it one of the most sought after raw materials of the industrial revolution.

It was this substance, called latex, that lured the grandfather of Chico Mendes and tens of thousands of other men to the Amazon rain forest in two waves over the past hundred and twenty years. Called *seringueiros,* these men settled in the forests around ports like Xapuri and worked in solitude, fighting to make a life from the living forest—and fighting to free themselves from bosses who saw to it that they remained enslaved by their debts. Recently, as outsiders intent on destroying the forest began to invade the Amazon, the *seringueiros* had to fight once again. This time, they were fighting to save their homes, their livelihood, and the rain forest around them.

In leading this struggle to preserve the Amazon, Chico Mendes had made a lot of trouble for a lot of powerful people. He was to the ranchers of the Amazon what César Chavez was to the citrus kings of California, what Lech Walesa was to the shipyard managers of Gdansk. The Xapuri Rural Workers Union, which Mendes helped found in 1977, regularly sent swarms of demonstrators to thwart the ranchers' chain saw crews. The rural workers had driven two of Brazil's biggest ranchers clear out of Acre—a man nicknamed Rei do Nelore (King of Cattle) and Geraldo Bordon, the owner of one of Brazil's biggest meat-packing corporations. With his aggressive tactics and affable, plain-talking style, Mendes had then attracted the attention of American environmentalists, who invited him to Washington and Miami to help them convince the international development banks to suspend loans that were allowing Brazil to pave the roads leading into the Amazon. Mendes made friends abroad, but he made more enemies at home.

One of his most dangerous foes was Darly Alves da Silva, a

rancher who had come north to Acre from the state of Paraná in 1974. Alves lived on a 10,000-acre ranch with his wife, three mistresses, thirty children, and a dozen or so cowboys, most of whom the tappers considered little more than hired killers. Alves and his family had established a tradition of murder as they moved from state to state, starting in the 1950s. When somebody bothered the Alves family, somebody usually turned up dead—if he ever turned up again at all. Darly's scrappy father, Sebastião, once spent four and a half years in jail in the south for the murder of a neighbor. He only served time because he had had a vision from God that told him to confess his crime. There were many other, unsolved murders that were allegedly his work.

A fourteen-year-old boy named Genézio, who lived at Alves's ranch, later testified in court about fourteen murders that had been committed on the ranch or by the family. For instance, one day he saw some *urubu,* vultures, circling over a little-used pasture. He waded into the weeds and saw a charred corpse. A wooden post, still smoldering, was embedded in the smashed rib cage. Two weeks earlier, a workman named Valdir had disappeared after arguing with one of Darly's sons, Oloci. Another time Raimundo Ferreira, a worker at the ranch, asked to marry Darly's nine-year-old daughter, Vera. Oloci told his father that Raimundo was "trying to joke with Darly's face." Later, Oloci and his half brother Darci asked Ferreira to go with them into the jungle. After a few days, word got around that the brothers had cut off Ferreira's ear and nose and then shot and stabbed him to death.

The Alves clan had threatened Mendes many times, and more than one attempt had been made on his life. But this time was different. With his *empates,* Mendes had prevented the Alveses from taking possession of a tract of forest that Darly wanted to add to his holdings and convert to pasture. The *empates* were a frustration, but what really infuriated Darly was that Mendes had forced him and his brother Alvarino into hiding back in September, after a lawyer working with the tappers found a fifteen-year-old arrest warrant from the family's days in the south.

Darly did not look dangerous. His eyes swam behind the thick lenses of bulky bifocals that overwhelmed his narrow face. Bony legs and arms dangled from thin shoulders and hips, as if someone had cut the strings on a marionette. His ill-fitting black mustache seemed pasted on. It was his voice, a thin, wispy voice, that hinted that this was a man to handle with care. Quick streams of words had to slip out around teeth that were always clenched. Darly swore that this was the last time Mendes would ever bother him. "No one has ever bested me," he told a friend. "And Chico wants to do that."

Darly was confident he could act with impunity. His brother worked in the Xapuri sheriff's office, just forty paces from Mendes's front door, and the sheriff was a good friend of the family. The main reason Darly had moved to the Amazon was that it was one of the last places where might still made right. In that sense, it differed little from the American West of the nineteenth century as described in 1872 by Mark Twain in *Roughing It:* "the very paradise of outlaws and desperadoes." In the Amazon, when you ask people about *justiça,* justice, they simply chuckle in a sad kind of way; most of the men in the prison cells are sleeping off a drunk, having had several too many slugs of the blazing, strong sugarcane rum called *cachaça,* which is sold for pennies a glass. In fact, more than a thousand people have been murdered in land disputes in rural Brazil since 1980, and Amnesty International estimates that fewer than ten of the killers have been convicted and sent to jail. (And not one *mandante,* mastermind, of a murder has ever been tried.) Sometimes the gunmen meet resistance; there is hardly a rubber tapper's shack that does not have an oil-stained spot on the wall where the shotgun is hung. But usually the professionals prevail. In this anarchic atmosphere, the *pistoleiros* often assume the look of their imagined Wild West predecessors, strutting through town with a revolver stuck in the waist of tight jeans, boot heels raising red dust.

Thus it was that in the latter half of December, the threats against Mendes had been replaced with death pronouncements. "Threat" implies that death is only a possibility; in Mendes's case, imminent death was a near inevitability. Mendes told his brother Zuza about a series of ominous telephone calls to the union hall and his neighbor's house (Mendes did not have his own telephone). "Zuza," he said, "you watch out because things are getting very hot. I have a feeling I'm not going to make it to Christmas."

Mendes and his guards finished their domino game and moved to the front room to catch the end of *Anything Goes.* Everyone jumped slightly each time a seed pod dropped onto the tile roof from the huge *benjamin* tree that took up most of the small front yard and overhung the house. Finally, dinner was ready. Ilzamar set out a platter of fish and pots of beans and rice. When the table was ready, the two guards sat down on the small wooden stools, along with the wife of one of Mendes's friends, who had stopped by to chat. The guards were not required to stay with Mendes after dark, but they were friends of the family—and they enjoyed dominoes and home cooking. Normally they ate in the Military Police barracks, several blocks away.

By now, the insect symphony outside had reached *fortissimo,* a layered blend of high-pitched hums and creaks and rattles that muffled human speech. Ilzamar took her plate to the front room to eat with the children. Even though he was wearing only a pair of white shorts, Mendes was hot and uncomfortable. Telling everyone else to eat, he threw a towel over his shoulder and opened the back door to head to the outhouse to splash down with cold water. The powder blue towel, decorated with a rainbow and musical notes, had been a birthday present.

As he had many times before, Mendes muttered about how dark it was in back. He had talked to friends about stringing a new wire for an outdoor light bulb; someone had cut the wire the last time they tried it. They had agreed to do it *amanhã,* tomorrow—a word that is heard often in the draining heat of the Amazon. Grumbling as he shut the door, he went into the bedroom and picked up the small black flashlight with the high-intensity beam that had been a gift from Mary Allegretti, an anthropologist from the south who had worked with him for years, trying to help the rubber tappers.

Opening the door once again, Mendes flicked on the flashlight. The narrow beam swept the darkness. It is possible that he saw the two figures crouched by the palm tree in the corner opposite the outhouse. But no one will ever know, because in that instant one of the men pulled the trigger on a .20-gauge shotgun.

In the darkness, the light blue towel must have made a good target. That is exactly where the load of buckshot struck. A tight pattern of sixty pellets buried themselves in Mendes's right shoulder and chest and sent him tottering back into the kitchen. He screamed once and said no more. Trailing blood, he staggered toward the bedroom, possibly in an attempt to reach his revolver; he had kept the weapon even though the police, who had openly sided with the Alveses, had taken away his permit early in December. But his body suddenly went limp, and Mendes fell into the arms of one of the guards, Roldão Roseno de Souza, who had been with him since late October. Mendes crumpled to the floor on the threshold of the bedroom door.

He took very little time to bleed to death; later, forensic analysis showed that eleven pieces of lead had found a lung. His blood spread a dark stain across the rough plank floor and dripped through the cracks onto the earth below. The towel, riddled with holes, lay beside him.

Now all the dogs in the neighborhood were barking. Roseno cradled Mendes's head. No one dared open the back door a second time. The other guard, who had only a five-shot revolver, jumped through a window facing the street and sprinted to the military barracks to get help and grab a machine gun. Friends came running with weapons of their own, knowing as soon as they heard the shot what had happened.

Ilzamar bolted into the street, screaming, "They've killed Chico!" But the regular gaggle of policemen and hangers-on sitting outside the sheriff's office just yards away did not stir.

The funeral of Chico Mendes was held on Christmas Day. Through what the tappers call *radio cipó*—vine radio, the rain forest version of the grapevine—word of the murder quickly spread. Hundreds of rubber tappers hiked for many hours through the forest to attend the wake and funeral. On Saturday night the church bell again rang a call to mass; one by one, the rubber tappers filed past Mendes's body and spoke of how he had changed their lives. Hour after hour they shuffled by, and the singing of hymns went on into the evening.

By Christmas morning, more than a thousand people had crowded around the church. The rains had returned in force, drenching the mourners who followed the casket to the cemetery on the road leading out of town. At the head of the cortege, a young man studying for the priesthood held aloft a wooden cross with a painted portrait of Mendes fastened to the middle. The painting had been done in 1987 by an artist named Jorge Rivas Plata da Cruz. That was the year Mendes first traveled abroad and began to make headlines for his environmental work. In the painting, his mustache and hair are carefully coiffed and pure black. There are no worry lines around his smiling eyes. He is wearing the first suit he ever owned, the one he wore on his first trip abroad. It had been in a batch of clothing sent from Italy for the poor of Xapuri.

Along with the hundreds of rubber tappers and small farmers in the procession were dozens of Mendes's friends from the other Brazil. The funeral brought together the two sides of his life—the people from the forest and those from the outside, who had found in this simple rubber tapper an indispensable ally. Mary Allegretti, Mendes's first friend from the world outside the forest, had flown down from New York City, forcing her way onto a booked flight to get to Xapuri on time. Now she stood holding her umbrella over Ilzamar and the children, although it had little effect in the driving downpour. A contingent of labor leaders, celebrities, and leftist politicians from São Paulo and Rio had flown up for the funeral, headed by Luis Inácio da Silva, better known as Lula, the gravel-voiced socialist who later came close to gaining the presidency of Brazil. Surrounding the crowd were dozens of journalists, many from overseas. An international version of vine radio had efficiently disseminated the news of the killing.

Luis Ceppi, Xapuri's priest, presided over the service. Ceppi, who was Italian and a member of Italy's Communist party, had helped the rubber tappers' movement get European support. As he gave the benediction, rain and tears streamed down his cheeks and soaked his white robe. The casket was placed in a brick crypt next to that of Ivair Higino de Almeida, the union member who had been brutally murdered in June—allegedly by Darly Alves's sons and hired gunmen. A mason closed the crypt and troweled the cement flat. White porcelain tiles were then applied over the bricks. Mendes had told friends, "I don't want flowers at my funeral, because I know that they would be taken from the forest." Nevertheless, someone piled freshly picked blossoms on his grave that day.

The murder of Chico Mendes might well have been an unremarkable event. He was the fifth rural union president murdered in Brazil that year, and just a week later another president of a rural union, in eastern Brazil, was blasted in the face with a shotgun in front of his family. But over the previous three years, Mendes's close relationships with environmentalists, labor organizers, and human rights advocates from Brazil, the United States, and Europe had focused increased attention on the struggle of the rubber tappers. His *empates* and organizing skills had brought him awards from the United Nations Environment Program, the Gaia Foundation, and other groups. As a result, this murder deep in the Amazon rain forest—where it once took three weeks for news to travel down the river—instantly became an international story, making the front page of newspapers around the world.

The significance of his murder was further amplified by the disturbing environmental anomalies of 1988. The scorching summer in the United States that year had motivated politicians and the media for the first time to pay serious attention to the greenhouse effect: the theory that billions of tons of gases released each year by the burning of fossil fuels and forests are trapping solar energy in the atmosphere and disastrously warming the planet. And just as the heat was breaking records and fires were ravaging Yellowstone National Park, the television networks got detailed satellite photographs of the Amazon burning season—thousands of fires burning simultaneously. It almost felt as if the heat and smoke generated in the forests were being inhaled on the baking streets of Los Angeles, Washington, and New York.

Then came the slaying of Chico Mendes. In the months that followed, dozens of television crews, photographers, and reporters from around the world would take the six-hour, four-stop flight from São Paulo to Rio Branco, the capital of Acre, then bounce for four more hours along the rutted, dusty, partly paved road to Xapuri. The Hotel Veneza, the only hostelry in town with a bathroom for each room, quickly filled up. Those turned away had to walk down the block to Hospedaria Souza, where an oversexed rooster liked to start crowing at 3:00 A.M. and one of his hens had a habit of laying eggs on the floor of the outhouse, then roosting behind the toilet.

The citizens of Xapuri gradually adjusted to all the attention. After a while, the woman who ran the Veneza learned that Americans do not like heaps of sugar brewed directly into their coffee, as is usual in the Amazon. So many journalists wanted to be taken to Seringal Cachoeira, the rubber tapping area where Mendes and the tappers had their showdown with the Alves family, that the tappers started charging $200 to truck the visitors in and put them up for a day or two in tappers' homes. Mendes's house was turned into a small museum, and the guest book filled with a thousand, then two thousand, then—by the end of the dry season of 1989—four thousand names.

Visitors who stayed long enough to walk for a time in the surrounding forest discovered the bounty of the ecosystem that Mendes had died defending. It was a place of spectacular diversity and vitality. Turn over a log and find 50 species of beetle. Survey an acre and find 100 species of butterfly. In the Amazon, one type of rubber tree has exploding fruit that flings seeds 20 yards; three-toed sloths harbor dozens of species of insects and algae in their matted fur; river porpoises are cotton-candy pink. It was a living pharmacy that scientists had only just begun to explore. A fourth of all prescription drugs contain ingredients derived from tropical plants—malaria drugs and anesthetics and antibiotics and more—and less than 1 percent of the Amazon's plants had been studied.

It became clear to outsiders that the murder was a microcosm of the larger crime: the unbridled destruction of the last great reservoir of biological diversity on Earth. Just a few centuries ago, the planet had 15 million square miles of rain forest, an area five times that of the contiguous United States. Now three Americas' worth of forest were gone, with just 6.2 million square miles left. A third of the remaining rain forest was in the Amazon basin, and over the past decade alone, chain saws and fires had consumed about 10 percent of it—an area twice the size of California.

The aggression against the forest was therefore a many-layered tragedy, causing human deaths, killing millions of trees and other organisms, and resulting in the extinction of several species of plant and animal life each day—most of which had not even been noticed, let alone catalogued or studied. In some ways, Chico Mendes and the rubber tappers were simply another endangered species, as much a part of the ecosystem as the trees they tapped, the birds in the branches, or the ants underfoot.

But the tappers were a species that was fighting back.

Chapter 2
Amazonia

XAPURI AND THE HUNDREDS of other human settlements in the Amazon are like tiny islands scattered in a great green sea. Some are linked by roads cut through the wilderness; others can be reached only by boat or airplane. Even Manaus, once the gleaming center of the rubber boom and now a noisy, polluted city of 700,000, is like an island, connected by only one road to the developed south of Brazil. Overall, despite the devastation around the edges and the fishbone pattern of open space that eats into the trees wherever a network of roads is built, the overwhelming majority of the region remains virgin forest. From above, it seems to be a uniformly mottled green carpet, touched here and there with pink or rust or yellow where a particular tree species is in flower. On a thousand-mile flight over the undeveloped parts of the basin, you look down on nothing but that carpet, the only distraction being the occasional glint of the rivers, which coil and twist like a spilled spool of silver ribbon, or here and there a clearing where an Indian tribe or rubber tapper community has carved out a small patch in which to raise crops.

Just as the forest itself can only be described in superlatives, the same is true of the geographical setting. The dimensions of the Amazon basin are unlike those of any other river valley in the world. The conventional conception of a river valley is of a meandering

depression that drops steadily toward some sea or lake, some desti-
nation where water can find its own level and come to rest. But the
Amazon basin is a great flat plain, shaped more like a crepe pan than
a bowl, that covers an area nearly the size of the contiguous United
States. The preponderance of the river system lies within Brazil, but
the Amazon's tributaries extend into eight other countries that ring
the basin from northeast to southwest: French Guiana, Suriname,
Guyana, Venezuela, Colombia, Ecuador, Peru, and landlocked
Bolivia. To the north and south, the basin is contained by the
Guyana Shield and the Brazilian Shield. These weathered uplands
were formed in the Archean era, more than two billion years back
in Earth's five-billion-year history. The rock, scoured by eons of
rain and wind, is some of the oldest material on the surface of the
planet. The western rim of the basin is the towering wall of the
Andes mountain range, which curls like a spine along the Pacific
coast of South America, never more than 100 miles from the ocean.
On the time scale on which geological changes are measured, the
Andes are newborn, having pushed upward some twenty to forty
million years ago when the plates of the earth's dynamic crust
beneath the Pacific collided with the continent.

There is geological evidence that before the Andes rose, much of
the basin drained west into the Pacific. Once the mountain chain
blocked that route, the basin filled with water and became a brack-
ish, landlocked lake. Over time, hundreds of feet of sediment accumulated on the bottom. Then, somewhere around the site of
the present town of Obidos, this inland sea broke through and
forged a route east to the Atlantic, carving a channel that now is
more than 200 feet deep in places, making the Amazon the deepest
river in the world. Today, the Amazon has its beginnings in the
snows of the Andes. Some 18,000 feet above sea level, at a place in
southern Peru just over the continental divide from a river that cuts
westward down to the Pacific coast, a lacy network of ice-fed
streams joins in a downhill rush to form the most distant headwaters
of the river. Although it starts its life just 100 miles from the Pacific,
the river seeks its lowest level in the opposite direction and must
travel 4,007 miles before it reaches an ocean. The river is perpetually

replenished by the water vapor that sweeps west from the Atlantic, falls as rain, evaporates from the forest's own humid mass, blows farther west, and then finally collides with the mountains and falls as precipitation once again.

After its initial plunge—some 16,000 feet in the first 600 miles —the river steadily gathers strength from a widening system of tributaries and takes on the name Solimões. The Solimões, which at its source rips away at the young, crumbling rock of the still-rising Andes, is so heavily laden with silt that it is opaque. It settles down as it reaches the flat basin, and the rest of the way to the Atlantic is barely a downhill ride. In fact, over its final 2,000-mile run to the ocean, the total vertical drop of the Amazon is just a little over 100 feet.

Near the geographical center of the basin, the Solimões is joined by a major river running south from the ancient Guyana Shield, the Rio Negro. The Rio Negro is clear but as dark as strong tea, containing little sediment but many dissolved organic compounds leached from rotting vegetation. (The similarity to tea is no accident; among the dissolved compounds are tannins, the same organic acids that give tea its hue.) Once these two great streams are joined, the river takes on the name Amazon and acquires a pale tan hue.

For the next 600 miles, the distance between banks is often 5 miles or more, occasionally 18 miles. In the widest stretches, it is difficult to see the riverbanks from the deck of a small boat in the central channel. Parallel to the river, the land appears to have been scratched deeply by the claws of a gargantuan cat. The furrows, many of them flooded, are created during the wet season, when the water overflows the banks and scrapes away at the landscape.

The mouth of the Amazon is incompletely plugged by a grassy island the size of Switzerland. There is no way to visualize the volume of water that flows past this island; suffice it to say that it is greater than the combined flows of the next eight rivers on the ten-biggest list. It is a fifth of all the fresh water flowing from all the world's rivers into all the world's oceans. Where the river reaches the coast, a tan stain blossoms over the blue ocean, billowing outward as if someone has just spilled a great pot of tea with milk. More than 100 miles from the coast of South America, the silty exhalation of the river still flows fresh and unmixed atop the denser salt water. It was this freshwater outflow that in February of the year 1500 caught the attention of the first European to find the river—a Spanish sea captain who had previously sailed with Christopher Columbus. Vincente Yanez Piñon followed the freshwater current to the mouth of the river, which he named the Sweet Sea, failing to conclude that it might be a river because it so dwarfed any he had previously seen.

Although the forests of the Amazon cover little more than 2 percent of the earth's land surface, they account for 15 percent of the total terrestrial plant biomass—trunks and stems and leaves and roots. The ecosystem is a high-revving photosynthetic engine, fueled by the steady, seasonless tropical sun. The plants are in metabolic overdrive; everything is either in a state of birth or death, growth or decay, attack or defense. Where one tree has fallen to crumble and rot, dozens of green seedlings and saplings suddenly spring up to vie for the blast of sunlight entering the hole in the canopy.

Despite the seeming extravagance, it is an efficient, miserly system that picks up after itself and wastes nothing. Anything that dies is quickly dismantled and reabsorbed. The Amazon forests must be self-sufficient, because the ancient soils beneath most of the basin have long ago been leached clean of minerals and nutrients. Only 4 percent of the Amazon has what agronomists consider fertile soils.

Water that evaporates from one leaf soon condenses again and falls as rain. The dense sieve of roots and fungi that carpet the forest floor allows few of the nutrients in the rainwater to escape into the streams, rivers, and eventually the sea. Indeed, stray compounds have been so completely filtered from some Amazon tributaries that the water is almost as pure as if it were distilled.

The vastness of the Amazon rain forest contributes to the impression that it is a continuous, unchanging mass of jungle. But the region actually includes many forest types. When the rains of the wet season combine with the maximum snowmelt, the rivers of the

Amazon basin rise 40 feet or more, inundating enormous stretches of forest. This seasonally flooded forest—called *várzea* or *igapó,* depending on which part of the basin you are in—makes up only 2 percent of the total forest area. Even so, a majority of the Amazon's human population lives in the flooded portions, probably because that is where the soils are regularly enriched by silt and because these areas are close to the rivers. Until roads were cut into the forest, almost all significant human settlement occurred within a few miles of the rivers.

The flooded forest is an ecosystem all its own, where plants must survive for months underwater and fishes swim for part of the year through the treetops, eating fruit and playing an important role in distributing seeds. The *terra firme*, firm ground, that makes up the rest of Amazonia tends to have aged soils that have been washed clean of nutrients over millennia. In some areas, there is natural savanna, in others, low forests that are little more than a tangle of lianas. But huge swathes of *terra firme* support rich rain forest. This forest has evolved in such a way that it is nearly independent of the substrate. The system feeds itself and waters itself, recycling nutrients and holding water in its biomass like an enormous sponge. It is somewhat like hydroponic agriculture, in which plants can thrive on sterile sand—or even suspended in racks—as long as they receive moisture, nutrients, carbon dioxide, and sunlight.

Within any single patch of rain forest, there is also an initial impression of monotony: all you see are columnar trunks, thickets of vines and creepers, mats of decaying leaves. It is only after you have walked for a while in a mature stand of rain forest that individual elements begin to stand out: trees with flying buttresses, hanging plants, climbing plants, plants with fruit clustered high in the air, or plants—like cocoa—in which the fruit grows directly out of the tree trunk. You notice that your feet are intermittently shuffling through foot-long canoe-shape leaves, then plate-size hand-shape leaves, then a dusting of purple flower petals dropping from unseen blossoms 100 feet above. A Morpho butterfly flits past, like an animated origami masterpiece folded from a sheet of electric-blue foil (one naturalist described these seven-inch forest dwellers as "the bluest things in the world"). As you walk on, a tree above you clacks quietly in the wind and a woody pod falls at your feet. It is the seed pod of *Cariniana micrantha,* a relative of the Brazil nut. Out of its end pops a perfectly fitted cap. In the exposed cavity you see tightly packed regiments of seeds, each with a feathery tail that would have allowed it to soar away from the parent tree—if the monkey that dropped the seed pod had left it on the tree to ripen a little longer.

The dizzying complexity of the forest exists at all levels. Every time you turn to focus on a particular object, perhaps a rotting log, that object then splits into individual elements—fungi, beetles, ants, and a pile of aromatic wood dust where a nest of termites has been hard at work. Look even more closely, and those fragments would split apart yet again. The leaf-cutter ants crossing the log are carrying chunks of plant material into their subterranean fungus garden. Spores of the fungus are planted on this food source, and later the ants harvest the fruiting bodies that the fungi produce. The ants cannot digest the leaves themselves, and the fungi have evolved to an extent that they can no longer live anywhere but in nests watched over by ants. Meanwhile, the termites' guts harbor bacteria without which they cannot digest the tough cellulose skeleton of the tree. The beetles are attacking a pile of monkey droppings. And, at the point where the log appears to be slowly sinking into the earth, a thick mat of fungal threads called mycorrhizae are reducing the dead wood to its chemical constituents. These constituents include traces of minerals such as phosphorus, a coveted commodity in Amazon forests.

The fungi have a symbiotic relationship with the surrounding trees, and if you were able to trace the strings from which that fungal mat is woven, you would see that they emanate from nearby shallow tree roots. Although the fungi are a separate organism from the tree, neither can thrive without the other. Where the fungus interlaces with the tissue of the tree root, there is an ongoing exchange of goods. The tree provides the fungus with carbon-based compounds that help it grow, and the fungus provides the tree with recycled phosphorus and other minerals. Slowly, as you absorb more and more of the details around you, the spectacular complexity and interrelatedness of the rain forest become overwhelmingly apparent.

Even so, that which can be seen at eye level or on the forest floor is just a taste of the richness of the forest. It is in the canopy—the topmost layers of branches and foliage 100 feet or more above the floor—that the incredible biological bounty is most apparent. Many researchers have noted the similarity between tropical rain forests and coral reefs. In both ecosystems, life occurs in strata, with the richest array of life forms in the layer closest to the sun. In the case of a coral reef, that is the shallowest part, where innumerable fishes and invertebrates rely for their food on phytoplankton and corals sustained by photosynthesis. In the rain forest, it is the canopy. This stratum has been called the last great unexplored frontier of the natural world. While the coral reef has been made accessible by scuba gear, there is still no simple way to wander through the treetops. In the shadows beneath the canopy, less and less grows and thrives until finally—on the equivalent of the deep sea floor, where little light penetrates—there is the thin brown layer of rotting mulch and the tangle of runners and buttressed tree roots, much of which is simply there to support the rich community far above.

The forest's layered look has been determined by the location of the crucial fuels that it needs to thrive. The architecture of the forest has resulted from a sort of tug-of-war between the need to absorb water and nutrients from the earth below while competing with neighboring plants for the light coming from the sun above. The elevated canopy came into being as competing plants evolved different ways of reaching above each other. Even though the tropics are bathed in almost twice as much sun as regions at the latitude of Paris, there never seems to be enough to go around.

Evolution has solved this dilemma in several ways. The most straightforward is the tree trunk. The forest giants, such as the Brazil nut tree, rise twenty stories or more, hoisting their foliage above the main mass of the canopy. In these enormous trees, water and nutrients are pulled up through the trunks by the vacuum created as water evaporates from the surface of leaves far above; the pull of the vacuum can exceed 2 to 3 tons per square inch. Farther down, in the understory, is a mixture of palms and slimmer trees that tolerate perpetual twilight. There are palms on stilts, palms covered with spines, palms that climb like vines, palms with berries, and palms with nuts. And the forest floor is covered with saplings and seedlings that remain stunted until some tall neighbor comes crashing down and allows a flood of sunlight to pour onto the plants below.

The large trees expend an enormous amount of their productive energy in getting their green leaves as high as possible. Other plants have different strategies: climbing or perching. Myriad epiphytes —air plants—grow high in the canopy, their dust-fine seeds having lodged in the crooks of tree branches. They include ferns, orchids, peppers, and even cacti. The epiphytes are not parasites; they derive their nutrients from the rainwater coursing down the tree trunks to which they cling. Normally, rainwater alone contains insufficient nutrients to nourish a plant. But in the rain forest, as the rain splashes onto a leaf or dribbles down a stem, it absorbs organic and inorganic compounds from the surfaces of the plants or from excrement deposited by the many animal residents of the canopy. Thus, by the time a raindrop reaches one of the suspended epiphytes, it may have concentrations of nutrients such as nitrogen, phosphorus, and potassium that are anywhere from fifteen to sixty-five times higher than in normal rainwater. Some epiphytes— particularly the bromeliads, relatives of the pineapple—have evolved fleshy, waxy leaves that form a rosette which catches rainwater and organic debris that falls from the tree crowns farther up. Some of these reservoirs can hold as much as 10 gallons of water. These living cisterns have in turn become a home for frogs—and there are species that live only in certain bromeliads.

Other plants, such as the lianas that form an impassible tangle in parts of the Amazon, use larger trees as a ladder on which they climb toward the sun. Some of these coiled vines would measure up to 3,000 feet if straightened out. They have evolved some intricate strategies for reaching the sunlit heights. A botanist named Tom Ray studied the climbing behavior of a vine species with the ghoulish name *Monstera gigantea;* he found that as a seedling, this vine initially grows toward the *darkest* place within reach. Most of the time, the darkest spot in the forest is the base of the largest tree. Once the vine finds a tree, somehow it changes strategies and begins to seek sunlight.

Then there are the true parasitic plants, such as the strangler fig, which begins its life as an epiphyte high in the canopy where it first lodged as a seed excreted by a bird or monkey. The young plant unreels long, thin roots that resemble dangling bungee cords and spreads its parasol of leaves to catch the sun. If a root touches down in a spot relatively rich in leaf litter, the plant begins to thrive as nutrients get pumped up the roots. Quickly, more roots descend. Over a period of years, the thickening mass of dangling roots begins to fuse and can eventually completely encase the host tree, as if it had been dipped in cement. The mummified host dies and rots, providing a rich source of nutrients for the fig, which has made the transition from something you might see hanging in a macramé sling in a garden shop into a massive, 150-foot-tall giant.

To anyone from a temperate latitude, it is a bit startling to learn that a veteran tropical botanist can come upon an Amazonian tree and matter-of-factly state that he does not know its species. Yet it happens all the time, and it is a testament to the diversity of living things in a rain forest that such confusion still reigns. The Amazon is one of the few places on Earth where the description of a new species is not something to shout about. One icthyologist, Michael Goulding, has described 400 species of fish from the flooded forests around Manaus—a fifth of the 2,000 known Amazon fish species (and there may well be 3,000 or more in all). While the most diverse forests in the world's temperate zones, in Appalachia, have no more than 25 species of tree, one 2.5-acre plot of rain forest outside Manaus was found to harbor 414 tree species. And a single tree has been shown to hold 1,500 species of insect. The Amazon basin has 20 percent of the world's bird species. Overall, biologists have not even determined to a factor of ten how many species of plant, insect, fish, amphibian, reptile, bird, or mammal inhabit the Am-

azon basin. As recently as 1983, some were estimating that there are
1 million species of Amazonian plants and animals; more recent
estimates top 10 or 15 million.

Alfred Russel Wallace, the nineteenth-century evolutionary the-
orist and Amazon explorer, described the subtle complexity of
the Amazon forests in the book *Tropical Nature:* "If the traveller
notices a particular species and wishes to find more like it, he may
often turn his eyes in vain in every direction. Trees of varied forms,
dimensions and colors are around him, but he rarely sees any of
them repeated. Time after time he goes towards a tree which looks
like the one he seeks, but a closer examination proves it to be
distinct. He may at length, perhaps, meet with a second specimen
a half mile off, or he may fail altogether, till on another occasion he
stumbles on one by accident."

Wallace's point has since been borne out scientifically: although
there is an abundance of species, there is usually a paucity of individuals of each species. Moreover, a species may inhabit only a
tiny part of the total forest mosaic. In a study of rain forest plots
around Manaus, for example, forest tracts that were 50 miles from
each other shared only 1 percent of their species. It is this characteristic of the rain forest that has biologists so convinced that species
are becoming extinct each day. The felling of a few acres may
destroy all the individuals of a species, obliterating forever that bit
of Earth's archive of genetic possibilities.

Theories attempting to explain the origins of the biodiversity of
the Amazon have changed dramatically in the past couple of decades. Twenty years ago, it was common to see texts authoritatively
state that the richness of species in the tropical rain forest was due
primarily to the unchanging nature of the region. For 65 million
years, climatic conditions remained remarkably constant, the story
went, allowing organisms to evolve extremely specialized adapta-
tions to tight ecological niches that all fit together seamlessly, like
the pieces in a jigsaw puzzle. The Amazon rain forest was considered
a classic "climax" community, a system that had reached a pinnacle
of maturity, apportioning every resource, with not a leaf out of
place. Now, though, this concept has lost ground to a competing

theory that is almost its opposite: the species of the Amazon are numerous and diverse because the ecosystem is constantly in up-heaval—changing all the time and at every scale of time and geography.

On the greatest scale—that at which global geology changes—there may well have been a long stretch of time during the Cretaceous period, between 144 million and 65 million years ago, when the region now called the Amazon had a stable tropical climate. In fact, much of the planet's exposed land was covered by tropical forests during that period. Fossilized pollen grains have shown that tropical forest plants once thrived in Alaska, for example. That period also saw the evolution of the major families of plants. Then South America, North America, Africa, and other continental chunks—which had been joined into a single landmass—began to drift apart, causing the evolutionary paths of organisms on different continents to diverge as their environments diverged. The three major regions of rain forest today—the Amazon, equatorial Africa, and equatorial Asia—share many families and genera of plants and animals, possibly because those general types of organisms evolved before the continents moved away from one another. But only a few *species* of rain forest organisms exist on more than one continent. Thus, the explosion of species in the Amazon and other rain forests seems to have occurred fairly recently in geological time.

In the Amazon, the burst of species formation may have been the result of changes that started to take place late in the Miocene period, some 25 million years ago. The earth began to slide into a climatic cycle of ice ages and brief warming periods, a cycle that dramatically altered the face of the Northern Hemisphere. (Right now, we are at the end of a 9,000-year warm interlude.) During the ice ages, mile-thick glaciers scraped across the continents of the Northern Hemisphere. Even now, vestiges of the last ice age, which peaked just 22,000 years ago, persist; among them are the Great Lakes and Long Island, which is simply a big moraine, a great heap of dirt and rock that was pushed ahead of a glacier. Conditions changed in the tropics as well—not as drastically, but enough to have a substantial impact on life forms there. Affected by the gla-

ciers to the north, the climate of the Amazon basin periodically
became cooler and drier, perhaps twenty times or more, over the
past 3 million years.

Some scientists believe that with the onset of each ice age, the
cooling and drying of the Amazon caused savanna-like conditions
to spread and the rain forests to retreat. But one theory holds that
there were always some wet pockets, called refugia, in which the
basic rain forest ecosystem was able to persist. Wherever there was
sufficient rain and warmth, the churning biological engine of the
tropical forest was sustained, idling, ready to break out as soon as
favorable conditions expanded. Dispersed across the region, these
refugia contained similar stocks of plants and animals. Because
there was no genetic mixing among refugia, over time each group
of animals and plants evolved along an independent pathway.
Much of the support for the refugia theory comes from studies of
the variations in wing patterns of passion-flower butterflies and the
variations in color schemes in toucans, the resplendent family of
fruit-eating birds with oversize beaks. As warm, moist conditions
returned to the entire basin, all these types of insect, plant, and
animal could colonize new terrain, evolving further to suit new
niches, then bumping up against their now-different counterparts
from other refugia. The result is a mosaic of variations on themes.

On the regional scale, variation in species in the Amazon was
probably promoted by the disastrous floods that occasionally seem
to have swept over vast areas of the basin. Kenneth Campbell, at
the Natural History Museum of Los Angeles County, has been
studying sediments in western Acre; he posits that this part of the
Amazon was hit by an enormous mass of water that may have
broken through some temporary glacial dike in the Andes. By
scouring large areas, such events would have created a clean slate
upon which species would be jogged into competing and adapting
to new conditions.

On the local scale, rivers are constantly changing their course,
eating their way crabwise through the forest, destroying established
biological communities ahead of them and creating new opportunities as shallow silty beaches are deposited in their wake. Boats

navigating on Amazonian rivers constantly scrape against the submerged trunks of massive rain forest trees, whose shallow roots have been undermined by the water's steady advance. On the upper reaches of the Juruá River, a traveler is likely to meet *ribeirinhos*— the farmers who live by the river and plant their corn and beans on the rich silt exposed during the dry season. One such farmer is Manuel de Caro de Souza. He had to move his entire house and manioc mill twice in ten years to stay near the river, which was shifting away from his tract 30 feet each year.

Another phenomenon that can disrupt a biological community at the local scale is the occasional windstorm. The Amazon almost never sees the tornadoes and other violent storm conditions that sweep North America when a cold front clashes with warm air. But every few years a strong *friagem,* cold front, makes it all the way up to the tropics from Antarctica. When such a weather front barrels through, it can topple trees and rend the normally tightly knit forest canopy. Again, animals and plants are thrown into an unbalanced situation that favors change. In August 1989, Xapuri lost much of its tin roofing in a sudden blast that was stronger than any wind the townsfolk could remember. Such gusts can reshape a forest, even if they occur only once a century.

Finally, there is the scale of the reach of an individual tree. When a tree falls, it can create in microcosm the same kind of disruption caused by a strong storm. Such tree falls may be a crucial element in shaping the mix of species in the forest. A tropical forestry scientist named Gary Hartshorn studied tree-fall rates around the tropics and found that in many areas, the time it takes for a section of forest to be completely replaced can be as little as eighty years. The overall effect is that the forest is perpetually off kilter, in a continual state of recovery but never quite returning to some inanimate state—a condition that opens up opportunities and lets no organism settle too comfortably into a static niche. And it creates a kind of biological disarray that is bound to mystify scientists.

There is ultimately something about the elaborate, evanescent kaleidoscope of life in the tropical rain forest that almost taunts biologists who attempt to master it. Generations of scientists have

been lured by the biological marvels of the Amazon. Those with
the hubris to go home convinced that they have solved the region's
riddles almost invariably end up humbled. The better ones go away
with more questions than they had when they arrived. The closer
one gets, the more intertwined things become. Brush against a slim
plant on the forest floor and a flood of biting red ants streams from
the plant's hollow stems, ready to kill anything that might attack.
The plant's defenders are rewarded with a specialized home and
feeding center that sustains them.

When one comes across a three-toed sloth, a slow-moving vege-
tarian mammal of the canopy, one is struck by its greenish cast,
which is imparted by the algae that live in its matted fur, along with
several dozen species of mite, moth, and other organisms. The sloth
has an odd habit: rather than defecating randomly from its perch
—like monkeys and birds—once a week or so, it descends to the
ground and deposits its feces in a hole it digs near the base of the
tree in which it spends the most time. Perhaps this strategy has
evolved as a way of returning some of the nutrients it took from the
tree by eating its leaves. Whatever the reason, it must be pretty
important; venturing onto the forest floor is a risky business for an
animal that can barely drag itself across a flat surface. Thus, the sloth
itself is an almost incomprehensibly intricate biological system.

Fifty miles from Manaus, scientists have taken 250 acres of rain
forest and imposed a Cartesian grid on it. Every 65 feet they planted
a plastic pipe in the ground. Each pipe is identified by a letter and
a number, instantly telling visitors where they are. As various teams
of botanists, mammalogists, entomologists, and other specialists
come through, they are mapping the location of individual organisms. One palm specialist, Andrew Henderson, from the New York
Botanical Garden, spent three weeks counting 6,476 palms, of 29
species, in just 25 acres. His goal was to understand the distribution
of the species in light of underlying conditions, such as soil type
and elevation. One could only wish him luck and endurance. Even
if he came to understand that tiny slice of Amazonia, he might not
know much about the next slice, let alone a piece of forest on the
far side of the basin. When Henderson later traveled up the Moa

River in the westernmost part of the state of Acre, in a matter of days he counted 69 species of palm. Just a few hundred miles away, he was in an entirely different biological galaxy.

Until the murder of Chico Mendes, Acre was off the beaten track for most scientists. Research had generally been concentrated along the main branches of the Amazon, which were relatively accessible. When the killing drew attention to the rubber tappers' proposal for extractive reserves, the remote state suddenly became something of a Mecca for botanists and graduate students studying everything from palm tree diversity to the woman's role in rubber tapper society. In the summer of 1989, there were so many foreign researchers in the area that disgruntled ranchers began to spread rumors that female American graduate students were prancing naked through the forest and having sex with tappers.

Douglas Daly's students were doing no such thing. On a hot morning in the dry season eight months after Chico Mendes's death, Daly—a colleague of Andrew Henderson's from the New York Botanical Garden—led a group of graduate students and government technicians into the rain forest a few miles up the road from Xapuri. Daly's group was part of a larger, twenty-day course on tropical ecology funded by American organizations ranging from the U.S. Fish and Wildlife Service to the Jessie Smith Noyes Foundation, a private philanthropic organization that supports environmental activities in Latin America. Like Daly, most of the other teachers were American. Oddly, Americans and Europeans have been teaching Brazilians about Amazonian biology for many years. Until recently, Brazil focused most of its funding for scientific research on applied sciences such as agronomy and electrical engineering; tropical biology was merely an incidental pursuit, supported only to the extent that it furthered research in cocoa or rubber cultivation. It is only the wealthy, developed nations that have had the luxury of funding pure research.

Daly and his students were dropped off by bus at the entrance to a 25,000-acre rubber tapping estate called Seringal Triunfo, about 40 miles from the network of trails where Chico Mendes once tapped rubber trees and organized the fight for the forest. It was forested tracts such as this one that Mendes had hoped to convert to protected extractive reserves. The other students in the course had been split into small teams. One group went by boat up the Abunã River, which is part of the Bolivian border in eastern Acre, to observe birds; another headed off in search of monkeys and marmosets; a third took several dozen small cage traps into the forest to survey the population of small, ground-dwelling mammals. The plan was for all of the students and teachers to go over their findings that evening back at a bar in the border town of Plácido de Castro.

Daly and his team would spend the day identifying plants, particularly those that were useful as food or had possible medicinal properties. They began by hiking to the *barracão,* the central compound of the rubber estate. They were met by two tappers who, for $2 apiece, would act as guides for the day. The compound seemed rundown, and there was little rubber in sight. The group was told that the owner was not concerned about falling rubber production; his main goal these days was to let time pass. The value of the property was steadily rising, and soon he could sell it at a huge profit to a rancher or investor who would cut down the forest. This *barracão* was something of a zoological garden, very much of the inhumane kind. One wooden cage held several monkeys. Two adult jaguars, caught as cubs but now well over 100 pounds each, paced in a cramped stockade built of heavy wooden posts and shaded by a thatch roof. One of the spotted cats scowled and screamed and raked a broad paw at the air between two posts. Despite the rush of roads and deforestation, jaguars were still fairly common in eastern Acre, although the only ones you were likely to see were in captivity.

The clearing was achingly bright and shimmered in the 90-degree heat, even though it was only eight o'clock in the morning. The blond grasses and red earth were bleached and desiccated. One tapper, a slim, dark man named Ilson, took the lead. Daly and the rest followed, and the second guide brought up the rear. The class left the scorching pasture and plunged into the forest. The effect was like diving into the sea after baking on a tropical beach. The temperature instantly dropped ten degrees and the abrupt change from light to shade hurt everyone's eyes as tightly constricted pupils were suddenly forced to dilate. As the students' eyes adjusted to the dimness, their minds too began to adjust, very slowly, to the landscape.

It was the dry season now. Leaves crackled underfoot as the group hiked along one of the *estradas,* rubber trails, that were hacked out of the forest by the tappers to get from one rubber tree to another. Fine red dust covered the foliage on each side of the trail, and unseen snakes and lizards scuttled loudly away from their basking spots as the group passed. The trail wound over humps and down into gullies. Each low spot was slightly damp, and dazzling butterflies congregated on the moist mud, lapping up leached mineral salts with their proboscises, which unrolled like tiny New Year's Eve party favors. Every hundred yards or so, the students passed a rubber tree, whose bark bore the corrugated marks created by year after year of cuts from a special tapper's knife, a *faca de seringa.* Periodically, Daly stopped to ask Ilson the tappers' name for a certain plant or to make a point to the class.

Daly considered Ilson a true *mateiro,* a master woodsman. If he did not recognize a tree instantly, he sliced lightly into the bark with his machete and broke off a sliver. He sniffed the wood and examined any fluid that oozed out. One tree, *limãozinho,* had a distinctive lemony fragrance. When the papery bark was peeled from another tree, it smelled like garlic. Tropical cedar emitted the familiar pungence of its northern cousins, although it had a very different shape, with sweeping buttresses—winglike masses of wood that jut out around the tree base—that are thought to provide structural support in lieu of deep roots. Ilson claimed that the forest contained *pau brasil,* brazilwood, which quickly blushes to a deep red color after it is cut. But there Daly disagreed. True *pau brasil,* he said, existed only in the coastal rain forests of Brazil, which once ran in an unbroken swath from São Paulo to Rio. It was this tree that gave the country its name. During the colonial era, the sixteenth through eighteenth centuries, brazilwood was heavily harvested for the valuable purple dye that could be extracted. Now the tree, and the coastal forests themselves, are all but extinct.

Daly was a slim sprite of a man and wore slightly crooked gold-framed glasses. His twelve years of experience in the Amazon showed in his wardrobe, which was perfect for the jungle: light cotton trousers, heavy boots, and a long-sleeve shirt, to keep the insects at bay. His pack seemed too large for his body; he carried a camera and a tripod as well. A student carried a press for botanical specimens—wooden racks held together by straps—and a pile of old Acre newspapers. On the top of the stack was a picture of a bikini-clad contestant in the upcoming beauty pageant sponsored by the state bank of Acre, Banacre. The newspapers would be placed between the samples of stems, flowers, and seeds that would be squeezed and later dried in the racks.

After an hour of hiking, it was time for the first break. Ilson took off his sweat-stained baseball cap and retrieved the crumpled pack of cigarettes tucked inside. He lit one, then crouched down on his haunches. A student asked him about some hard brown pods he had found in the leaf litter. Ilson said, "Aricuri." He picked up one of the pods—it was about the size and shape of a small cigar—and set it on a half-buried tree root. It rattled slightly. "Delicious," he said, smiling. Then he took out his machete and, steadying the nut with his left hand, began lopping at one end with the heavy blade, precisely missing his fingertips by a fraction of an inch despite his hammerlike strokes. The pod's fibrous coat was remarkably tough. Once he had cut his way through, three cavities could be seen running the length of the pod, one held dense white nut meat; two were hollow but rattled. Ilson tapped the end of the pod with his palm and out popped two small, pale, leathery grubs. Called *gongo,* they have the texture of a roasted chestnut and take on the flavor of the nuts on which they subsist. Tappers prefer to pick out the slightly rotten nuts and eat the grubs; the nuts themselves are simply too hard to extract from the pods.

The class resumed its hike, and soon Daly had the familiar experience of coming upon a tree that he could not even place in a family, let alone a genus or species. It was time for the first arboreal ascent of the day. He sat down, unhitched his backpack, and pulled out a pair of tree-climbing irons—curved, pronged pieces of metal. He strapped them onto each foot with the prongs facing inward so that he could get up "where all the action is"—into the canopy. In the rain forest, it is only in the canopy, where the flowers and fruit are, that you can start to tell the trees apart. The trunks are often quite similar, frequently with a smooth bark that provides no easy foothold for parasitic plants. The leaves, too, are often nearly identical. Many rain forest trees, even those from disparate families, have oblong leaves with shiny surfaces and a sharp point called a drip tip; both features encourage rainwater to slide off the leaf quickly, keeping nutrients from leaching away.

The tropical forest canopy poses harrowing challenges to the most adventurous of biologists. In addition to its great height, it is thick with marauding columns of ants, clouds of stinging wasps, and venomous spiders and snakes, among other pests. Investigators have tried to use systems of gondolas, catwalks, and pulleys—even hot-air balloons, which could be set down atop the canopy—but all of these strategies are either too dangerous, too limited, or too disruptive to the ecosystem to be of great use. Even so, scientists keep trying new tactics; one team in Panama has proposed using a construction crane to lower a gondola into the forest. But many still rely on that old standby—climbing.

Daly started to clamber up a tree, ignoring a thin rivulet of ants. He had a loop of rope around himself and the tree and alternated moving one foot up, then rising, shifting the rope up, then moving the other foot. He had to ascend about 50 feet before he got to the first branches—and this was a small tree, whose top lay in the middle zone of the canopy. Daly had just about disappeared into the foliage when he found what he was looking for: a branch with fruit on it. A hack of a knife sent the branch floating gently to the ground. It was only later, when the samples were hauled back to Rio Branco, that the tree, with its small, tart orange fruit, was identified as *Lacunaria,* in the Quiinaceae family.

Daly descended the tree and led his class deeper into the forest.

Suddenly they came to a place where the shadows gave way to a blinding patch of sunlight. In the depths of a rain forest, it is easy to forget about the sun. The canopy, whose leaves have fifteen times the surface area of the forest floor below, efficiently catches most of the sun's rays. As a result, the patch of light ahead—the result of a recent tree fall—was almost startling. Insects floated like white sparks against the surrounding black shadows. Daly and his students broke into dripping sweats as they clambered onto the broad trunk of the fallen giant and felt the day's blast-furnace heat. Teetering along the trunk was the only way to get across the chaotic mass of thorny undergrowth. A false step surely would result in ripped flesh and a broken ankle. Here was the dynamic, unbalanced forest in action. Vines and runners and small shrubs were exploding in a tangle of photosynthetic action, sparked by the unfamiliar but welcome touch of the full intensity of the sun. Insects and animals were feasting on the verdant new shoots.

Near the end of the day, as the class began to swing back through the forest toward the central compound, two students lagged behind and sat silently while the rest moved ahead along a trail. The forest closed in around them, and soon there were no human sounds. A breeze stirred some branches high above, and the slow, steady drizzle of leaves and flower petals turned into a shower for a brief moment. Vaguely, clouds could be seen drifting above the canopy. The occasional call of a rain forest bird echoed through the trees. A *seringueiro* bird sang its hypnotic, three-note song. It was a simple minor-key *do-re-mi* that was repeated at odd intervals and sometimes had an extra silent beat thrown in—*do . . . re-mi.* The tone was that of Pan pipes, ethereal, sourceless, and soft. Earlier in the day, several students had found themselves absentmindedly whistling an imitation.

The puffy cumulus clouds grew taller and taller, as if someone were making an extra large ice cream cone. The clouds were growing as they always do in the afternoon, when the sun causes millions of tons of water to evaporate from the forest below. The evaporation from the leaves helps keep the forest cool, just as the evaporation of sweat from your body keeps you from frying in the summer sun.

Distant, muffled thunder added to the faint music of the rustling leaves and bird calls and the steady trill of cicadas and other insects. Even in the dry season, sooner or later several of these mountains of mist always burst. Sure enough, a brief torrent of dime-size raindrops soon battered the canopy. Down on the forest floor, the rain was hardly perceptible. Almost all of the water was intercepted by leaves and branches and epiphytes. There is often a ten-minute delay between the time a downpour starts and the time water actually begins to hit the forest floor.

As the shower passed, there was a scattering of high-pitched chirps from the canopy. But they were not from birds. A half-dozen slim, tan monkeys leaped through the treetops. "*Saguinus labiatus*," said one of the students. These skilled climbers, with their prehensile tails acting as a fifth limb, sought their sustenance up where the sun was creating new growth.

Then a different sound intruded, a distant, grinding roar that grew louder and louder. Gears clashed as someone fought with a truck's balky clutch. Ten more minutes of walking brought the class to another blaze of sunlight. This time it was no tiny tear in the forest fabric, but a straight, sharp rip that started over a hill and disappeared toward the opposite horizon: a new road through the heart of the forest. It had been graded flat so that it ran through a shallow canyon as it cut across the variegated topography of that part of eastern Acre. A notched tree trunk made a ladder that the students clung to as they descended to the road.

The pavement was black and broiling. The class crossed the road and picked up the trail on the other side. They spent another hour hiking through thickets and swampy spots and one remarkably tall stand of virgin forest that was dense with rubber and Brazil nut trees. They cut through a tangle of *taboca*—a spiny, bamboo vine —and drank some of the pure water that flowed from the slashes in the woody tubes. Eventually they made their way to the *barracão* and guzzled tepid soda.

That night, in Plácido de Castro, they traded stories with the other teams over Antarctica beer and plates of rice, beef, fish, and beans. The mammal team had found seven different types of shrew-

like animal in one acre and could not place four of them in a genus,
let alone species. Others got out their botanical and wildlife guides
and debated Latin names and seed types. As the researchers talked
on, one of the exhausted boys who had been serving food and drink
since six that morning suddenly grabbed a broom and started slapping at something on the wall behind Douglas Daly. It was a fleeting
gray form about four inches long. With a quick lunge of the broom
handle, the boy knocked it from the wall and then squashed it. One
of the scientists who had jumped up gave it a quick look. "*Pho-
neutria*'s the genus," he said. "One of the most venomous spiders
in Brazil."

The life ebbed out of the conversation. The mood had already
been soured after someone brought up the subject of the blisteringly
hot asphalt of the road they had come upon during their walk.
Something about the shallow red canyon that the bulldozers had
carved into the earth did not leave them. The students understood
now why the *seringal* was run-down, why many of the scars on the
rubber trees were growing over and others were encrusted with
sun-cured ribbons of aging latex. They knew now why no stacks of
rubber were seen on the veranda of the *barracão*. With the coming
of the road, the owner no longer cared about a few tons of rubber
or nuts. Now the value of the property would skyrocket, just as it
had wherever a road had been cut into the forests of the Amazon,
offering profits of 400, 600, and not uncommonly 1,000 percent.
The future of those towering trees, the chirping monkeys, the
Lacunaria, and the *gongo* was sealed. The road determined the fate
of that land as assuredly as a diagnosis of AIDS dictated the fate of
a man.

Chapter 3
Weeping Wood

SINCE EUROPEAN EXPLORERS first confronted the daunting expanse of the Amazon, the region's thick forests have been perceived as shielding a hidden treasure. The carving of roads into this tropical wilderness in recent decades has merely been a continuation of centuries-old efforts to exploit its presumed richness. The only people who made no effort to dominate the land were the Indians, who arrived some ten thousand years before the white men, spreading southward from the isthmus of Panama, sticking to the highlands first, then infiltrating the depths of the rain forest. Hundreds of independent Indian cultures evolved. Somewhere between three and five million Indians in all were scattered throughout the Amazon, hunting, fishing, cultivating pumpkin, corn, manioc, and many other crops, and harvesting cocoa, palm and Brazil nuts, medicines, resins, and other products from the forest.

With a relatively low population density, they had little destructive impact on the surrounding ecosystem. Despite regular harvests, the rivers were still thick with turtles. Small plots were slashed and burned for farming, then intentionally abandoned to nature before the fragile soil was damaged. Deposits of charcoal have been found buried almost everywhere that scientists have looked, implying that much of the Amazon has burned at one time or another, but in small enough doses that the forest has recovered. In some areas, such as Pará in the eastern Amazon, unusually dense stands of Brazil nut trees are thought to have been planted by the Indians, supporting the theory that they were—and in some areas still are —sophisticated managers of the forest, not merely opportunistic gatherers. It was this lifestyle and ethic that were later passed on to the rubber tappers and formed the basis of the extractive reserves that Chico Mendes promoted.

In the first half of the sixteenth century, when Europeans began to venture into the basin, the light touch of the Indians quickly gave way to the heavy hand of the conquistadors. After the conquest of the Incas by Francisco Pizarro in 1532, myths sprung up that the wealth of this Andean civilization paled beside that which might be found in the mist-shrouded forests to the east. There, an Indian kingdom with a capital called El Dorado was said to be ruled by a monarch who was anointed daily with fragrant oil, then dusted with powdered gold. He was reputed to bathe in a spring, the bottom of which was encrusted with gold dust that had washed from his body. The forests were fragrant with the coveted spice cinnamon. Pizarro's brother Gonzalo, along with Francisco de Orellana, led an expeditionary force in 1541 down the eastern slope of the Andes to seek out and conquer this hidden empire and plunder it for spices and gold. The main force of the expedition was bogged down as it attempted to cross the frustrating network of rivers that covers the basin. Eventually, Pizarro was defeated by the jungle, which provided constant obstacles and little food. As the Spaniards resorted to boiling their belts and found their Indian bearers deserting, Orellana and a crew of fifty forged ahead on several small boats to find food. They never returned; later Orellana was branded a "despicable traitor" by Pizarro, who retraced his steps back to Peru.

Orellana had continued downstream, making what turned out to be the first descent of the great river system by a European. It was this expedition that led to the name "Amazon," after an account of the trip was published by Friar Caspar de Carvajal, who accompanied Orellana. Among myriad accounts of battles and extraordinary adventures—in which hyperbole and fact were inextricably mixed—he claimed that they had encountered fierce Indian tribes in which women directed the battle and clubbed to death any warrior who might be tempted to flee. As he recounted, "These women are very white and tall, and have hair very long and braided and wound about the head, and they are very robust and go about naked [but] with their privy parts covered, with their bows and arrows in their hands, doing as much fighting as ten Indian men, and indeed there was one woman among these who shot an arrow a span deep into one of the brigantines, and others less deep, so that our brigantines looked like porcupines." The resemblance to the Amazons of Western mythology was noted, and the name stuck.

Unfortunately, the shrubs containing a cinnamon-like essence were dispersed throughout the forest—following a pattern set by many plant species in the rain forest, where insects can overwhelm plants of one kind that are too closely packed. And no city of gold was ever found. That did not discourage future generations of explorers from hacking their way into the forests. It took more than two centuries for the myth to wear thin.

The conquistadors were followed in the eighteenth century by the *bandeirantes,* Brazilian pioneers who fanned out from the southern city of São Paulo in search of slaves, gold, and simply the glory of expanding Portugal's holdings. By the nineteenth century, the original concept of El Dorado had been tempered into a more figurative pot of gold; great profits could be reaped in the burgeoning trade in turtle oil, Brazil nuts, cocoa, fragrant oils and rare woods, and minerals (gold was finally found, although not in so convenient a form as the original explorers had hoped). Many forest products were brought to light by the hundreds of Indian cultures in the region. The Indians showed the white people the strong fibers of jute, the elastic gum called chicle, which formed the original base of chewing gum, and quinine, the first remedy for malaria. In his 1847 account *A Voyage up the River Amazon, Including a Residence at Pará,* the American naturalist William H. Edwards described the brisk river trade: "Coarse German and English dry goods, Lowell shirtings, a few descriptions of hardware, Salem soap, beads, needles, and a few other fancy articles, constitute a trader's stock. In return are brought down balsam, gums, wax, drugs, turtle-oil, tobacco, fish and hammocks."

By the mid-nineteenth century, the Amazon had become a favorite collecting spot for "naturalists"—a new breed of scientist-adventurer. Most of them were self-taught generalists, eager to explore and classify the natural world and attempt to comprehend the laws governing its workings. Among this peripatetic band were Charles Darwin and Alfred Russel Wallace—whose intellectual competition would produce the theory of natural selection—Richard Spruce, and Henry Walter Bates. It was Edwards's book that sparked Bates and Wallace, both in their twenties, to make their famous collecting foray to the Amazon a year later. After four years without serious mishap, Wallace sailed for England, but his ship burned and foundered. He himself survived, although his thousands of specimens and notes were lost. Bates returned to England after eleven years in the Amazon, with a collection totaling 14,712 species, 14,000 of them insects. Some 8,000 species had never before been described in Europe. Bates was paid the equivalent of 20 cents apiece for thousands of his insects; he estimated that he cleared only a few hundred dollars after more than a decade's work —not that it mattered. The naturalists had come for biological riches, not financial ones. For this group, the Amazon was a different kind of El Dorado altogether. It was, according to Edwards, "the garden of the world."

Despite the increasing attention from both scientists and merchants, the Amazon remained a lazy, undeveloped backwater. Products were collected upstream by Indians and a scattering of *ribeirinhos,* families who settled along the river. The harvest then made its way to civilization via a tenuous chain of peddlers and middlemen. Almost nothing was cultivated, and then only for local consumption. There was no urge to develop the area because southern and coastal Brazil still provided enormous stretches of fertile farmland.

The second great wave of change came over the Amazon late in the nineteenth century, all because of an inconspicuous tree whose only distinguishing characteristic is that it bleeds a milky white sap when its soft bark is scratched. The 100-foot-tall rubber tree, with waxy leaves and a soft bark, is a member of the euphorbiaceae family, which includes species ranging from manioc—the starchy root, also known as cassava or tapioca, that has spread through much of the tropical world—to the poinsettias that decorate shopping malls at Christmas.

The exudate, called latex, is thought to have evolved as a protection against termites and other boring insects. It flows through laticifers, fine tubules a half inch or so beneath the bark. When something invades the bark and breaks this layer—be it a termite or the blade of a *faca de seringa*—the tree immediately begins to bleed. Along with its gummy quality, which can quickly clog the mouth of an invading insect, the latex also has natural insecticidal properties. Like other plants that inhabit regions where nutrients are scarce and threats are many, the tree expends a lot of energy producing this chemical defense. It is analogous to a country's defense forces—expensive and rarely used, but crucial to survival.

Latex is a polymer of isoprene, which is a hydrocarbon, a molecule comprised solely of carbon and hydrogen atoms—just like oil, natural gas, and the cellulose making up this book. "Polymer" means that many isoprene units are linked together in chains. The fluid remains a liquid when the chains are short, but it starts to thicken when reactions with air and heat or the addition of chemicals cause more isoprene units to join a chain. In coagulated latex, the average is five thousand links per chain. These chains, in turn, are coiled, nested, and woven together; here and there, they are tacked to each other by weak bonds. The tight coils and cross links give a hunk of coagulated latex its remarkable elasticity. When tugged, the coiled molecular chains will stretch to more than twice their length, but the cross-linked chains ensure that when the tension is released, the molecules will revert to their original shape.

Dozens of species in at least six other families of tropical plants have evolved similar systems of chemical weaponry to defend themselves in the endless battle that is tropical existence. For cen-

turies, the Indians had used the latex exuded by a variety of plants
to make everything from unbreakable bottles to torches, shoes to
soccer balls. But it was mainly *Hevea brasiliensis* that suited the
white man's needs. By the end of the nineteenth century, what had
once been an obscure substance harvested by a handful of Indians
had become one of the essential ingredients for the automotive and
electrical power industries and one of the underpinnings of the accelerating industrial revolution. Eventually, a trillion dollars' worth
of rubber was extracted from the Amazon. It was rubber that created Xapuri and almost every other settlement in the far reaches of
the basin. In the process, it created one of the strangest, most brutal
forms of labor exploitation in modern history.

The entire history of the rubber trade seemed to hang in the dusty
air of Guilherme Zaire's warehouse, which was on the waterfront
in Chico Mendes's hometown. The air smelled strongly of smoked
latex, an aroma that initially had a pleasant, tarry pungency but
after an hour or so tended to numb the nose. Zaire, who for forty
years had been one of the leading rubber merchants in Acre, sat
just inside the heavy wooden door that was swung wide open,
allowing a few rays of the afternoon sun to penetrate deep into the
dim interior. He smiled as he recounted his long involvement with
this strange, wonderful substance with many uses and just as many
names: *borracha, seringa, caoutchouc.*
 Zaire had also had a long career in local politics, including stints
as state representative and mayor of Xapuri. He was born in Xapuri in 1921 to a Syrian father and an Italian mother. "My father
was a *regatão*," he said, a river peddler. (The word has its roots in
the Portuguese word for "haggle" or "bargain," *regatear.*) "He came
rowing up the river in a canoe in 1903, right around the time Acre
was conquered by Brazil." Zaire sat behind his heavy wooden desk,
which came up close to his armpits, and sketched the shape of Acre
on his blotter. The skin on his hands was pale, almost transparent,
but his nose suffered from an excess of tropical sun and was swollen
and reddened and precancerous. His gray eyes, enlarged by thick

bifocals, were the same shade as his silver hair, which he combed straight back and slicked down to his scalp.

As he spoke, he kept an eye on the parade of laborers who made a steady circuit from the dimly lit depths of the building out into the bright sun, each balancing a 100-pound slab or ball of natural rubber on his head with his arms up at each side, centering the load. The stronger workers tended to carry the slabs, because they could stack them on their heads and heft two or even three at a time. Their neck muscles and blood vessels bulged. Under the strain, one man's face puckered like Dizzy Gillespie hitting high C. Some of the men sweated profusely, while the dark skin of others had a dry, satiny sheen.

They were loading a heavy flatbed truck with rubber that had been brought into town by riverboat from the rubber estates all around Xapuri. As each worker approached the truck, he stepped onto a plank that rested on a chunk of rubber. The rubber compressed a little, giving the man a bit of a springy boost as he grunted and heaved his load over the side of the truck and onto the growing pile in back. There was little small talk. The only sounds were the steady shuffle of thongs and callused feet on the worn, shiny cement floor, the creak of the springy plank, the grunt, and the dull thud as another chunk of rubber was sent on its way down the dusty highway to a factory in Rondônia, the rapidly developing state to the south where the forest was falling at a record pace. Thirty-three thousand pounds of rubber were to be loaded today, and no one was taking it slowly.

Zaire drew what looked like a stretched-out *W* with a line across the top—something like the open wings of a butterfly. The strange shape of the state had been sculpted by the struggle for rubber. In the mid-1800s, Acre was Bolivian territory, with the straight line on the *W* being the border with Brazil. The border was simply drawn because much of the region at that time was still terra incognita. In fact, the western end of the line was only an approximation because no one had charted the headwaters of the Javari River, which separated Brazil and Bolivia from their common neighbor, Peru. It was unknown because no one had much of a reason to be there—at least until the rubber boom began.

As the demand for rubber crested in the latter half of the nineteenth century, Brazilian rubber tappers swarmed into the region. Word had spread that the valleys of Acre's two main rivers, the Purus and Juruá, were the best places in all Amazonia for rubber trees. Toward the end of the century, Bolivia made plans to exert more control over this far-flung territory. The tappers resisted and booted out the Bolivian tax collectors; in 1903, the territory was turned over to Brazil in return for a cash payment and a promise to build a railroad bypassing rapids that denied Bolivia convenient access to the Amazon River system.

Another part of Acre's anatomy was also shaped by this struggle. One of the rivers forming the border with Peru—the lower edge of the left butterfly wing—is something of a natural boundary between the species of rubber tree tapped by Brazilian *seringueiros* and a different type of rubber tree that was harvested by *caucheros*, Spanish-speaking rubber harvesters. South of the Breu River, the *caucheros* harvested latex from *caucho* trees by ringing the bark completely or even chopping the tree down, draining 100 pounds of latex in one operation—but killing the tree in the process. (*Breu*, meaning tar, is the Brazilian term for this different type of rubber tree.) The *caucheros* were aggressive itinerants, who left their families behind and scoured the forests. North of the river, Brazilian *seringueiros* settled in one place and tapped latex in a way that allowed a tree to live a long , healthy life. The tappers thus established strong ties to the land. In this way, the Breu became a battle line, defended staunchly by the *seringueiros*.

The legacy of this history is that in Acre, unlike in any other state in Brazil, the mainstay of the economy has always been rubber. The whole state is occupied by tappers. Flying over the forest, you see a scattering of small clearings, each the home of a tapper.

As the parade of rubber through the warehouse continued, Zaire talked and sketched, adding to his map the courses of the Juruá and the Purus. The Juruá and its many tributaries drain the western wing of the state, flowing north to join the main trunk of the

Amazon. The Purus leaves the state at its midsection, but all its tributaries, including the Acre, drain the eastern wing. Before a highway to Rondônia was cut through the forest, these two rivers were the only two ways to get to Acre, Zaire explained.

His father headed up the Purus and settled for a time in Bôca do Acre (Mouth of the Acre), then pushed on to Xapuri. "My father came to the Amazon because, in Syria, they said it was El Dorado." He set up shop and began buying rubber from the surrounding rubber estates and selling dry goods and other imported supplies that were brought upriver from Manaus and Belém. "There were lots of traders, mostly Syrian, Portuguese, and a few Japanese. At that time, an English company controlled the whole network of rivers. The big, wood-burning steamships would come up the river every January," Zaire said. That was when the rivers rose 30 or 40 feet above their average depth, swollen by the deluges of the rainy season. "In March, they'd make a second trip. We would get supplies for the whole year because soon the river would drop." If a pilot miscalculated the season or there was an unexpected change in the depth, a ship would become stranded for an entire season. "Sometimes, six or seven ships would get stuck in the mud."

Zaire was the only one of three sons who followed his father into the river trade. One brother became a lawyer, the other a rancher. Zaire had received a degree in accounting in Belém and was also studying medicine, but when his father had a stroke in 1943, he took over the business. One of the rubber estates he controlled was Cachoeira, where Chico Mendes had grown up and come of age. Zaire had known Mendes since he was a child, and when Mendes moved out of the forest and into Xapuri in 1971, it was Zaire who gave him his first job—as a salesman in his shop. Seeing that Mendes was keenly interested in politics, Zaire played a key role in launching Mendes's political career as well. In 1977 he sponsored Mendes, along with two other employees, as a candidate for the town council. It is an indication of Zaire's power in the town that they all were elected.

As he reminisced and watched his workers load the rubber, he could not help but smile, displaying a Cheshire cat grin that exposed small, even teeth. Zaire had had a good run of it. When rubber was bad, Brazil nuts were good. There was always something to be traded, some way to make money. He had a daughter living in Santa Barbara, California, a place he had visited twice—"such a beautiful city," he said. He had also been to New York and Las Vegas, and he traveled frequently to Rio de Janeiro. He wore a Rolex watch. Along with the stacks of rubber, his warehouse bulged with canned goods and dry goods bound for the rubber estates. Zaire also had a coffee exporting business as well as several other investments in Rio Branco. In general, rubber merchants are both hated and tolerated by tappers. They are seen as exploitative plunderers but also as the only link to distant markets. In Xapuri, Zaire somehow avoided being reviled. Everyone considered him to be a fair man.

For three hours straight, the laborers made their mesmerizing circuit in and out of the warehouse. As Zaire talked, the piles of rubber in the back room shrank and the mountain on the truck blocked the sun. The pile of rubber quivered slightly as each new ball tumbled into place.

The look, feel, and smell of the hunks of smoked latex seemed antiquated, anachronistic. It was a material from another time, but in the Amazon all times overlap. Here, rubber tappers still live as they did in the nineteenth century while ranchers hop to their properties in sleek, twin-engine planes and watch television via satellite. The different eras not only overlap but are tightly linked. This latex, collected from trees dotting the world's least trammeled forest—collected in the same way for a hundred and twenty years—was going into automobiles and surgical gloves, even into the tires of the space shuttle.

Zaire was tiring of the rubber trade. "The risk is very high, and you're not guaranteed anything," he said. "It's not like it used to be." He hoped to have his *seringal* disappropriated by the government and turned into an extractive reserve. "To me, the land is worthless. I can't sell it to a rancher, because it only has value to a rancher if it's deforested. And no rancher wants to buy land that has tappers on it because there will be a fight to get them out. My

money is made by selling the product, not the land itself." This
was exactly the point that Chico Mendes had tried to make—the
point that got him killed. "All this trouble, just over rubber," Zaire
said.

The workers were done now, and in the back room they splashed
themselves down with buckets of water drawn from a cistern. After
the accounts were tallied, the heavy Mercedes diesel fired up, and
the truck rumbled on its way up the rough, cobbled lane toward
the road to Rondônia, the dark, resinous load jiggling back and
forth.

The unlikely transformation of a tree's natural insect repellent into
the white gold of the rubber boom began nearly five hundred years
ago. European explorers in the New World began making sporadic
anecdotal references to the Indians' use of a bouncy, resilient material derived from juices bled from trees. But the first scientific
appraisal of the material did not occur until 1736. As with many
scientific discoveries, the first study of rubber was a serendipitous
digression from an assigned mission. An expedition had been sent
to South America by the French Royal Academy of Sciences to
resolve a debate about the shape of the earth: Newton's law of
gravitation predicted that the planet should not be a perfect sphere,
but rather somewhat flattened at the poles and fat at the equator.
The idea was to make precise celestial measurements along the
equator and then compare them with measurements taken by a
team of scientists at the Arctic Circle, deep in Lapland.

Charles Marie de La Condamine, a thirty-five-year-old geographer and naturalist, and Pierre Bouguer, a thirty-eight-year-old
astronomer, mathematician, and hydrographer, planned to head
inland from the Peruvian coast to accomplish the equatorial end of
the task. The two men stayed for several weeks at a village at the
river mouth, waiting for their guides to arrive. They remarked on
the means used to light their rooms at night: a 2-foot-long torch
that produced a bright, steady light, did not run like a candle, and
was only half burned after twelve hours. It was a stick of a black,
resinous material, wrapped in a banana leaf. On their subsequent

trip inland to the city of Quito (later the capital of Ecuador), they found the material used for many purposes. On June 24, 1736, La Condamine sent samples of the material back to Paris along with a note. As translated by Austin Coates in *The Commerce in Rubber: The First 250 Years*, the note said:

> In the forests of Esmeraldas province a tree grows which the natives of the country call Hhévé (the Spaniards write it Jévé); simply by an incision it lets flow a white resin like milk; it is collected at the foot of the tree on leaves specially spread out for it; it is then exposed to the sun, whereupon it hardens and turns brown, first outside, and then inside. Since my arrival at Quito I have learned that the tree which discharges this substance grows also along the banks of the *Amazon* river, and that the Maïnas Indians call it *Caoutchouc;* moulds of earth in the shape of a bottle are covered with it; they break the mould when the resin has hardened; these bottles are lighter than if they were of glass, and are in nowise subject to breakage.

It later turned out that La Condamine had confused two different types of rubber trees: the Peruvian *caoutchouc* was a different tree from the one in the Amazon, which was *Hevea*. Even so, the word *caoutchouc,* which meant "weeping wood" to the Indians, traveled with his samples to Europe and was thenceforth applied to this odd new material. La Condamine quickly took advantage of one of the local uses of the substance, coating some cloth with latex to make a waterproof cover for his delicate instruments.

Not until 1743 was the French team able to complete its original mission. (As it turned out, the world was indeed flatter at the poles and fatter at the equator; Newton and gravity had stood up to the test.) Afterward, La Condamine chose to return to France by way of a trip down the Amazon; he provided the first scientific survey of the river. As he traveled on the river, he found that the Portuguese—who had gained control of most of the region that is now Brazil—had already established a widespread trading system for cocoa, which had become a popular drink in Europe. Along with the cocoa grown on plantations around Belém, beans were also being gathered in upriver villages for shipment 2,000 miles downstream to the town, where cocoa was the accepted currency. A century later, the same links became the basis of the blossoming rubber trade.

When he reached Belém in September of 1743, La Condamine saw that the Portuguese colonists there had already picked up a few uses of latex from a local Indian tribe, the Omagua. Liquid latex was poured into molds or over forms, then cured over a smoky fire. As each successive layer was added and smoked, a thick, resilient wall was built up. One of the articles produced this way was a flexible squirting bottle, something like a modern baster. A pear-shape rubber reservoir was fitted onto the end of a hollow wood stem. These "syringes" (*xiringa* in old Portuguese) were used to serve drinking water. It was this association that led to the Portuguese names for rubber, the rubber tree, and rubber tappers— *seringa, seringueira,* and *seringueiro,* respectively.

The English word "rubber" was derived from one of its first uses in Great Britain—to rub off unwanted pencil marks from a sheet of paper. (By a circuitous linguistic trade route, this use also produced a synonym for *seringa* in Portugal and back in Brazil— *borracha,* which means "rubber" and also "eraser.") By the late 1700s, many types of rubber articles were finding their way to Europe and the United States. One of the first was rubberized fabric. The most dramatic use of this material was in the hot-air and hydrogen balloons that began to soar over Paris in 1783. The Montgolfier brothers and a scientist named Jacques Charles had a bit of a competition. Charles did far better with his hydrogen balloon, constructed of silk coated with a thin varnish of rubber.

By the early 1800s, syringes, bottles, and rubber boots by the thousands were being exported to New England and Europe. Almost all of the articles were manufactured in the Amazon, mostly in and around Belém (then called Belém do Pará). There was one significant drawback to this otherwise miraculous material: it grew brittle and stiff in winter's cold, sticky and soft in the heat of summer. That posed a problem for some customers, such as the fishermen of Massachusetts, who needed their boots year-round.

Because of the limitations of the unmodified material, rubber goods remained something of a curiosity until a trio of tinkerers—

a Scot, an Englishman, and a New Englander—put their minds to making durable goods from the substance. Two of them would live in perpetuity, for their names became synonymous with their products. The Scot, Charles Macintosh, devised a system for laminating rubber between two pieces of fabric, leading to the macintosh raincoat. Charles Goodyear, the struggling son of a Connecticut inventor, stumbled onto the chemical process for giving rubber durability; his name is still embossed on millions of automobile tires each year. Goodyear, who lived in Philadelphia in the 1830s, was in and out of bankruptcy constantly as he tried to market various products, including his father's inventions. He became preoccupied with the possibilities of improving rubber, even as the young American rubber industry crashed in 1837 when investors pulled out because of the persistent problems with brittleness and gooiness.

Goodyear scraped by, borrowing heavily, purchasing scraps of rubber, and experimenting with various solvents and processes for making rubber products. In 1839, a partner found that sulfur improved rubber. When Goodyear accidentally dropped a piece of the sulfur-infused rubber onto a stove, it did not melt. In fact, when heated, this treated rubber seemed to take on all the qualities that natural rubber lacked. At last, rubber kept its bounce in heat or cold.

Ironically, the man who most fully refined the process and reaped the greatest financial reward was Thomas Hancock, an Englishman whose name is virtually unknown. When Goodyear had been unable to find financial backing in America because of the crash, he sent some samples of the treated rubber to England in search of licensees. One of the samples reached Hancock, who had already patented many machines for processing rubber. Hancock was unaware of the source of the rubber or its composition; he only knew that it had the properties he was desperately trying to create. It took him more than a year to close in on the ideal temperature and sulfur-rubber mixture that produced what he called simply "the change." This change soon laid the groundwork for a boom in the uses of rubber and led tens of thousands of men into the Amazon, where they created splendid cities in the jungle.

While Goodyear struggled and fiddled and wrote up a patent that included an extra, unnecessary ingredient, white lead, Hancock went about perfecting his process and had it independently confirmed by other scientists. His patent was registered in London on May 21, 1844, one month before Goodyear's American patent. The owner of a firm that manufactured rubber bottle stoppers then suggested to Hancock a more lively name for "the change": vulcanization (after Vulcan, the Roman god of fire). The two inventors began marketing products independently in their respective countries. They clashed in court when Goodyear tried, unsuccessfully, to extend his patent to England. Even though he died bankrupt and Hancock prospered, it is Goodyear whose name is associated with vulcanization. As Coates puts it in *The Commerce in Rubber,* "Charles Goodyear was to be gathered among the immortals of America, while Thomas Hancock received English treatment: due respect while living, fading notice when dead, and on some suitable centenary thereafter, a postage stamp."

Quickly, European and American factories began churning out new lines of durable rubber products. As the industrial revolution gathered momentum through the mid-1800s, an increasing number of uses were found for the new material: gaskets in steam engines, bumpers on rail cars, condoms. Between 1827 and 1850, the amount of rubber shipped down the Amazon rose from 34 tons to 1,500 tons a year. Ironically, just as the boom began, the Amazon's own rubber industry—the small manufacturers of shoes and bottles in Belém—floundered and failed, faced with the superior vulcanized product made north of the equator.

In typical fashion, the developed countries were turning to a colony only for the raw material on which industry relied. Even though Brazil had gained its independence from Portugal in 1822, for another century it remained a classic colony—a place from which things were taken, with little returned. Indeed, even today, the Amazon is dominated by the economics of extraction—whether the extracted substance is rubber, timber, or gold; the region serves as a colony both for the industrial world and the industrial south of Brazil.

Exports of raw rubber continued to increase through the 1850s and 1860s, but, before the jungle could really boom, vast new markets had to be created. Sure enough, in the 1870s came the widespread use of electrical power, which required rubber for electrical insulation on cables; and, in 1888, a Scottish veterinarian named John Dunlop crafted hollow tires filled with air for his son's tricycle. Until that time, bicycles had been equipped with solid rubber tires that sent every bump in the road straight up the rider's spine.

In the 1890s, Europe and the United States were swept by a bicycle craze that sent the demand for rubber soaring. And then came the automobile, whose tires soon created an enormous demand for rubber. They became the chief product made of rubber and remain so today. Even with the advent of synthetic rubber during World War II, natural rubber's unequaled resilience and ability to shed the heat of friction maintained its demand. Today's most sophisticated radial tires have sidewalls of natural rubber; the tires on the space shuttle fleet are 100 percent natural rubber.

With demand soaring from 1870 on, the Amazon rubber boom began in earnest. The equatorial forests of Africa and Asia also contained tree species that produced types of latex, and other trees around Central and South America produced useful latexes. But the best quality came only from *Hevea brasiliensis,* which grew only in the Amazon.

By 1875, the area around Belém swarmed with an estimated 25,000 rubber tappers. Initially, the tappers were free-lancers who hunted for *Hevea* in the unclaimed forests a few days by canoe from Belém; they collected and smoked the latex, then paddled back to town to sell the rubber. The more aggressive tappers soon laid claim to swathes of forest and began to employ others to do the tapping. The landholders then acted as middlemen, collecting rubber from their tappers and paying them with goods from the merchants back in town.

The rubber merchants and representatives of foreign capital, mainly British, began looking farther and farther up the Amazon for untapped trees, for the trees near Belém were already being excessively tapped. Little care was employed in such boom times; the tappers often used a simple hatchet to scar the bark, and their sloppiness killed many trees as the deeper sapwood was struck. The river system was already being scoured by fleets of canoes carrying peddlers, who actively traded with the Indians, mixed-blood *caboclos,* and *ribeirinhos* who inhabited the banks upstream. The river trade in rubber evolved from this network.

The only thing lacking was a supply of labor. In some areas, Indians had been enslaved or forced to collect latex, but most tribes were either slaughtered or withdrew farther into the forest as the quest for rubber moved up the Amazon. As the price of rubber steadily rose, workers from Belém and the surrounding state of Pará abandoned other enterprises, such as agriculture, to head into the forests after latex. In 1854, the president of Pará complained that the state now had to import food that had once been grown there because so many men were heading into the forest. In *Amazon Frontier: The Defeat of the Brazilian Indians,* John Hemming writes that the president said the rubber trade "is leading into misery the great mass of those who abandon their homes, small businesses and even their families to follow it. They surrender themselves to lives of uncertainty and hardship, in which the profits of one evening evaporate the following day."

Between 1850 and 1900, the number of men harvesting rubber in the Amazon rose from 5,300 to 124,300. Once the immediate labor pool was exhausted, agents for the rubber estate owners sought a new source of would-be *seringueiros.* They found it 600 miles southeast of Belém, in the parched state of Ceará, which occupies the bulge of Brazil that protrudes into the Atlantic Ocean. This state once had richly forested uplands, called the *sertão.* But by the 1850s, the forests had been razed and replaced with cattle pasture.

A steadily worsening cycle of drought had begun to affect the region every decade or so. (It is thought that the deforestation may have amplified the effects of the drought.) The cycle reached one of its worst peaks between 1877 and 1879. Crops and cattle died; famine followed. Thousands of people fled from the desiccated hills of the interior and swarmed to the coastal towns, particularly to the port of Fortaleza. But there was no work, and soon the region became the poorest in Brazil. The agents had no trouble luring tens of thousands of desperate men into the rain forest. Word of the white gold that was harvested simply by cutting tree bark had already spread. Even now, in places like Acre, there are few rubber tappers who are not *nordestinos,* northeasterners, with their roots in Ceará. The music of the Amazon and the names for foods and dances are all from the northeast coast.

These workers were loaned the cost of their passage into the Amazon, so even before they left Ceará they were saddled with debt. This was their first contact with the system of *aviamento,* advances, under which they suffered for a century. The debts that were incurred at the start only compounded, never diminished. The farther upriver a tapper settled, the longer the line of middlemen standing between him and the market for the latex.

The system started on the *seringal,* a large tract of forest owned or claimed by someone who lived there, in a nearby town, or a thousand miles downriver in Manaus—which was still 1,000 miles upstream from the mouth of the great river. Almost always, the *seringal* was on a river or stream, so that rubber could be shipped to market. (Many of the smaller streams disappeared completely during the dry season, cutting the tappers off from the outside world for months at a time.) The lowest rung on the ladder was the *seringueiro.* A tapper and his family, or sometimes several single men, lived deep in the forest, in a clearing at the center of a cloverleaf of two or three trails, called *estradas,* each of which wound through the forest past 100 to 200 rubber trees. The clearing and trails together were called a *colocação,* collection area.

The tappers scored the bark of the rubber trees, and the latex bled into a cup propped against the tree. The liquid latex was brought back to the tapper's shack, then ladled onto a paddle as it was rotated over a smoky fire. The latex congealed, layer after layer, forming a dark brown ball. A tapper was given the right to tap trees on the *seringal,* but he could only sell his latex to the *patrão* of the estate. (*Patrão,* which literally translates to the beneficent-sounding "patron," may seem an odd choice to describe these bosses who robbed the tappers blind.)

The neophyte tappers were also advanced the necessary gear for living in the forest and collecting latex: a machete, a *faca de seringa,* and a cheap rifle. Back in Europe, flimsy weapons were manufactured specifically for the rubber trade and, as one historian of the time put it, were good for only "half a hundred shots" before the barrel fell apart.

The bosses controlled every aspect of the tappers' lives, and the results were brutal. Thousands of the men died each year from malaria, yellow fever, intestinal diseases, and accidents. From 1900 to 1910, the toll ran so high that between 10,000 and 14,000 new workers had to be recruited each year from Ceará. In many cases, the tappers had to pay in rubber for women (many were prevented from taking their families when they fled the northeast). The bosses and their foremen and hired thugs forbade the tappers from growing their own food or finding other markets for their rubber. Tappers who violated these rules or tried to flee without paying their debt occasionally found themselves ringed with strings of flammable rubber, doused in kerosene, and set afire.

The exchange of rubber for goods took place at the *barracão.* There, the boss would advance goods to the tappers at the beginning of the dry season and would collect balls of smoked latex in payment at the end of it. (During the rainy season, the latex became too diluted with water, and the trails of a *seringal* were nearly impassible.) An energetic tapper could harvest more than a thousand pounds of rubber a year. But it would invariably be bartered away at an impossibly low rate of exchange, leaving a gaping deficit. The deficit was increased by rampant cheating; it was not even necessary for a boss to tamper with the scales because most of these *nordestinos* were both illiterate and innumerate. On top of this mounting debt would be added the annual rent for the use of the trees, which typically was 130 pounds or so per *estrada.* Tappers buried under this sort of debt referred to themselves as *cativeiro,* captive. Euclides da Cunha, a Brazilian journalist who powerfully documented the inhumanity of the rubber boom, wrote that the *seringueiro* "comes to embody a gigantic contradiction: he is a man working to enslave himself!"

The bosses on the rubber estates had far better lives than the tappers, but they too were usually in debt. Most of them were simply agents or lessees, indebted to the actual owner of the land, the *seringalista,* or to *aviadores,* the creditors and rubber barons back in the quickly growing rubber trading ports of Belém and Manaus. Every time a ball of smoked latex changed hands as it moved downstream, its value increased. Close to the export docks, where the risk was lowest, the profits were greatest, and astronomical fortunes were made. The *aviadores* of Manaus began an intense competition with those from Belém, downstream, for control over the flow of rubber from Acre and other far-flung regions, and both groups vied to exceed each other in lavish expenditures. Baroque cathedrals and mansions, museums and monument-studded plazas, sprung up hundreds of miles into the Amazon—islands of opulence in the dark jungle. Laundry was sent by ship back to Europe for cleaning. Manaus had electric trains before Boston.

No greater monument to that explosion of wealth exists than the domed Teatro Amazonas, the Manaus opera house, a garish palace perched on a hill overlooking the broad Amazon. Its construction started in 1884, when Manaus was a city of 45,000. Almost all of the materials were shipped from Europe and painstakingly assembled over a period of years. The blue and gold tiles that made the Moorish dome gleam were from Alsace. Crystal chandeliers were imported from Venice. The cobblestones around the opera house were replaced with rubber tiles, to quiet the noise from carriage wheels. The only feature built of materials from the Amazon was the main staircase—and that was because the ship carrying the commissioned Carrara marble staircase from Italy sank in a storm shortly before the theater's opening date, December 31, 1896. Artisans rushed to carve a replacement from tropical hardwoods. By the inaugural performance, the Italian Lyric Opera Company's *La Gioconda,* Manaus was a dynamic city of 75,000 (three times the concurrent population of Houston, Texas). But there was something about the almost desperate, profligate indulgence of the rubber barons that implied that the boom could not go on forever.

Indeed, even as the boom was reaching its peak, the groundwork was being laid for its demise. In 1877, the same year that drought struck Ceará and sent thousands of men up the Amazon, twenty-two seedlings of *Hevea brasiliensis* arrived by ship in Singapore, having taken a circuitous route. They had started out as a handful of seeds among a batch of 70,000 that had been smuggled out of the Amazon by one Henry Wickham, a British traveler and opportunist. Wickham had carefully wrapped the seeds in banana leaves, stashed them in cane baskets, and stowed them in the hold of the steamship *Amazonas*. They were taken across the Atlantic to Liverpool and then to London and the Royal Botanical Gardens at Kew, a repository and laboratory where botanical samples from around the world were studied and cultivated both to satisfy scientific curiosity and to uncover any commercial value. Some of the seeds had then been sent on to Ceylon, and from there they hopscotched their way to the Far East.

Since 1857, the British had been mulling over the idea of cultivating the best rubber tree species on British colonial soil. The man who proposed the idea was Thomas Hancock, Goodyear's competitor. The demand for rubber was skyrocketing, and the trees around Belém were dying from overuse. The flow of rubber from deep in the Amazon was still irregular. Moreover, Brazil and Great Britain were not on the best of terms. In 1863, Brazil severed diplomatic relations with Britain for five years after the Royal Navy imposed a blockade on Rio de Janeiro in a trade dispute.

A young geographer with the British East India Company, Clements Markham, had at this time just successfully transplanted *chinchona*, the tree from which quinine was extracted, from Peru to India—through the Kew Gardens. He was convinced of the importance of securing a permanent—and British—supply of this vital material. In 1876, Markham contacted Wickham, who was considered an authority on the Amazon. Wickham had already tried to develop a rubber plantation in Brazil, but had failed when disease struck the densely packed trees. Almost every attempt to cultivate plantations of the trees in their home range fared no better. It seemed that diseases, including a fungus that was a particular scourge of *Hevea,* quickly grew to epidemic proportions if the trees were grown more densely than their natural distribution. Like most of the large tree species of the Amazon, *Hevea* is widely dispersed in the forest. Rarely is there more than one tree per acre. Wickham agreed to the plan and smuggled his batch of seeds to England. Once in Singapore, those twenty-two seedlings soon became the basis for dense, healthy plantations of rubber trees. It was clear that the fungus had not followed the trees to their new home.

The first shipment of Asian rubber, a mere 4 tons, arrived in London in 1900, marking the beginning of the end for the Amazon boom. As the coming of the automobile caused the demand for rubber to explode, the price reached $3 a pound in the early 1900s. But the Amazon could not keep up with the demand, and its output peaked in 1910, at 62,891 tons. In contrast, production in Asia steadily climbed. The Asian supply began to catch up with the demand, and world prices fell. With them fell many of the Amazonian *aviadores,* who as middlemen had built their fortunes on nothing but credit in one direction and debt in the other. In 1913, Asian production exceeded Amazonian for the first time. By 1919, the harvest from Asian rubber plantations had soared to 350,000 tons, whereas Amazonian production had slid to 43,720 tons. Brazil briefly tried to stem the crash by creating a program to encourage investment in the Amazon, called Defense of Rubber. But that failed too.

The fabulous mansions of Manaus and Belém began to crumble; the forest reclaimed dozens of rubber estates when their owners and bosses were wiped out. The *seringueiros* in the forest either scratched out an existence by farming and collecting rubber, died of malaria, or drifted downriver. The Amazon basin settled back to its quieter roots, with small-time *regatões* once again frequenting the backwaters in their canoes, bartering machetes, shotguns, and dry goods for rubber, Brazil nuts, palm oils, and other forest products. With the failure of so many middlemen and bosses, on many rubber estates the tappers were finally allowed to cultivate their own crops and sell their production to more than one buyer.

By an odd twist of industrial history, a crucial raw material for technological development had come, not from a hole in the earth or a chemist's lab, but from the scratched bark of trees widely dispersed through a vast tropical rain forest. An illiterate army of workers had been pushed into the forest, exploited, enslaved, and ultimately abandoned. By the end of the boom, the *seringueiros* who were still alive were hardened survivors. The same laws of natural selection that had evolved the chemical weapons of Amazonian plants, the razor teeth of the piranha, and the killing coils of the anaconda had now given birth to a tough breed of men and women who would not be so easily pushed off their land. Thus the end of the Amazonian rubber boom contributed to the genesis of independent tappers.

One of those men was Chico Mendes's grandfather. Around the turn of the century, he had moved from Ceará to Pará to cut rubber. He returned to Ceará, married a young Portuguese woman, and fathered six children. In 1925, as yet another drought ravaged the coast, he took his family up the Amazon, past Manaus to the Purus, then up the Acre River to Xapuri. One of Chico Mendes's uncles recalled the departure vividly: "Our father said to us, 'My children, let's go make money in Acre.'" They packed up their few belongings and boarded one of the small steamers. This time there was no turning back. Chico's father, Francisco Alves Mendes, was twelve years old when they began the journey.

Chapter 4
Jungle Book

T HE FAMILIES WHO MOVED FROM Ceará into the Amazon had to adapt to a shockingly different environment from the one they had left behind. The northeast had been hot, dry, scrubby, windswept. The Amazon was humid, dark, closed—an insect-ridden wilderness. Disease was rampant. There were no hospitals, no schools. Even though Brazil had been collecting millions of dollars in taxes on the harvested rubber, the government had put nothing back into the region. Every aspect of life presented a new challenge. Families were dispersed through the forest, often separated by four- or five-hour hikes. Isolation required self-sufficiency, so each family hunted and gathered what could not be grown or bought from the traveling merchants.

Even hunting for game to supplement the limited stores of rice and beans presented novel difficulties. Many tappers, for example, tell similar stories about the first time they shot a monkey, an act that became a sad rite of passage into *seringueiro* society. Inevitably, the stories focused on the moment after the tapper raised his shotgun and fired, and a wounded monkey tumbled to the forest floor. As the hunter approached, the monkey's face contorted in pain. The animal stared uncomprehendingly at its torn flesh, then turned to stare imploringly at the startled hunter, who was horrified to notice for the first time just how human a monkey looks. Then the tapper remembered his children crying of hunger; although repulsed at his own actions, he reloaded and shot again.

Despite the hopes of Chico Mendes's grandfather, when he and his family settled on Seringal Santa Fé, just a few hours' walk from Xapuri, a tapper could no longer make money there. The price of rubber had been depressed by the bountiful supplies from Asia. The rubber estates were barely scraping by. The amount of rubber produced in the Brazilian portion of the Amazon had dropped from its 1912 peak of 31,000 tons to 17,000 tons. And, despite the depression, *aviamento* was still in place. Each tapper got his shotgun, machete, cooking pots, rubber knife, and other necessities on credit; it was usual to start work at least a year's worth of rubber in debt. The system had become a bit more liberal: the tappers could now grow some of their own food instead of buying everything at inflated prices from the boss. And they could supplement their income during the rainy season by gathering Brazil nuts; the Acre and Purus river valleys were blessed with some of the Amazon's densest populations of both rubber and Brazil nut trees. But there was no avoiding the burden of perpetual debt.

The rule on the *seringal* was for sons to follow their father into the forest to learn how to cut rubber. Francisco, Chico Mendes's father, had trouble keeping up with his brothers. He had club feet; his mother always attributed the deformity to a fall she had suffered during her pregnancy. But he pushed on without complaining and was able to learn the routine of the tapper's life. By the time he reached adulthood, he had also learned to read and write, which set him apart from many of the other tappers. When his father died, only Francisco stayed on at Seringal Santa Fé; the rest of the children drifted to other rubber estates. He met and married Irace, who was widely admired for her beauty. They made an odd couple. He was a typical *nordestino*, dark and compact; only his light brown hair was slightly unusual. She was tall and fair and had bright blue eyes —all rare traits in Acre. People recall her as almost a stately presence. Francisco was a serious man, according to people who grew up nearby. He disliked parties and preferred talking politics to spreading *fofoca,* gossip. And he hated *aviamento*—the rubber bosses and the rent.

The Amazon rubber trade limped along through the 1930s, and Xapuri and the rubber estates around it were an unchanging world. Between 1900 and 1940, the population of Acre dropped from 100,000 to 79,000, as many northeasterners headed downriver and tried to go home. Then came a brief reprieve. During World War II, the demand for Brazilian rubber rose sharply when the bustling rubber estates of Southeast Asia were threatened by Japan. The Allies desperately needed a secure source of this crucial material, so the United States turned to Brazil. The resulting enlistment of an army of *soldados do borracha,* soldiers of rubber, was one of the strangest, saddest chapters in the strange, sad saga of the Amazon.

The revival of the rubber trade began when the Japanese attacked Pearl Harbor on December 7, 1941, and soon after attacked Singapore and the rest of peninsular Asia. The United States still had no factories producing synthetic rubber. England had access to rubber plantations in Ceylon and India, but it was estimated that they would meet only a tenth of the Allied demand. The importance of rubber to the war effort is best illustrated by remembering that gas rationing in the United States was not so much an effort to conserve fuel as to conserve tires.

The United States had already been studying ways to boost the production of rubber in the Western Hemisphere—for example, by developing blight-resistant strains of rubber trees for plantations. But the long-term research was meaningless in the face of this crisis. What was immediately relevant was a report by an American survey team in the Amazon. It calculated that there were perhaps 200 million rubber trees in the wild that could be tapped and, given a large enough labor force, could produce as much as 100,000 tons of rubber a year. At an estimated production rate of a ton per rubber tapper per year—an ambitious estimate, to say the least— a work force of 100,000 tappers was needed.

A special American committee was convened to study "the rubber situation"; it concluded that Brazil's northeast could again, as it had during the first rubber boom, serve as the source of the new rubber tappers. Agreements were signed with Brazil that guaranteed a high price for rubber for five years in return for exclusive rights to Brazil's production. Brazil in turn would create agencies to recruit "soldiers of rubber," to transport them into the forest, and to offer supplies and medical care—and a postwar pension.

At first, the American officials in the Amazon tried to set up their own system of boats and warehouses with which to collect the rubber directly from the tappers. The idea was to offer a higher price than the old bosses and *seringalistas* and thus stimulate the tappers to produce more rubber. It was a logical idea, but logic does not apply in the Amazon. Quickly it became apparent that the project was being sabotaged at every turn by the established middlemen of the old system. Furthermore, a lack of river craft hobbled the effort. In 1943, as rubber shipments to the United States barely grew, the American embassy in Rio recommended that the whole project be turned "back to the Brazilians." In *Brazil and the Struggle for Rubber,* Warren Dean cites a document in which the embassy reported that it was impossible to bypass "the established society, with its century-old tentacles stretching up all the thousands of tributaries." The established suppliers should be used, the document said, even though no "darker picture exists anywhere of what in more progressive societies we choose to call corruption and exploitation."

During the last few years of the war, posters sprung up in the towns of Ceará: "March to the West," read one. "While our soldiers are fighting in Italy, you are fighting in the trenches for rubber," read a second. Another devastating drought, in 1942, helped recruitment. The *flagelados,* the ever-suffering people of Ceará, were lured with deceptive propaganda. Some were told that rubber grew on the trees in 130-pound balls. All they needed to do was jump up and grab it. As one tapper, Jose Silvério, recalled to the Brazilian reporter Malu Maranhão, "There was training that we did: you had to jump very high, holding a rope. We were told that that way we can get these balls. We were promised medical assistance, money, and a uniform—a white shirt, pants, and a hat. The trip was a torment: a ship to Belém, riverboats to Manaus, then many days walking to the *seringal.* Then things got worse. There, we could see that the balls of rubber only existed in the heads of the people who told us this. When I saw how the rubber left the tree drop by drop, and took all day to fill a cup, I realized that I was never going back to Ceará."

Despite plans to ship as many as 50,000 men up the Amazon, only a fraction of that number actually went—estimates range from 9,000 to 24,000. Of those migrants who made it all the way upriver to the rubber estates, almost half died of tropical diseases. Silvério said, "The first year, thirty of my friends died. The only medical help was Doctor Malaria. Those who didn't die went crazy. A friend, Tenório, spent all day biting his belt and talking with a girlfriend he left in Fortaleza."

Germany was sufficiently concerned about cutting the Allies' rubber supplies that submarines were sent to sink the ships carrying rubber soldiers. One woman in Xapuri, who was fourteen years old when her father took the family to the Amazon from Fortaleza, recalled a night when a submarine was spotted as their ship was heading toward the mouth of the Amazon. The passengers, crammed deep in the ship's hold, were told to climb to the upper deck and don life jackets. They watched as minesweepers and dive-bombers tried to sink the attacking submarine. Months passed before that family was deposited at the mouth of the Acre River, where they had to wait a few months more before they were taken to a *seringal*. Then came the inevitable disappointment when the stories of a healthy lifestyle and easy labor were replaced by the reality of living in debt in the forest.

After the war, despite the promise of pensions, the *seringueiros* were forgotten and abandoned—just like the previous wave of settlers after the first rubber boom crashed. Nonetheless, they remained proud of what they considered patriotic service to their country and the free world. Many of the rubber tappers still proudly sing ballads that were originally anthems for the rubber soldiers. More recently, these songs have become a rallying cry for the rubber tappers' movement that Chico Mendes led. The lyrics reflect something of the plight of these displaced people, many of whom still live in the past:

One day, when the splendid rays of victory
come to our country, you will see that your
efforts, ensuring this freedom, will make you so
happy.
　If you suffer from the darkness and the
solitude, one day, free from this prison, you
will sing the glory of the nation.
　Cheers, Brazilian soldier, your product will
be useful all over the world.
　Cheers, Brazilian soldier, your product will
be useful all over the world.
　At the moment you join the ranks of the
forest battalions and think about the victory of
Brazil and forget about your dangerous life,
courageous soldier, you will triumph.
　Cheers, Brazilian soldier, your product will
be useful all over the world.

On December 15, 1944, toward the end of the second, smaller rubber boom, Irâce Mendes bore a son, Francisco "Chico" Alves Mendes Filho. The *seringal* where he was born, called Porto Rico, is now partly deforested ranchland. Life for the Mendes family differed little from that of their neighbors. Almost everything that was needed could be grown in the clearing around the house or harvested in the forest. Over the preceding decades, the *seringueiros* had evolved a remarkably uniform lifestyle. Each family received from the estate boss an identical kit of implements and a fairly uniform plot of forest—often about 700 acres. Also, most rubber estates at that time had a *mateiro,* who was employed by the boss to ride herd over the tappers. Often a veteran tapper, he laid out the *estradas* and determined which rubber trees should be tapped and which should be allowed to recuperate. He often taught the tappers about the medicinal qualities of various plants, most of which he had learned from the Indians. In many cases, the tappers had intermarried with the Indians, creating another conduit for passing forest lore to this new, hybrid culture.
　The Mendes *colocação,* or collecting area, was called Bom Futuro,

Good Future. One family's *colocação* was just like another's, right
down to the finest details—and most of these details remain the
same today. The family compound is called the *centro,* the center,
and it is indeed the heart of the family's existence. Everything
outside the *centro* is the *rua,* the street. (Today, when a tapper
ventures into town or a child grows up and moves out, he is said to
have gone to the *rua.*) The compound consists of a rectangular
house, called a *tapiri,* and sometimes a separate shed for animals.
The buildings are raised about a yard off the ground. This is not
just to avoid flooding but to allow the pigs and chickens to circulate
beneath the house. The structures are built of one species of palm
tree, the *paxiúba.*

Paxiúba is a remarkably versatile tree. It produces edible nuts
that also can be pressed for oil. But its main value is in construction.
The tree became the basis of *seringueiro* carpentry because nothing
more than a machete was required to cut down even a large specimen—and few tappers had much more. The tree's trunk does not
thicken as it nears the ground; instead, it is held up by clublike,
thick roots that descend in all directions from about a yard up the
trunk. One need only hack at these individual supports for the tall,
slim trunk to come crashing down.

The house is built on thick stilts made from sections of tree trunk.
A smaller chunk acts as a step leading to the entrance. Almost all
the tappers' homes have an entry that leads into an open room that
is a covered veranda. In houses that are more exposed to the elements or that have a bad insect problem, this room is walled in with
thin battens of *paxiúba,* which are produced by splitting a tree
trunk, then pounding the fibrous wood flat. When guests stay
overnight, this area is often filled with swinging hammocks, strung
from the *paxiúba* rafters. (Hammocks were invented by the Amazonian Indians and have been universally adopted by the tappers,
although the husband and wife in a family frequently have a traditional bed in their bedroom.)

The roof is a double layer of palm thatch separated by an air space
that keeps the entire roof from rotting when the outside layer gets
wet. Also, the wind can sweep in beneath the roof, keeping the

house cool. Before the fronds are plaited into mats to make the roof, they are left to dry "until they make noise," as the tappers say.

Inside, the house is split into several bedrooms and an eating area. The floor is made of half-rounds of small *paxiuba* saplings, but the sections are never so close that crumbs of manioc flour and rice cannot fall through to the ground below. The kitchen, in a separate wing, has a wood-fired stove made of clay dug from the stream beds. The stove is waist high, and a chimney made of sections of tin cans shunts about half of the smoke from the fire obliquely through the nearby wall. The rest of the smoke rises to the rafters and soon blackens the underside of the thatch. Every kitchen has a wooden platform, called a *jirau,* that juts out from the house; there, dishes are washed and food is prepared. Water and scraps fall to the ground below. Herbs and scallions are grown near the house in a hollow log, or sometimes an old dugout canoe, that is filled with soil and propped up on stilts to keep the rats and pigs away.

A tapper's house is something like the surrounding forest. It is an efficient system, designed so that the water dripping from the kitchen or the rice grains falling through the cracks in the floor are not wasted. The water forms a puddle for ducks and a wallow for pigs; the rice is soon gobbled by the ever-present flock of fowl.

Childhood for Chico Mendes was mostly heavy work and, when there was some free time, a little play—kicking a handmade rubber ball or plucking at his father's guitar. If all of his siblings had lived to adulthood, Chico would have had seventeen brothers and sisters. As it was, conditions were so difficult that by the time he was grown, he was the oldest of six children—four brothers and two sisters. In the more remote rubber estates of Acre, even today it is not uncommon to meet a mother who tells of the loss of more than half her children without batting an eyelash. Most of the deaths are ascribed simply to "fever."

When he was five, Chico began to collect firewood and haul water. A principal daytime occupation of young children on the *seringal* has always been lugging cooking pots full of water from the nearest river or *igarapé*—the tappers' term for the spring-fed streams in the low sections of the rain forest. Another chore was pounding freshly harvested rice to remove the hulls. A double-ended wooden club was plunged into a hollowed section of tree trunk filled with rice grains, like an oversize mortar and pestle. Often two children would pound the rice simultaneously, synchronizing their strokes so that one club was rising as the other descended.

By the time he was nine, Chico was following his father into the forest to learn how to tap. It was important for Chico and his brothers to learn tapping because their father simply could not walk fast enough, with his crippled legs, to tap efficiently. Francisco wanted to let his sons do the tapping so that he could concentrate on tending the beans, rice, and corn that were vital to the family's existence. So every April, as the *estradas* began to dry out after the rainy season, the boys would follow their father each day as he made the rounds of the trees.

Well before dawn, Chico and his family would rise. His mother would brew some thick, strong coffee, and he and his father would quickly eat some manioc flour and maybe some dried meat. Then they would grab the tools of their trade—a shotgun, a *faca de seringa*, a machete, and a pouch to collect any useful fruits or herbs found along the trail. They left before dawn, because that was when the latex was said to run most freely. Although most tappers now carry a chrome flashlight, when Chico was young his father wore a *poronga*, a sheet metal hat that held a kerosene reservoir and a wick and had a curved wind guard. In the flickering light from this headlamp, they started their rounds.

They circled the trail quietly, purposefully, the silence of the forest broken only by the steady slap of the machete on the thigh and the brisk padding of feet on the trail. As they reached each tree, the elder Mendes grasped the short wooden handle of his rubber knife in two hands, with a grip somewhat like that of a golfer about to putt. The palm of the right hand would apply even pressure as the short blade dipped into the corky bark, routing out a shallow channel. It was important to get the depth just right: the ducts that produce the latex are in the layer just outside the cambium, the generative tissue where the growth of the tree occurs. A cut that is too deep strikes the cambium and imperils the tree; a cut that is too shallow misses the latex-producing layer and is thus a waste. That same kind of subtlety extended to the entire complicated biological system that was Chico's only school.

There were different styles of cuts. The flag style was considered the best—an oblique gash that ended in a little downward twist. At the beginning of each tapping season, the first gash would be made high on the tree. Each successive cut would be just below the last one. As the seasons passed, a tree's bark would come to read like a calendar kept by a prisoner on a cell wall. Each gash represented another day of tapping. In areas where the trees are over-worked, the tappers often have to use a ladder, made of a sapling with steps notched out of it, to reach uncut portions of the tree trunk. In parts of Acre, it is common to see ladders with thirteen or more steps. It is also common to meet tappers with a perpetual limp or back problem that resulted from a 20-foot fall.

Tappers feel strongly that the trees come to know the touch of individuals. Even the sophisticated Guilherme Zaire, who had been the *seringalista* to both Chico and his father, agreed on this point. "Every time a new tapper starts cutting a rubber tree, the tree has to get used to the guy," he said. "Otherwise the tree doesn't produce very well. A tree feels who's doing the cutting. Every tapper has his own style, his own *amaciamento de seringa.*"

Chico learned how to position a tin cup, or sometimes an empty Brazil nut pod, just beneath the low point of the fresh cut on a crutch made out of a small branch. Two or three spare cups were always hung on top of a stick embedded in the ground near each tree. The white latex immediately began to dribble down the slash and into the cup. But by then Chico and his father were already walking briskly down the *estrada* to the next tree.

Chico quickly adopted the distinctive, fast stride of the rubber tapper. Tappers have a unique way of walking. Their legs swing straight from the hip and pump incessantly, regardless of the steepness of the trail or the slickness of the footing. Their stride bears some resemblance to that odd Olympic sport called race walking but is more graceful. The pace has evolved from the nature of the tapper's day. The 150 to 200 rubber trees along an *estrada* are exasperatingly spread out. A simple, minimal bit of work is required at each tree, but there is often a 100-yard gap between trees. Thus, a tapper's morning circuit can be an 8- to 11-mile hike. And that is just the morning. Many tappers retrace their steps in the afternoon to collect the latex that has accumulated from the morning cuts.

A crucial part of the morning circuit is the hunt. Chico loved hunting. The larger the game the better—that was the rule in a place where a shotgun shell cost two or three pounds of rubber. Most of the shell casings were reused, packed by hand with black powder and lead shot. Tapir were at the top of the list of available game. These calf-size, ancient cousins of the horse followed a predictable routine, so a tapper could hide at known wallows or near a tree that was dropping its fruit. Often tappers had mental calendars of when a particular tree would be ready to drop its fruit and so knew when to watch for animals attracted to the feast. Occasionally, the tapping routine would be interrupted by signs of a particularly prized animal. In such an instance, as one tapper explained, "you follow the tapir and attack when she goes to sleep. She walks a little differently when she is getting ready to sleep. She eats different things, then takes a bath, cleans herself, and then sleeps. That is when you shoot."

When a tapper is on the trail, his peripheral vision and ears are continuously scanning his surroundings for a different kind of noise from the usual trill of birds and buzz of insects—a rooting peccary or armadillo, a rat porcupine or monkey high in a tree. When he notices something, he freezes. High above in the canopy, some branches sway as if caught in a zephyr. But there is no wind. In a seamless instant, he slips the shotgun, which has been slung over his shoulder, into his hands and points it at the treetops. "Points" is the right word; a forest dweller does not aim along the barrel. His whole body seems to lean toward the movement in the branches, and the shotgun is more an extension of his hands than his eyes. A tapper rarely misses.

Chico's intimate knowledge of the rain forest was gained in those early mornings with his father. As they walked from tree to tree,

Chico learned the names and uses for dozens of jungle plants. The bark of the yellow-flowering *ipê* tree was said to fight cancer. The hard, tumorlike termite nests that grow out of the sides of mature forest trees were ground and brewed in a tea taken to cure pneumonia. The heart of a plant called monkey cane made a tea taken for heartburn. This forest lore was later studied by a new breed of scientists called ethnobotanists, who sift through the pharmacopoeia of the forest in search of useful drugs. Tappers have been found to use sixty-seven different plants for a wide variety of purposes. Some Indians have been known to recite the names and uses for two hundred plants.

The forest itself was an effective, unforgiving teacher. One of the first lessons that Chico would have learned is to look before touching. Along with products that human beings find useful, such as latex, the forest is also full of defense systems that can be dangerous. Walking through the jungle, you find yourself staring down at your feet and then glancing up quickly to avoid the draping lianas and newly fallen tree trunks that are always threatening to engulf any trail. As your feet rise over rotting logs or slither along the narrow sapling bridges that the tappers build to cross swampy spots or gullies, your hands are always tempted to seek support on the surrounding trees and vines. But many trees are decidedly unfriendly to fingers. *Astrocaryum* palms, for example, bristle with bands of black spines the size of toothpicks but sharper than sewing needles. Evidently this is an adaptation that wards off climbing mammals that might otherwise eat the palm fruit—which in one common species happens to be three times higher in vitamin A than carrots.

The hazards are both animal and vegetable, and the more famous jungle denizens, such as snakes and tarantulas, are not nearly as common as some of the more subtle threats. There is *Lonomia achelous*, a green caterpillar the size of a cigar. The caterpillars spend the night feeding on leaves in the canopy, protected by darkness from bird predators. At dawn, they descend on the tree trunks and congregate at or below eye level. Their long, branched hairs hide delicate spines that exude a chemical remarkably similar to tissue

plasminogen activator, one of the new wonder drugs that can save
the life of a heart attack victim by dissolving a blood clot in a
coronary artery. It is not rare to hear of a tapper who has brushed
up against a mass of *Lonomia.* Within moments, every orifice of
the body streams blood; any cut begins to bleed. (Douglas Daly,
the botanist from New York, has collected *Lonomia* for a biochem-
ist working on new heart drugs.)

By the time Chico and his father came full circle on an *estrada*
and returned to the house, it would be close to midday, time for a
lunch of beans, rice, manioc flour, and maybe some meat—depending on how the hunt had gone the previous few days. Then,
they would retrace their steps on the same trail, to gather the latex
that had flowed from the trees during the morning. Only rarely
would they return home before five o'clock. By then, they would
be carrying several gallons of raw latex in a metal jar or sometimes
in a homemade, rubber-coated sack.

When latex is collected the same day that a tree is cut, it is still
liquid. The very best rubber is produced when this pure latex is
immediately cured over a smoky fire. The smoke particles prevent
the growth of molds or fungi that can degrade the rubber. Thus
this rubber will bring the highest price.

The smoking of the latex was done in an open shed that was
always filled with fumes from the fire. The smokier the fire, the
better. Usually, palm nuts were added to the flames to make the
smoke extra thick. Chico would ladle the latex onto a wooden rod
or paddle suspended over a conical oven in which the nuts and
wood were burned. As the layers built up on the rod, the rubber
took on the shape of an oversize rugby football. The smoking
process would continue into the evening. After a day's labor of
fifteen hours or more, only 6 or 8 pounds of rubber were produced.
The tappers often developed chronic lung diseases from exposure
to the dense, noxious smoke.

This was the only method of curing latex when Chico was a child.
Lately, it has been replaced by coagulation with acetic acid (vine-
gar). Rubber produced by the new method does not fetch as high
a price. And the worst rubber is produced when the latex is not

collected the same day. After two or three days, it coagulates on its own and must be peeled out of the collection cup. The result resembles half of a soft yellow-brown rubber ball, but it can be full of impurities, such as insects—not to mention chemical contaminants that can leach out of the container itself. This presents a problem for manufacturers in the factories down south, and often such rubber—called *biscoitos,* biscuits—is rejected. At best, it can be sold only at a discount to factories producing cheap goods such as sandals.

Once the smoking of the latex was finished, the Mendes family ate dinner. The tapping routine was repeated three or four times a week but along a different *estrada* each day, to allow the trees that had just been tapped to rest. Tappers with three *estradas* could simply progress daily from one trail to the next. By the time a tree was visited the second time, it would have had at least three days without a cut. In this way, no tree would be drained of its vitality.

Before climbing into his hammock each night, Chico frequently convinced his father to give him a few reading lessons. They sat on the veranda and squinted by the glow of one of the smoky oil lamps that are still the major light source in tappers' homes. Chico would finally fall asleep, only to be awakened the next morning long before the roosters began to crow.

By the time Chico was eleven, he was harvesting rubber full time. The family moved to Seringal Equador, next to Cachoeira. They lived and worked on a *colocação* called Pote Seco, Dry Pot. Chico could now read a newspaper aloud to other tappers, earning him a reputation as an unusually intelligent boy. Francisco Siqueira de Aquino, a friend of Chico's father's, recalled that the youngster presented a contrast. He had a look that was somewhat daft, but he was clearly gifted. "As a kid, you'd never have thought that Chico could grow up into such a man. He used to walk around with his mouth hanging open, and he drooled. But he fooled you. Everyone admired how such a small kid could read so fluently."

Chico learned more than simple reading skills; he also began to learn the arithmetic of debt. The rubber collected through the dry season would be taken to the *barracão* toward the end of the year, when the boss would subtract any debts that were owed and the rent for each *estrada;* he also cut the weight by 10 percent to account for any water that might be trapped in the balls of rubber. Francisco always chafed about paying the rent and having the weight of the rubber reduced. Often, little was left for the tappers.

Toward December, with the return of the rainy season, the tappers stopped harvesting latex and began collecting Brazil nuts. The nuts, each about the size and shape of an orange section, are sheathed in individual shells and encased in hard, softball-size pods — about a dozen nuts to the pod. The pods are collected only after they have fallen to the ground from the high branches of a *castanheira,* Brazil nut tree, one of the tallest species in the rain forest. Biologists were long puzzled by the heavily armored casing of Brazil nuts. It seemed impossible for any animal but a man with a heavy machete to break open such a pod. The question was, how are the nuts liberated and dispersed? By careful observation, it was found that the agouti, a rodent like a beaver, is able to gnaw through the casing. The rodent then does what North American squirrels often do with a hoard of food: it buries the nuts in scattered locations up to 150 feet from the source. Many of the nuts are later uncovered and eaten, but enough survive that the tree's progeny are effectively spread throughout the rain forest.

During the rainy season, the Mendeses often crouched on their haunches around a pile of Brazil nut pods, hacking off the top of each one with a sharp machete blow, then tossing the loose nuts onto a growing pile. For tappers in regions with Brazil nut trees, the nuts can provide up to half of a family's income. One tree can produce 250 to 500 pounds of nuts in a good season and some tappers' trails pass enough trees to allow them to collect more than 3 tons of nuts each season. While that might sound like a potential windfall, even as late as 1989, tappers received only 3 or 4 cents a pound for the harvest—which later sold for more than $1 a pound at the export docks.

When the Mendeses were not harvesting latex or nuts, they tended small fields of corn, beans, and manioc. The family followed the Indian method of cultivation, periodically abandoning one

clearing and cutting another. The rhythm of the rubber tappers'
life was thus harmonious: they extracted value from the forest
without devastating it. This is not to say that they had no impact;
the pressure from hunting usually caused the largest mammal species to diminish, particularly such valued prey as tapir. But unlike
the *caucheros* of neighboring Peru and Bolivia, who killed the trees
and moved on, Brazil's *seringueiros* lived in relative balance with
their environment. Ninety-eight percent of the average *colocação*
remained covered by forest. Overall, these were people who walked
softly on the land. It was this instinctual respect for the forest that
caused such anger to rise in Chico Mendes when he was later confronted with a flood of newcomers bent on destroying the forest.

Chapter 5

Coming of Age in the Rain Forest

A FOUR-WHEEL-DRIVE Toyota flatbed truck bounced along the rugged white clay trail leading to the rubber estate called Seringal Cachoeira. The trail wound across a blackened, smoldering pasture like a chalk squiggle on a blackboard. It was September 7, 1989, Brazilian Independence Day, and the burning season was well under way in much of Acre. Humpbacked white cattle, the long-faced Nelore breed known for its resistance to the rigors of tropical life, nuzzled through the ashes in search of a few green sprigs. The air was a hazy tan color that dimmed the sun to a flat disk. Each pothole and rut threatened to shatter the bottles of *cachaça* that jiggled in cartons in the back of the truck. Sacks of rice, tins of cooking oil, and other goods heaved back and forth, as did several rubber tappers, who were hitching a ride out to the *seringal* from Xapuri.

Stashed among the food was a roll of freshly printed posters depicting the smiling face of the slain rubber tapper Chico Mendes. The truck belonged to the rubber tappers' cooperative in Xapuri that Mendes had helped create in the last year of his life. With their own truck, the tappers could take their rubber to markets themselves, bypassing middlemen and using the savings for books and medicine and other necessities. On the return trip later that day, the truck would carry a load of empty bottles, recycled tins, and heavy slabs of rubber bound for factories in the south.

The truck passed through several wooden cattle fences; at each one, a tapper jumped down, opened and then carefully closed the gate, politely adhering to a universal law of ranching etiquette. Finally, it left pasture behind and entered the deep shade of the forest. Traveling around eastern Acre was a bit like crossing the checkerboard landscape of *Alice in Wonderland*—forest, field, forest, field. As the truck was engulfed by the forest, one of the tappers riding in back smiled and said, "This is Cachoeira." A cousin of Chico Mendes's, his name was Sebastião Mendes.

Cachoeira was very important to the rubber tappers of Acre. Before Chico Mendes had moved to Xapuri in 1971 to pursue a career of union organizing and politics, he had spent a decade tapping in these forests. His youth had been spent on the network of winding trails that linked Cachoeira with the surrounding rubber estates. It was in these forests that his life course was determined when, as a teenager, he met a stranger with different, radical ideas who taught him that the rubber tappers did not have to tolerate the cruel conditions under which they worked. And it was here that events mounted to a crescendo and led to his death. This was the forest tract fought over by the tappers and Darly Alves da Silva, who had hoped to turn the land into something resembling the blackened landscape that the bouncing truck had just left.

The truck leaned dangerously to one side as the teenage driver negotiated a sagging bridge built of heavy split logs. Then it swam through a flooded section of road that looked like one of the snaking oxbow lakes that parallel river bends in the Amazon basin, marking the former course of a river. On straightaways, the driver floored the accelerator, and those in back had to duck quickly to avoid getting snagged on the dangling vines, some nicely barbed, that festooned the forest. All along the road, tendrils and roots had crept onto the bare clay; they needed to be trimmed back every month. Here men had to work hard to hold back the forest.

In the dry season, Cachoeira was an hour from Xapuri by truck or most of a day's walk. In the rainy season, it could only be reached by boat. The *seringal* sprawled over 61,000 acres, 98 percent of them forested, and ran up to the banks of the little Xipamanu River where it formed a portion of the border with Bolivia. Sixty-seven rubber tapper families lived in the forest, including quite a few Mendeses—all relatives of Chico's.

The truck emerged into the smoky sunlight and squeaked to a halt under a lonely Brazil nut tree. The tree's 150 feet of height was exaggerated by the absence of anything around it except a field planted in head-high manioc shrubs. All across the Amazon, Brazil nut trees can be seen standing in the middle of otherwise denuded landscapes. The dispersed trees, many dead or dying, are a fitting memorial to the rain forests that once surrounded them. They illustrate vividly how no element of this elaborate biological system can thrive on its own. In 1965, Brazil created a forestry code that, among other restrictions, prohibited the cutting of Brazil nut trees. The government recognized that the economic value of the living tree far outweighed the value of the timber or pasture; tens of millions of dollars' worth of Brazil nuts are exported each year, mostly to the United States.

But the problem is not solved so easily. To produce nuts, the trees have to be pollinated. Biologists have since found that large euglossine bees, which are the commonest pollinator of Brazil nut trees, cannot thrive outside the forest. Male bees can only catch the attention of females for mating by gathering in a dense swarm. And the only way the males can find each other is for each bee to collect an aromatic compound from certain forest orchids. When a Brazil nut tree is isolated, the progression is simple: no forest, no orchids; no orchids, no aroma; no aroma, no swarm; no swarm, no mate; no mate, no bees; no bees, no Brazil nuts. Even though the trees are no longer cut, they no longer produce nuts. Moreover, most slowly die as fires are set every other year or so in the surrounding pasture, for the fire steadily chars the bark around the base of the tree.

At Cachoeira, fortunately, most of the Brazil nut trees, unlike the solitary giant at the entrance, were still surrounded by thick forest. Beyond the tree, the rutted track straggled to a dead end, where it dropped off into something resembling a diorama of the Grand Canyon—a network of steeply eroded gullies of orange-stained clay leading 20 feet down to a slow stream, one of the hundreds of spring-fed rivulets that laced most of the region. During the rainy season, the gouge in the earth filled with a foamy torrent that gave the *seringal* its name (*cachoeira* means "rapids" or "waterfall"). It was at this spot that the confrontations with Darly Alves and his workers and the police had taken place.

Across the stream and up a hill was the central clearing of the *seringal.* Four tappers' houses ringed several acres of pasture. Nearby was a schoolhouse named for Ivair Higino de Almeida, the twenty-six-year-old member of Xapuri's rural workers' union who had been killed six months before Mendes. This *seringal* no longer had a boss. For years now, the tappers of Cachoeira had been able to sell their rubber directly to a variety of merchants. One was the Syrian Guilherme Zaire, who owned the *seringal* until 1968. Another buyer lived on the *seringal,* in a pink house on the far side of the pasture that was once the boss's house. This buyer paid less for the rubber than Zaire, but he transported it to town himself.

The house of Mendes's uncle and aunt, just uphill from the stream, served as a sort of gateway for visitors to Cachoeira. During the weeks-long confrontation with the Alves family, the house was taken over as the commissary for the *empate.* Several women had cooked day after day while several hundred tappers occupied the *seringal* to block the Alveses' chain saws. The house was a typical *tapiri,* but the spot in the woods out back, where the family did its bathing and laundry and got its drinking water, was unusually beautiful. The *garapé* ran clear and cold over a packed bottom of white sand. The banks were lined with ferns. A small grove of citrus trees stood nearby—a refreshing sight and a rarity on *seringais.* Although lemons and oranges can grow easily in the tropical climate, they are not commonly cultivated; the tapper culture that evolved out of a century of debt bondage still has not developed a balanced diet. In contrast, the original diet of most Indian tribes in the Amazon was well rounded; they cultivated and harvested dozens of fruits and vegetables along with such basic crops as manioc.

Sitting in the common room of the little house was Joaquim Alves Mendes, a younger brother of Chico Mendes's late father. He sat at a roughly crafted table and began to shuffle dominoes beneath a shred of cheesecloth. His head had just a faint dusting of white hair. Even though, at seventy-five, he was one of the oldest men on the *seringal,* Joaquim was still lithe and bright-eyed. He and his wife, Cecília, had lived in this house since 1968, after moving from another *seringal,* Santa Fé. Cecília was in the kitchen, scraping the skin from some hunks of manioc root. She had aged beautifully, as, it seems, did many rubber tappers' wives. Her thick silver hair fell below her shoulder blades.

Joaquim explained to a visitor that everyone was taking it easy today because of the holiday. As he started slapping dominoes onto the kitchen table with some friends, he explained that at Seringal Cachoeira, for as long as anyone could remember, Independence Day marked the official start of the burning season. By waiting to light their fires until the holiday, the tappers could combine work and pleasure. In the rain forest, fire is a form of celebration—the celebration of man's ability to control nature. The tappers and Indians have always cleared small plots and burned them to make room for crops; such clearings eventually grow back, having little impact on the rain forest. It is only in the past two decades that the ranchers have used fire to attack the forest as a whole.

As if to underscore Joaquim's remarks, popping and crackling sounds echoed from the forest behind the clearing where the family grazed its animals. A thin brown cloud billowed above the treetops where Joaquim's son Sebastião was clearing a newly cut forest patch to plant some manioc. Smoke began to filter through the walls, through gaps in the makeshift wallpaper of pages from a child's textbook.

The conversation slowly shifted to Chico Mendes, to the time when he was entering his teens, about to become a man. Cecília and Joaquim had known Chico as well as anyone; they had watched him grow up. Joaquim explained how Chico's father, Francisco, hampered by his crippled legs, began to turn over more and more responsibility to Chico and his older brother, Raimundo. Early one evening in 1956, when Chico was twelve, the course of his life—which might have simply followed that of his father and every other tapper—changed forever.

Chico was helping his father cure a batch of latex that they had collected in the afternoon. As they sat ladling the white "milk" over the slowing rotating ball of coagulating latex, a stranger hiked up to the family compound. He gave the traditional rubber tapper greeting, a solid clapping of the hands three or four times, to announce his presence without alarming anyone. The man was different from any *seringueiro* Chico had ever seen. Of medium height, he was stocky and square and heavily muscled, not slim and taut like most of the tappers. He had a full dark beard, a mane of thick black hair, and a stentorian voice that carried far in the forest. Most unusual, he had a sheaf of newspapers—a rare item—stuck in his pocket.

The man did not bother to introduce himself by name; in fact, even to the handful of friends he made around Xapuri over the next few years—even to the common-law wife whose house he shared for four years—he never spoke much of his past. He told them he had recently moved from Bolivia to a *colocação* not far away. That was all he said initially, but in the relaxed rhythm of the Amazon, where nothing can be rushed, the conversation slowly opened up.

They began to discuss the articles in the old newspapers, which the man read with remarkable fluency; "he did not stutter in front of a newspaper," recalled a tapper on Cachoeira. Chico's father was impressed with the man's knowledge of politics, and Chico was intrigued by his broad awareness of the outside world and his ability to read so effortlessly. Chico and Francisco said they would visit the man at his hut the next weekend.

In the following weeks, they paid regular visits to the stranger, who lived a three-hour walk from Pote Seco. His *colocação* had been abandoned for years when he bought it, so he had to "clean" it—tapper parlance for opening up the trails between the rubber trees. He had stacks of old newspapers, some books, a locked suitcase, and not much else. He was not adept at keeping house and hardly knew how to cook. Often, he would head out in the morning after eating a breakfast consisting only of large lumps of *açúcar negro,* the brown sugar that is considered a special treat on the *seringal.* Sometimes he would eat sugar for dinner, too. Despite his athletic build, he disliked heavy work, preferring to spend his days tapping the trees and his nights reading.

Chico convinced his father to let him spend each weekend with this man to take more reading lessons. In those days, not one *seringal* had a school. The *seringalistas* feared that if the tappers knew how to read and do arithmetic, they would not be so easy to cheat. And few tappers could afford the luxury of sending their children to school in Xapuri; the extra hands were needed for tending fields and hauling water.

Chico made the trek to the man's *colocação* every Saturday and generally returned in the darkness early on Monday morning, in time to start his chores along an *estrada.* He became fascinated with this stranger and hovered around him, eager to learn about the outside world. Although the man was clearly a loner, something in Chico's attitude—and possibly his being one of the few youngsters who had already learned the rudiments of reading—convinced him to work with this youth. None of the other children on the *seringal* interested the man, and he interested none of them.

Over the course of their first year together, the man gradually opened up to Chico and told him something of his life. Every Saturday night, they would sit and read newspapers and talk late into the evening. Only after many months did the man tell Chico his name, Euclides Fernandes Távora. Like most of the tappers of Acre, Távora was from the northeast—but not from the drought-ravaged countryside. He came from a relatively well-to-do family in the coastal city of Fortaleza. In the early 1930s, after completing a university degree and five years of military training, he attained the rank of first lieutenant in the army.

The 1930s were a tumultuous time in Brazil's history, one of the many peaks in a cycle of military rebellions and coups d'état that began with the overthrow of Brazil's emperor in 1889, marking the birth of the republic, and only ended in 1985. The rise and fall of various governments was caused as much by regional and class rivalries and power struggles between the branches of the armed forces as by any real need for change. In its first years, the republic was ruled by a coalition of wealthy Portuguese industrialists and coffee barons from the states of São Paulo and Minas Gerais—the same clique that had ruled the empire of Brazil. In contrast, the army drew its leadership from a broad range of classes and ethnic groups, including men of mixed race from the northeast—men like Távora. As a result, the army deeply resented the power of the ruling class.

Even as the republic began to mature through the turn of the century, the economy benefited only the ruling class. Almost as soon as it became a republic, Brazil began to borrow heavily from European banks, mostly British, to pay for new roads, harbors, warships, and railroads. The growing debt forced the government to expand its exports, such as coffee (Brazil already dominated the world market), so that foreign earnings could pay the interest on the loans. The result was economic growth that benefited lenders and the industrial and landowning elite and eluded most of Brazilian society. Fueled by this inequity, Brazil's first Communist party was founded in 1922 (today there are two Communist parties). The army became closely aligned with the political left and, in 1924, a column of rebellious officers rose up in the south and began a three-year, 10,000-mile march—often compared to Mao's Long March in China—that crisscrossed the countryside, encouraging revolt.

A charismatic leader of the rebellion was "the Horseman of Hope," Captain Luís Carlos Prestes. One officer closely aligned with him was Juarez Távora, a cousin of Euclides's. This legendary guerrilla force, later called the Prestes Column, fought fifty-six battles with government forces, organized "shadow" states, and befriended Indian tribes as it cut through the wilderness to avoid the enemy. Prestes's band made it to Belém, then headed up the Amazon to the Bolivian border. The rebels failed to overthrow the government but gained an enormous public following. After fleeing into Bolivia and then Argentina, in 1931 Prestes went to Moscow, where he became a communist.

In 1930, a military coup had put Getúlio Vargas in power. Vargas was the governor of the southernmost state of Brazil, Rio Grande do Sul, where broad, fertile plains were covered with cattle ranches. He was a charismatic *gaucho,* southern cowboy, whose supporters were driven by the desire to expel the *paulistas.* Just before the coup, Vargas sought the cooperation of Prestes, whom he saw as an ally. Prestes refused to cooperate. Although several members of his guerrilla band (including Juarez Távora) had returned to positions in the military establishment, Prestes was not impressed by the change in leadership and was still determined to make trouble. In 1935, using a false passport, he returned to Brazil to coordinate an uprising that had been planned in Moscow.

Euclides Távora told Chico that this was when he became involved. He had grown up detesting the enormous, persistent gulf between the haves and have-nots that had always characterized Brazilian society. So, along with many army officers of his generation, he was drawn to the political left and eventually to communism. In November, Távora and other young officers in the northeast and in Rio de Janeiro joined Prestes in a violent revolt. Within weeks, the rebels were defeated in bloody street fighting that claimed the lives of dozens of civilians. Vargas personally led his troops against the rebels. A state of siege was declared, and hundreds of suspected communists were rounded up, jailed, and tortured. Along with Prestes, Távora was among those arrested.

As the crackdown on communists continued, Vargas canceled the long-awaited presidential election of 1937 that would have returned Brazil to democratic rule. Instead, he proclaimed a new constitution and made himself head of a regime—the Estado Novo, New State—in which he was granted dictatorial powers. Vargas abolished all political parties, and the repression of radical elements was intensified; police raided bookstores and confiscated materials ranging from the novels of Jorge Amado to a translation of *Tarzan the Invincible,* by Edgar Rice Burroughs. Nevertheless, he was popular with a broad segment of Brazilian society. His

Constitution did grant some labor reforms, although they were modeled after labor codes established by Mussolini in Italy. (One indication of his force of character is that on his birthday, despite his flirtation with fascism, labor groups today still lay wreaths at some Vargas monuments in the south of Brazil.)

Brazil became swept up in Vargas's call for national unification. The goal was the rapid development and consolidation of the country's far-flung, independent-minded states, especially those in the Amazon. In a public display, Vargas made a bonfire of Brazil's state flags. In ten years, he doubled the country's network of roads and increased the number of airports from 31 to 512. This expansion was no accident, for Vargas was an avid amateur pilot. By 1940, he had logged some 80,000 miles, flying to every corner of the country, including all of the Amazon except Acre. Perhaps it was his aerial view of the forested frontier that gave impetus to his call for a "March to the West." In a speech delivered in Manaus in 1940, he described what he called the highest task of civilized man: "to conquer and dominate the valleys of the great equatorial torrents, transforming their blind force and their extraordinary fertility into disciplined energy."

As he consolidated his dictatorship, Vargas had to deal with the burgeoning population of political prisoners. In 1938, the government created an agricultural penal colony on Fernando de Noronha Island, a dot on the chart in the Atlantic 300 miles off the coast of the northeastern hump of Brazil. The rocky, mountainous island is studded with seventeen forts dating from the sixteenth and seventeenth centuries—the legacy of its role as a jumping-off point for Dutch and French attacks on the Portuguese mainland. Soon, the new colony filled with hundreds of political prisoners from both the communist left and the fascist right, which had grown in Brazil as the Nazi and fascist movements grew in Germany and Italy.

Távora was among those who made the eight-day sea voyage from Rio to the island prison. The prisoners were stripped and forced to march 12 miles in the broiling sun to the distribution point for uniforms. The communists were kept apart from their fascist foes and spent their time raising chickens, farming, and making salt. It appears that the prison warden, himself a veteran of the Prestes Column, made life relatively easy for the communists. Indeed, quite a few of them made a decent living when, after impressing the warden by renovating a baroque church, they were hired to build new barracks (this capitalist act dismayed the more radical communists). The health of many of the prisoners flourished there as it never had back on the mainland, nurtured by sunbathing and frequent swims. (Because of its beaches and rich coral reefs, most of Fernando de Noronha and the surrounding twenty other islets was made into a national marine park in 1988.)

After World War II, Vargas got the same treatment he had given the *paulistas.* In 1945, he was deposed by his generals, who feared his excessive nationalism and wanted to return to democracy. Unlike most deposed dictators, Vargas did not disappear, nor was he reviled. In 1947, he campaigned against local candidates of the new government—next to his old nemesis, Luís Carlos Prestes. Showing incredible resilience, Vargas was *elected* president of Brazil in 1950. But in 1954, under intense pressure from the military, he shot himself in the heart, ending one of the most remarkable political careers of the century. (There remains a debate about the authenticity of a supposed suicide note that was left behind—and of the nature of his death.) But Vargas's death did not sway Brazil from the course it had embarked on: modernization, industrialization, and the development of the Amazon.

Through the terms of Vargas and his successor Juscelino Kubitschek, the philosophy of rapid development was unwavering. Only the slogans changed: from "March to the West" to "Fifty Years in Five." Nothing epitomized this period better than the crowning symbol of twentieth-century Brazil—its capital of Brasília. Kubitschek spent a billion dollars, mostly borrowed, to realize a long-held dream of Vargas's: to promote the taming of Brazil's interior by moving the capital from hedonistic Rio de Janeiro and its beaches to the dusty *planalto,* a high, windy, uninhabited plain filled with scrub forest near the geographical center of the country. Of course, such a move entailed building a city from scratch. Brazil has a penchant for big projects; sure enough, even though the materials

and labor force had to be shipped in from the coast, Brasília was
built in a thousand days. The city was planned down to the smallest
detail, with every element meant to herald the anticipated emer-
gence of Brazil as the first superpower in the Southern Hemisphere. Brasília's space age architecture was streamlined, forward-
looking, but ultimately sterile, not unlike the TWA terminal at
John F. Kennedy International Airport. Ironically, like all of Brazil's cities, the gleaming capital soon became fringed with slums.
Once the city was completed, there were few jobs for the workers
who built it—mostly men of the same *nordestino* stock who, a
century earlier, might have traveled to the Amazon in search of
rubber. Once again, they found themselves exploited and then
abandoned.

Some time before Vargas's island penal colony was shut down in
1948, Euclides Távora had escaped, aided by a wealthy aunt and his
cousin Juarez, by then a colonel in the army despite his leftist
stance. Távora later claimed to a tapper friend that he made his
getaway disguised in women's clothing and hid in the hold of a
ship that sailed for Belém. It makes a fine story, and the Amazon is
ripe terrain for the cultivation of such stories, but it is a bit difficult
to believe that this burly, hirsute man got away with impersonating
a female. One way or the other, Távora, now a wanted fugitive in
a police state, made his way to Acre and then Bolivia.

As Távora spun his tales of the class struggle—sprinkled with
references to Lenin and Marx—Chico Mendes was mesmerized.
Later he frequently referred to his time with Távora as a crucial
lucky stroke. During those late sessions by the light of an oil lamp,
deep in the western Amazon, a misplaced malcontent passed on to
this young rubber tapper a spark that would not be extinguished.

Through all his years in the rain forest, Távora cultivated a certain
mysteriousness. Most of the people around Cachoeira and Xapuri
remember him only as "a good man" or "a hard worker." He
distanced himself from the other people in the forest partly out of
fear of capture but also out of scorn. As one tapper put it, "He only
spent time with people he considered intelligent." Despite his com-

munist ideology, he was from a privileged, urban background and deep inside resented the fact that circumstances had forced him to hide out among an uneducated, ill-kempt culture. One man who did know Távora well was Francisco Siqueira de Aquino, an aging rubber tapper who taught this soldier how to slit the bark of the rubber tree and survive in the forest. It was Aquino who was later the link that brought Távora back to Cachoeira—and indirectly to his meeting with the young Chico Mendes.

The two men had met in Bolivia in 1952. Távora was hiding from the Brazilian authorities, and Aquino had moved to Bolivia from Cachoeira, where he was born. Tappers from eastern Acre frequently crossed into Bolivia to harvest rubber. The price for rubber was sometimes better there than back in Brazil. The only drawback was that Bolivia collected a "foreigner's tax" on the rubber harvested by Brazilians—if they were caught. The Bolivian rubber estates frequented by tappers from Xapuri were a ten-hour hike away, on the far side of the Xipamanu River.

Aquino, now sixty-four and a grandfather, clearly remembered the afternoon during the dry season when Távora walked out of the forest surrounding his *colocação* in Bolivia and asked for work. Aquino, twenty-seven at the time, was nervous. The stranger was in his forties and very sharp—and very much out of place wandering about a *seringal* in search of a job. The man had never tapped rubber before but seemed eager. Aquino recalled that his hands had thin skin, no calluses; he seemed to be a city boy. When the man said he did not drink, Aquino agreed that he could become a *meieiro*. A *meieiro* is someone who is taken on by the tapper who controls a *colocação* and shares the work and the rubber production.

Távora said little about his past, explaining only that he had been arrested because he was a communist and then he escaped. A cousin and an aunt had helped him get to Acre.

Aquino took the newcomer around the rubber trails and taught him the art of tapping. Távora learned the technique in one week, but it quickly became clear that he did not like any of the other aspects of a tapper's life—particularly anything that involved heavy labor. The only manual labor he did was cutting kindling for the fires used to smoke the latex. And despite his military background and familiarity with weapons, Távora hated to hunt. The only time Aquino ever saw him hunt was when he stumbled on a wild pig and killed it with his knife. Távora preferred to tap rubber, which he did six days a week, twice the work hours of the average tapper. He relished the solitude and the silence.

In 1954, Aquino returned to Brazil, where he planned to work on the *colocação* of his parents, back at Cachoeira. Távora stayed in Bolivia, and the two doubted they would meet again. But just a year later, Aquino was working one afternoon on his parents' rubber trails when a man came walking out of the woods. In what must have been a rather comical replay of the events in Bolivia several years earlier, Távora again asked him for work. He had learned where Aquino had gone through the long-distance links of the rubber tappers' network, *radio cipó*. Távora said that he had worked for another tapper for a while in Bolivia, then traveled to other parts of the country, where he had stirred up trouble trying to organize the tin miners into unions. Thus he was forced to return to Brazil.

But this time there was no work; Távora would have to find a *meieiro* position elsewhere. Apparently he had saved some money or received help from his relatives, for he bought a *colocação* of his own. After a couple of years he sold it and moved to the abandoned one in Cachoeira, where he was living when he met Chico. (Tappers could buy and sell their user's rights to a particular series of *estradas;* they could cost as little as $20, depending on the condition of the *colocação*).

While Aquino knew something of Távora's past, only one person in Acre really knew his character—Neuza Ramos Pereira, a woman who had been made strong by the jungle. Neuza met Távora in 1962, when she was thirty-four and recently widowed. Her first husband, who had been twenty years her elder, had suffered for a year and a half with intestinal bleeding. After she buried him, Neuza had to work their *colocação* herself, helped only by their four

children. But she quickly realized that she would need a man around
if she wanted to survive. Távora's *colocação* was next to hers, so she
made him an offer: she would help him with the work around his
fields if he would return the favor.

As the two started visiting each other's homes, gossip quickly
spread that the widow had found a new beau. They were indeed
interested in each other, although it was not for love; it was more
of a business arrangement. She needed a man's help, and he needed
someone to cook and help with the farming. Távora moved to her
colocação and lived there until just before his death in 1966. They
never married formally because he still feared that he would be
discovered by the Federal Police.

Their relationship was rocky from beginning to end. Távora used
to describe Acre women as *galinhas*—"women who get close to you
in two minutes," as tappers say. He would stay out of the house as
much as possible, harvesting rubber all day, six days a week. Once
home, he would quickly eat dinner and then sit on the veranda,
reading newspapers silently until late at night. He slept only a few
hours, then got up before dawn to tap. The couple had tempestuous
arguments.

By the time Távora moved in with Neuza, Chico Mendes had
stopped making his weekly visits. The main reason was that Chico,
at seventeen, had to work overtime now at harvesting rubber. He
and his family had been rocked by tragedy the year before. Chico's
mother was pregnant for the nineteenth time in her forty-two years
—with only eight children to show for it. Neighbors say that she
had not lost her beauty, despite the harrowing conditions and hard
life she endured. When she finally went into labor one night,
something went terribly wrong with the birth and she began to
bleed. The closest thing to medical help was the comfort provided
by a woman from a neighboring *colocação*.

Chico spent the night running along the trails, trying to gather
some men to help carry his mother out of the forest in a hammock, the stretcher of the Amazon. When he returned, just before
dawn, his mother was already dead. The men who had come to
help carry her ended up helping Chico and his father bury her.

That same year saw the death of one of Chico's sisters and his remaining older brother, Raimundo, the only other sibling regularly gathering latex. Raimundo tripped while hiking in the forest, and his shotgun discharged. The shot hit him in the ear, killing him instantly. To keep the family going, Chico's father had to turn all his attention to tending the crops—corn, beans, manioc, and rice. That left Chico to manage the tapping and to care for his five younger siblings. Chico harvested rubber six days a week; often he would be out until after dark. The next oldest brother, Zuza—who was nine at the time—started tapping, too. Chico became more familiar with the *aviamento* system, which made it so difficult for the tappers to save any money. At every turn, the tappers lost.

Chico's political apprenticeship with Távora continued, although now it was the teacher who came to visit the student. Távora frequently showed up at the Mendes house, sometimes late in the evening; it was a way to avoid his wife. He and the boy would stay up talking long after everyone else was asleep. With almost missionary zeal, Távora recited to Chico time and again the basic tenets of Marxism and the struggle that was needed to free the Brazilian underclass. As Neuza recalled it, Távora saw himself as performing a service by educating Chico; he felt it was a waste to have such an intelligent boy lost in the forest.

Távora dwelled on the deep roots of the divisions in Brazilian society. From its colonial beginnings, Brazil had been split between a profiteering class of merchants and landowners, originally from Europe, and an exploited class that varied over time but included Indian slaves, African slaves, peasants of mixed blood, and poor immigrants. (As the supply of Indian slaves dwindled early in Brazil's history, four million African slaves were imported.) With the abolition of slavery in 1888, the owners of Brazil's coffee, sugar, and tobacco plantations simply shifted to the *virtual* slavery of European immigrants. At the turn of the century, Brazil's reputation for barbaric work conditions spread across the Atlantic to Europe. For a time, Italy forbade its emigrants to go to Brazil.

On Saturday nights, Távora and Chico frequently met at the *barracão* of Seringal Cachoeira, where the boss, Francisco Camelo, owned something that Távora craved—a radio. Távora used to race through the forest after a day of tapping to get to the central compound in time to catch foreign broadcasts of the news, which usually started at around five o'clock in the evening. The radio was also a refuge for Távora as his domestic battles with Neuza became more intense. He taught Chico how to tune in the Portuguese broadcasts of Radio Moscow, the British Broadcasting Service, and the Voice of America. Radio Moscow came on first, followed by the other two on different frequencies. By comparing various accounts of world events, Távora infused in Chico a crude awareness of geopolitics and Brazil's place in the tug of war between communism and capitalism, which came to a head in the early 1960s as the Cold War raged. Chico preferred the BBC broadcasts, which, Távora pointed out, gave the broadest, least biased coverage. They would stay overnight, hanging their hammocks on the veranda.

From the radio, Chico also learned about national developments. In the wake of Vargas and Kubitschek, Brazilian industry was booming—although the concept of industry itself must have been hard to grasp for a young rubber tapper who had never been beyond the Amazon forest. Shipbuilding, automobile and appliance manufacturing, and other industries thrived as multinational corporations were induced to set up shop in this land of plentiful raw materials and labor that was so cheap it might as well be free. Brazil also became consumed by the allure of mechanized, chemical-intensive agriculture. What better way to pay off the ballooning foreign debt than to export agricultural production? Generous incentives encouraged the planting of great tracts of wheat, citrus, and soybeans, leaving little land for domestic food crops. Thus, although the holds of freighters leaving Brazil bulged, the piles of produce at local markets dwindled. Brazil eventually represented a glaring contradiction: it became second only to the United States in total food exports—even as more than half of its own population was undernourished.

As income and land became concentrated in fewer hands into the 1960s, more and more small farmers and squatters in the settled south were driven out, and a million people a year flooded into the swelling slums around Brazil's cities. Others followed dirt roads and cattle trails north and began to slash and burn their way into the delicate fabric of the Amazon as they scraped to find a plot of their own. It was from 1958 to 1960, under Kubitschek, that the first major road was carved into the heart of the Amazon—the Belém-Brasília Highway, the Highway of the Jaguar—heading almost due north from the sparkling new capital toward Belém, one of the old centers of the rubber boom, at the mouth of the Amazon. Quickly, the trees began to fall. This road was the forerunner of the destructive network of dirt tracks that soon filled the air of the Amazon with smoke.

In the early 1960s, Brazil's fragile political system began to unravel. President João Goulart, a Labor party politician, floundered in office and then drifted toward socialism as the economy worsened. Growth slowed, and inflation rose above 100 percent a year. The industrial trade unions, which had always been controlled by the state, began to chafe for independence. Activists and the Catholic church began pushing for education and the rights of rural workers. Landless peasants in the northeast began to organize and press for the redistribution of land, and—most disturbing to the military and Brazil's elite—Goulart himself began to talk of agrarian reform and splitting up *latifundia,* vast but unused tracts of privately owned land. All of these developments were intolerable to Brazil's generals, and on April 1, 1964, they deposed the Goulart government. The coup was enthusiastically supported by the United States; in the wake of Castro's ascendancy in Cuba, the U.S. administration was petrified of any move toward the left in Latin America. One day after Goulart fled from Brasília, President Lyndon B. Johnson sent a congratulatory telegram to the new leadership installed by the military.

The coup resulted in a broad crackdown on leftist activity and increased the pressure on fugitives like Távora. He became more agitated, paranoid, and violent. Often, when someone came out of the forest and walked toward his house, Távora would flee to some hiding place. One day, he returned from Cachoeira with a letter from his family that made him tremble and blanch and cry. He never shared the news with Neuza but became even more obsessed with staying in touch with the outside world, whether through radio, letters, or newspapers. The isolation of the forest ate at him like a disease.

His relationship with Neuza reached its low point one night in 1965, when Távora refused to pray with Neuza's son. She screamed at him in rage. He took his revolver and pointed it at her head, but she did not blink. She said, "If you were really a man, you would kill me." Távora then ran outside and was soon followed by all of his belongings. Neuza cut his hammock cords with a machete, broke the lock on his suitcase—which he had always assiduously guarded—and threw everything out the windows. Távora went storming back to his own hut, but two months later came walking out of the woods again, nearly in tears, begging her to take him back. She gave him a second chance.

They lived together for one last year. In 1966, Távora said he was going to move to a small farm; he had had enough of the forest. He took all of his things, including ten head of cattle. Neuza said she was staying. Three months later, he became racked with stomach pains and began to lose weight. He withered from his former burly self and seemed to age before people's eyes. Some say the illness started after Távora ate some spoiled deer meat. Others say it was an ulcer or stomach cancer, brought on by his horrendous diet and tobacco chewing.

When Távora first became sick, he wrote to his relatives in the south. They came up to Acre to try to convince him to get treatment, but he refused. He only agreed later, when he was in critical condition. Francisco Siqueira de Aquino saw his old friend for the last time while drinking a soda in a Xapuri bar. Távora, who was on the way to Rio Branco for an operation, seemed on the verge of death. He never came back.

Chico Mendes saw Távora for the last time two months before his teacher left Xapuri. Mendes was now twenty-two and eager to fight against the increasingly harsh military crackdown. Távora told him to slow down, that he could look forward to fifteen or twenty years of military rule in Brazil. Távora said that the young man could only help the rubber tappers effectively by joining a union; in isolation, he would never accomplish anything. Around that time, Távora gave Mendes a small battery-powered radio that he had recently bought.

Even though Távora had spent the final thirteen years of his life hiding in the rain forests of the Amazon, he still found a way to foment the revolution that brewed inside him. The leftist indoctrination he gave Mendes molded the young man's mind, just as a tapper molds a shoe or a sack out of congealing latex. Távora did not just teach Mendes how to read, he taught him how to think. Through an improbable conjunction of two disparate lives, a mysterious chemistry had formed between a cultivated, well-educated soldier from a prominent family and a rubber tapper who had never seen a school. Távora gave Mendes a mastery of the vocabulary of socialism and communism that primed him for the arrival of the union movement in Acre, a movement that ultimately evolved into the fight for the rain forest.

Chapter 6

Roads to Ruin

UNTIL THE MID-1960s, Chico Mendes and the other rubber tappers of the Amazon had only one foe: *aviamento,* the system of debt servitude. In those days, deforestation, *desmatamento,* was not perceived as a threat; it was not even a commonly used word. Through most of the river basin, rain forest covered the landscape from horizon to horizon. The only highways were the rivers. Where the dusty dirt road now runs from Xapuri to Rio Branco, the state capital—passing a landscape of scorched pasture—there was only a trail. In some places, the ten-story forest canopy closed over the trail like a vaulted green gallery.

All that began to change as the military government consolidated its power after the 1964 coup. Its key goals were to gain control over the country's vast, underpopulated frontier and to accelerate economic growth. The Amazon was crucial to both objectives, and an agency, INCRA, was created to oversee its occupation. The forests began to fall first along the Amazon's southern flank, as new roads and government incentives brought waves of settlers and ranchers to the states of Mato Grosso, Goiás, Pará, and then Rondônia. As the cutting and burning intensified through the 1970s and 1980s, only Rondônia stood between the tide of destruction and the rich rubber forests of Acre. Nowhere was the influx of people more intense than in this state. Nowhere were the fires of the burning season hotter.

And no one knew this better than a man who had just flown into Acre to film the extension of those same destructive roads into the forests that Chico Mendes had fought and died to preserve. On an evening in the dry season of 1989, Adrian Cowell sat down at an outdoor café in Rio Branco with a colleague and some friends. The fifty-five-year-old British filmmaker was finishing a documentary about the human invasion of the Amazon called *The Decade of Destruction.* Over the previous ten years, he and his cameraman, Vicente Rios, had shot millions of feet of film and flown hundreds of thousands of miles in their effort to chronicle the invasion of the Amazon orchestrated by Brazil's generals and businessmen. Much of Cowell's focus recently had been on the destruction in Rondônia, where a floodtide of migrants flowed north along BR-364, Acre's only link with the developed part of Brazil, and destroyed a fourth of the state's rain forests.

Dozens of filmmaking teams have come and gone in the Amazon; they fly in for a couple of days, catch quick shots of the destruction, then fly out to the editing room. The result is always the same series of vignettes: a chain saw crew topples a tree; flames engulf a field of stumps and trunks; herds of cattle graze in the charred landscape. (When one American network news team wanted a rancher to coordinate the burning of his land with the arrival of its film crew in September 1989, even the Acre government was outraged.) Cowell was different. With a monomaniacal focus, he scraped together funding so that he could patiently film the struggles of the Amazonian peoples not just day after day, but year after year. As an old friend and colleague put it, "He thinks in time scales that are vaguely Chinese." (In fact, Cowell was born in China, and Chinese was his first language.) Whatever it took to get the shot, he did. He bought an ultralight airplane so that he could swoop low over the red dirt roads and matchstick piles that once were forests.

With Cowell was José Lutzenberger, a maverick Brazilian agron-

omist who had become one of the leaders of an international ecological movement called Gaia, which posits that all life on earth
functions as a single organism: disrupt one component and you
threaten the entire system. He and Cowell had flown in for thirty-
six hours to get some footage of Lutzenberger out amid the red dust
and rumbling logging trucks of the unpaved BR-364 highway.
Cowell was hoping to capture on film Lutzenberger's wrath at the
destruction that would follow the paving of that stretch of highway between Rio Branco and Rondônia.

Cowell was slim and deeply tanned, and his white hair and closely
trimmed white beard glowed against his face. An exceedingly quiet
man, he slowly came out of his shell as, over a few beers, he talked
about how he came to join the fight for the rain forest. His passion
for the Amazon and its peoples dated from 1957, when he spent
seven months traveling with Brazil's legendary Villas-Boas brothers,
two explorers who became specialists at contacting hidden Indian
tribes. He returned in 1969 with a government team and tramped
through the wilds of Mato Grosso to film its efforts to contact the
Krenakore, a tribe whose only previous encounters with the modern world had resulted in deaths on one side or the other.

In Rondônia, Cowell and his cameraman had followed a team
from the government's office of Indian affairs, FUNAI, as it tried
for two years to make contact with the Uru-Eu-Wau-Wau, a tribe
that was blamed for kidnapping and murdering a rubber tapper.
The tappers and other settlers had moved into land that was part
of an Indian reserve. On an open patch of high ground, the FUNAI
investigators strung pots, pans, machetes, and mirrors on lines so
that they clanked hauntingly in the wind. Nothing happened for
months, then a fusillade of yard-long arrows with sawtoothed heads
thwocked into the ground around their huts. In a flitting, grainy,
ghostly frame of celluloid, Cowell captured the first picture of one
of the Indians—the bright blob of a face amid a swaying green
mass of forest.

As the Indians of Rondônia were steadily pushed back by the
government-sponsored land rush, Cowell turned his cameras on the
newcomers. Over a five-year period beginning in 1983, he chroni-

cled the hopes and heartbreaks of a family that claimed one of the 250-acre plots offered by INCRA. The film shows how, at first, the family displays a brave pioneering spirit as the father and children hack at the forest with axes and machetes, then set fire to the mass of fallen branches and vines. Soot and dust rise as the father pokes holes in the dry soil between the smoldering corpses of the trees, then plants seeds in each hole. Over successive seasons, the land loses its fertility. The family is forced to move on, leaving a barren tract behind.

By 1988, so many roads were being scratched across Rondônia that the state's forests were broken by a spreading grid of open space that, from the air, looked like ferns flattened between the pages of a book—main roads bristling with smaller feeder roads. Clouds of smoke so darkened the sky during the burning season that airports were closed for weeks on end. Government policies that were designed to encourage the orderly immigration of small farmers from the south instead created a virtual blitz that incinerated millions of trees and left little to show for it. Rondônia represented everything that the rubber tappers of Acre, just up the highway, most feared.

The conversation inevitably turned to Chico Mendes. Starting in 1986, Cowell had become one of his most trusted and influential friends from outside the Amazon. Without Cowell, Chico Mendes would likely have remained a small-time labor leader in the Amazonian backwater of Xapuri. But Cowell had recognized in Mendes's struggle an idea that might just save some of the Amazon from the chain saws. The key was to give Mendes a bigger audience, an audience outside the forest. Cowell had filmed Mendes almost continually from 1986 until his murder. Lutzenberger had also befriended Mendes, and he had seen to it that Mendes got some grants when his money ran out. Cowell and Lutzenberger were both depressed about the slow pace of the trial of the murderers.

As they talked into the night, Lutzenberger clipped articles out of a pile of newspapers with a Swiss Army knife. He enthusiastically described some new research that used computer models of the global circulation of clouds to show how moisture from the Amazon basin affects the weather from Argentina to France. "If you turn the globe and put the Amazon in the center, then you see its fantastic impact on places as far away as Europe," said the scientist, who had a distinctly avian appearance—partly due to his long face and neck and his habit of flapping his arms excitedly when making a point. His thinning blond-gray hair was slicked straight back and cropped off abruptly, so it hung like the tassels of a curtain behind his ears. "There is westward movement of clouds from the Atlantic Ocean to the Andes. Water gets cycled between the clouds and the forest six to seven times during this trip. Once the moisture reaches the Andes, a tiny bit gets up and over; some goes all the way south to Patagonia; the rest goes up north as far as Nova Scotia and thence over to Europe."

The solar energy that bears down on the Amazon and evaporates all that water is the equivalent of two or three million hydrogen bombs of heat a day, Lutzenberger said. "Suppose we destroy the rain forest? You don't get in its place sand dunes as in the Sahara or naked rock; you get poor scrub or bare soil." The thin vegetation contains little moisture, so "instead of the fantastic evaporation you see now, which keeps things cool, the soil will get real hot. Updrafts will destroy the clouds." Where the rain forest helped sustain itself, the new hotter, drier landscape will tend to make things even hotter and drier. As a result, if enough forest is cut, the scales may be tipped sufficiently that the system no longer needs human assistance and destroys itself.

Lutzenberger stopped for a moment to sip some more beer and ponder the full moon. "A complicated system can take a lot of abuse, but you get to a point where suddenly things fall apart," he said. "It's like pushing a long ruler toward the edge of a table. Nothing happens, nothing happens, nothing happens—then, suddenly, the ruler falls to the floor."

The assault on the Amazon that now raged in Rondônia and threatened Acre was a continuation of one of the most basic processes of civilization: the conquest of the wilderness. Wild regions of the earth have always been perceived by human beings as places to be tamed, settled, and then exploited. In his sensitive book *The*

Wooing of Earth, the scientist René Dubos noted that "the word 'wilderness' occurs approximately three hundred times in the Bible, and all its meanings are derogatory." Just as the word originally had negative connotations, so too did "jungle," which was derived during Britain's occupation of India from a Hindu word for "uncultivated land" or "wasteland." In fact, biologists are loath to use the word "jungle" when referring to rain forests because of its popular association with the perilous Hollywood back lots that were the home of Tarzan and bloodthirsty headhunting tribes.

It was not surprising that at some point Brazil—whose population was historically strung along the Atlantic coast, moving inland along only a few rivers—should see in the Amazon forests more than just the source of a few products. A century earlier, the same process of settlement had changed the face of the United States as the steadily advancing frontier ate through the continent's forests. (The title "Timber Capital of the World" was briefly held by towns such as Bangor, Maine; Albany, New York; Williamsport, Pennsylvania; Saginaw, Michigan; Eureka, California; and Portland, Oregon.)

The Amazon basin—undeveloped, open, virtually free for the taking—made up more than half of Brazil's territory. When the junta gained power in 1964, the Amazon remained largely untamed. Getúlio Vargas's call for a march to the west had remained mostly a slogan. The region had been in a steady decline since 1912, when the rubber boom collapsed. In 1960, there were only 200 miles of paved roads in the Amazon, and Belém and Manaus were still the only significant population centers. The snaking, slow rivers remained the only way to move substantial amounts of goods and people. Brazil had a population of 70 million, but the 2.5-million-square-mile region defined as Classic Amazonia had only 2.5 million inhabitants. In other words, half of the nation's land area had only 3.5 percent of the nation's people.

The military government soon recognized that the settlement of the Amazon could solve a number of problems. It seemed obvious that the region could serve as a social pressure valve, a repository for "surplus population"—the phrase used by planners to describe peasants who were being driven off the land in the developed south. They were being displaced by the spread of large-scale agriculture and the accumulation of vast land holdings by a few wealthy individuals and corporations. These displaced poor were now flooding into the cities or standing their ground and agitating for land reform. It was far simpler for the government to relocate them in some out-of-the-way place than to initiate any effort at land reform; that would entail splitting up the undeveloped property of Brazil's elite and distributing it to small farmers.

The Amazon could also help absorb "surplus population" from the overcrowded, permanently depressed northeast. Over the next two decades, some Brazilians would laughingly refer to the various schemes to help this desiccated region as the country's "drought industry." For the most part, the millions of dollars that were poured into resettlement and water projects and roads heading west into the Amazon benefited only construction contractors, real estate speculators, and corrupt government officials.

Most significant, the development of the Amazon suited the generals' military plans. The forests were an obstacle to their complete control over the land; moreover, Venezuela and Peru had already started programs to occupy their Amazonian territories. So the Brazilian junta, following established military doctrine, implemented its strategy of *ocupar para não entregar,* occupy so as not to surrender. One of the military's so-called Permanent National Objectives, drawn up by theorists at Brazil's leading war college, was the occupation of the hinterlands. A central architect of this strategy was General Golbery do Couto e Silva, a leading military planner who after the coup created the National Information Service, Brazil's version of the CIA. (He was an important figure in Brazil's military governments until General João Figueiredo began the process of *abertura,* opening, that led to a return of democratic rule in 1985.) The aim, Golbery said, was to "flood the Amazon forest with civilization."

In 1966, Golbery's plan began to take effect. A law passed in October created SUDAM, the Superintendency for the Development of the Amazon. This agency, run by a general, would oversee the planned occupation and distribute incentives for industrial and agricultural projects. In December, the junta inaugurated Operation Amazonia, a series of initiatives designed to promote investment in the Amazon and build roads toward the frontier. The two prongs of the plan encouraged investments in the Amazon by Brazil's rich and migration to the Amazon by Brazil's poor.

The incentives for the wealthy were hard to resist: among them were a reprieve from corporate income taxes for ten to fifteen years; the widespread availability of subsidized loans; sharp cuts in import duties on pesticides and any equipment needed to develop Amazonian land; and enormous tax credits, which companies could use to write off 50 percent of their income tax liability from enterprises outside the Amazon as long as the savings were invested in approved projects inside the Amazon. Corporations large and small—from banks and meat packers to manufacturers of car parts, from Xerox Brazil to Brazilian Volkswagen—jumped at the easy money. Most of the businessmen in the Amazon were *paulistas,* people from the elite class of São Paulo, and even those who were not were considered *paulistas* by the peasants of the north.

The military regime was particularly eager to push the development of cattle ranches. As one minister of the interior put it, "The steer is the great pioneer of this decade." The chief goal was not to increase exports. (Indeed, Brazil has never been part of the famous "hamburger connection," in which vast areas of rain forest are being cleared to make pasture to supply cheap beef to the American fast-food industry. That depredation has been largely confined to Central America.) The idea was to ensure plentiful supplies of inexpensive beef at a time when union wage hikes were curtailed to slow inflation. The availability of cheap meat was one of the few concessions the government made to appease the working class. Anyone who has ever been to a Brazilian *churrascada,* barbecue, where slab after slab of grilled meat is served until the guests reel and collapse in atherosclerotic ecstasy, understands the political significance of beef.

Besides making economic sense, ranching appealed to the sensibility of a large fraction of Brazilian businessmen, whose families made their fortunes on land in the south before they had moved to the cities. There was an appeal, a certain cachet, to being a *fazendeiro,* a rancher. In the first ten years of the government's program, three quarters of a billion dollars in tax rebates were doled out for 354 projects involving cattle ranching. But many of the *fazendeiros* were ruthless in their drive to acquire and develop the land. Attracted to Acre once the southern Amazonian states were overrun, they eventually hired *pistoleiros* to expel the rubber tappers from their forests and assassinate anyone who stood in the way of "progress"—including Chico Mendes.

At first, the new Amazonian landowning class simply hired local labor to slash and burn the forest cover. But their methods were inefficient; even with chain saws with blades a yard long, the forest giants such as *tarumã* and tropical cedar sometimes took an hour or more to bring down. Later, more efficient methods of deforestation were introduced, the most dramatic being the *correntão*— big chain—technique, in which a length of massive anchor chain was pulled through a stand of forest by two enormous bulldozers, toppling the shallowly rooted trees in a deafening chaos of sound as if they were so many toothpicks.

The cleared forests contained millions of tons of valuable hardwood, such as mahogany and cedar, yet the timber was almost always left to burn or rot. Economists now estimate that as much as $250 million worth of valuable timber was destroyed on SUDAM ranches alone. Herbicides were used on the smaller brush. Starting in the early 1970s, one of the most popular herbicides was Tordon, a potent defoliant sold by the Dow Chemical Company which had the same ingredients as Agent Orange—ingredients that Dow had in enormous quantities now that the Vietnam War was over.

After the cutting came the burning; soon the bright sunshine of each dry season became dimmed by a perpetual haze of smoke. After the fires died out, workers would spread grass seed in the new pasture and then turn a few head of cattle out to graze.

By the mid-1960s, the migration into the region had already begun of its own accord in chaotic fashion. Displaced small farmers and independent ranchers were pouring north along the Belém-Brasília Highway, in the eastern Amazon. In a 50-mile-wide corridor where the road cut through the states of Goiás, Maranhão, and Pará, millions of acres of public land were claimed, cut, and burned.

The settlers relied on the ancient *direito de posse,* right of possession, which has been recognized by Brazilian law since 1850 but dates from the colonial period. Under this rule, a *posseiro,* squatter, who stays unchallenged on a plot for a year and a day and puts it to some "productive" use gains the right to occupy up to 250 acres —or 7,000 acres if the land is not under any local or state control. After five years, he can acquire a paper title. In the Amazon, the simplest way for a settler to prove that land was being put to productive use was to cut down the forest. The area underwent explosive change. According to a study by Roberto Santos, a Brazilian economist and lawyer, between 1949 and 1953 the state of Pará sold 86,000 acres of land. Ten years later, between 1959 and 1963, the state sold 13.8 million acres of land. In the 1970s, somewhere between 200,000 and 400,000 people moved into the region along that first highway.

This first real land boom in the Amazon resulted in a climate of conflict, fraud, and violence that has been repeated wherever roads have been cut and continues today. Here the process of *grilagem,* land-grabbing through the creation of false land titles, was turned into a fine art. Offices holding real estate records mysteriously burned to the ground. Bribes were freely given and freely accepted. Sometimes titles were signed over at gunpoint. Soon, there were more titles to land in Pará than there was land. This phenomenon would spread to other parts of the Amazon. In Acre, the situation was made even more complex—and primed for fraud—by the existence of nineteenth-century *Bolivian* titles along with various layerings of Brazilian titles.

By 1970, much of the land along the Belém-Brasília Highway had been developed and then abandoned, as the settlers discovered that the underlying soils were too poor to sustain agriculture. Erosion set in, resulting in what one researcher called "a ghost landscape."

In theory, some limits were placed on the destruction. The Law of the Fifty prohibited a landowner from deforesting more than 50 percent of his property. But landowners soon realized that the law had a huge loophole. They could sell the uncut 50 percent to, say, a son; then the new owner could burn off half of the forest on his tract before "selling" the forested part to yet another "owner," and so on. Other supposed controls were placed on the conversion of land to pasture. If a company wanted to create a cattle ranch on a particular tract, it had to get a certificate from local officials indicating that no peasants or rubber tappers had squatters' rights to the land. And it had to have the new Indian agency, FUNAI, certify that no Indians occupied the site. In practice, the receipt of such certificates was more often the result of a few well-placed bribes than a field survey. Another alternative was to drive any inhabitants off the land with violence. As the pressure to develop grew during the early 1970s, the ranchers increasingly used bloody means to achieve their end.

Most of these SUDAM projects were developed along the southern flank of the rain forest, on the Pará–Mato Grosso border. The planners assumed that the presence of certain upland areas of savanna in this part of the Amazon basin was evidence that most of the region could support grassland. And then there was Marajó, the massive island in the mouth of the Amazon. Water buffalo had been raised on its grassy plains for centuries, so obviously the rest of the Amazon could support livestock. As had happened many times before when outsiders confronted the lushness of the region, the planners were fooled into thinking that the earth supported this biological richness; they never imagined that the forests might be great green castles built on sand. Even Alfred Russel Wallace, the naturalist, was duped. He wrote: "I fearlessly assert that here the primeval forest can be converted into rich pastureland, into cultivated gardens and orchards, containing every variety of produce, with half the labor, and what is more important, in less than half the time that would be required at home." As it turned out, of course, the planners—and Wallace before them—were wrong.

If all of these ranches had succeeded, the human, environmental, and economic costs of the Amazon development scheme might have been a little less painful. But most of the ranches never came close to reaching their planned potential. For one thing, SUDAM's hasty approval process neglected to assess carefully the nature of the underlying soil. The surveys that had been done were on too large a scale to discern the wide variations in Amazonian soil quality. (This was long before Brazil had ever heard of environmental impact reports. Even though such reports are now required for major Amazonian development projects, there is still no public debate, and projects frequently still receive a rubber stamp.)

As pointed out by Susanna Hecht, an agronomist who surveyed soils in the southern Amazon in the 1970s and who has since become one of the world's experts on the mismanagement of the region, in some areas the use of heavy equipment compressed the soil until it baked into brick-hard laterite. In others, the nutrient-hungry *capim* grass quickly sopped up many essential minerals. If fertilizers had been used, and other self-fertilizing plants mixed in with the grasses, the soil might have remained productive, but few ranches employed agronomists who might suggest such innovations, and the government failed to provide any technical assistance. And everywhere there was the incessant invasion of fields by inedible weed species and brush. The typical result was that after five years, pasture that might have supported one head of cattle for every 2.5 acres—a bad ratio to begin with—would drop to one head of cattle for every 10 acres. Soon thereafter, the land would simply be abandoned.

Most of the failures were downplayed in government statistics, and word that the Amazon in general was a bad place for raising cattle did not make it back down south. For some of the investors moving north to start cattle ranches, the low yield and bad soil were irrelevant; they were more interested in the rapidly rising value of the land itself than in the beef that might be raised on it. And everyone liked the idea of free money from the subsidized rural credit offered throughout Brazil. Often loans were available for ranchers at interest rates far below the rate of inflation. (In 1975, for example, when inflation was running at 35 percent a year, the interest rate charged on these loans was 7 percent.)

For every ranch funded by SUDAM, there were nine more that were created by independent ranchers, according to a report by Dennis Mahar, a World Bank economist. The independents were motivated by either the easy credit or the cheap land. Many of them were small farmers who chose to raise cattle because cattle require little labor, once the land is deforested, and they are a self-transporting commodity—they can walk to the slaughter-house. (Even among the rubber tappers, a few head of cattle are seen as desirable—as both a hedge against inflation and a way of carrying rubber out of the forest.)

The impact on the Amazon of the rush to raise cattle was calcu-lated by Robert Repetto of the World Resources Institute. By 1980, 35,156 square miles of forest had been converted to pasture, or 73 percent of the total deforested area of 47,718 square miles. When all of the subsidies and tax breaks and operating costs of the ranches were tallied, it turned out that the incentives to bring cattle ranch-ing to the Amazon cost Brazil $2.9 billion. And after all of that effort, the Amazon was (and still remains) a net importer of beef.

The ranches did nothing to boost regional employment, either. Studies show that the big ranches employed only one person for every 600 to 700 acres of pasture. And those who did work on the ranches could hardly make a decent living. Except for *boiadeiros* (cowboys) and *pistoleiros,* most ranch labor was picked up from contractors called *gatos,* cats, who would scour the flophouses in Amazonian towns, pay off the debts of unemployed migrants, and force them into indentured labor until they could repay the *gatos.*

One rancher after another discovered the disappointments and hazards of raising cattle in the Amazon. Along with erosion and bad soil, they had to cope with malaria, which often felled a third to a half of a ranch's labor force. Malaria tended to thrive in areas of fresh deforestation, where puddles formed and mosquitoes nor-mally restricted to the treetops descended to the ground. Typical is the story of a São Paulo businessman named Carlos Vilela de

Andrade, who bought 100,000 acres of untouched forest a few miles from the Belém-Brasília Highway in 1966. His workers quickly cut and burned the trees, but by 1975 weeds and brush were swamping the pastures and the soil was deteriorating. His initial euphoria had vanished. By 1979, he was broke; a corporate partner in the enterprise had taken over his shares and was trying to sell the ranch, with no takers.

Along with encouraging private development, the government's other major ploy to attract people to the Amazon was to build a vast network of roads. To shunt some of the newcomers away from the overburdened lands in the southeastern Amazon, the government hastened to complete the extension of BR-364, the highway that eventually snaked its way from the south of Brazil up to Acre. It was the stretch built from Cuiabá, the capital of Mato Grosso, to Pôrto Velho, the capital of what is now the state of Rondônia, that sparked most of the destruction. Even though the road was not paved until 1980, through the 1970s the population of the area grew at a dizzying pace.

Most of the migrants came from the south. Between 1970 and 1980, there was a net emigration of two and a half million people from Paraná, for example. Most went to the urban slums, but when word made it back to the south that there were substantial areas of fertile soil along BR-364 in Rondônia, the result was natural enough. Between 1970 and 1985, the population of Rondônia exploded from less than 100,000 to more than 730,000, with most of the new arrivals coming from the south. The state could not begin to support this flood of people—nor could the road. During the rainy season, buses were bogged down for days at a time. Along sparsely populated sections of roadway, there were reports of people dying in their bus seats. And for those who made it to Rondônia, the fertile land was long gone; INCRA was overwhelmed with applications for land. Those who grew tired of standing in line simply headed out beyond the planned grid of feeder roads and burned their way into the forest.

In 1970, not satisfied with the existing network, the government created a new program of road building and colonization that was intended to accelerate the development of the Amazon further. The so-called National Integration Plan was conceived by the military without any advice from Brazil's Congress. The plan was abruptly announced in June, after President Emílio Garrastazul Médici made a carefully orchestrated visit to the northeast at the height of an intense drought. There he found the justification to build a dirt highway to nowhere—the Transamazon—after seeing hordes of malnourished children and masses of homeless, hopeless peasants. Médici told reporters, "Nothing in my whole life has shocked and upset me so deeply."

The project called for the construction of a 3,400-mile highway running due west from the parched northeast bulge of Brazil, paralleling the main trunk of the Amazon River about 300 miles to the south. Other highways would run north and south. The goal was to lure 100,000 families into the Amazon within six years. It was hoped that 75 percent of those migrants would come from the northeast. Each family would be given title to a 250-acre lot, a prefabricated house, and a minimum salary, around $30 a month, for the first six to eight months. The road building would be coordinated with offers of land, cash, seeds, schools, and health posts overseen by INCRA. Villages, towns, and even small cities would be built from scratch. The government calculated the ancillary benefits: the process of building the roads would create jobs and the construction might uncover mineral deposits. To help sell the plan, the government devised the slogan "A land without people for a people without land."

After an initial burst of interest fueled by a barrage of propaganda, the effort fizzled and died. By 1980, only eight thousand families had settled in INCRA lots along the highway. Families who were accustomed to farming the open land of the south and northeast were flown by jet into the rain forest, where they scratched confusedly at the poor soil and watched as unfamiliar pests and weeds hindered their efforts. There was no consistent market for the crops they managed to raise. The oil crises of the 1970s made it too expensive to transport goods and crops from the Amazon.

Many colonists were felled by malaria. And the integration program failed to attract the very people it sought: less than a third of the settlers came from the northeast. Some of them began to call the Transamazon the "Transmisery" highway.

While the organized colonization scheme floundered, the road served a chaotic stream of thousands of settlers who cut their way into the forests and became *posseiros*. For every INCRA settler, there were four unofficial homesteaders. Ironically, many in this group fared better than those who moved within the system. According to Emílio Moran, an anthropologist who studied the highway project from its inception to the present, about 30 percent of the settlers were seasoned *ribeirinhos* or rubber tappers who followed the roads just as they once followed an Amazon tributary. By studying the character of the forest, they were able to locate distinctive plant communities that indicated the presence of *terra roxa*, a particularly fertile soil, and they staked their claims on these buried riches.

In the end, the Transamazon and the other roads of the National Integration Plan cost the Brazilian government about $39,000 for every settler relocated. No vast mineral riches were uncovered. The landscape of the Transamazon was not the flat plain the planners had presumed from inadequate surveys; it proved to be a nightmare of short, steep hills, resembling the corrugated tin roof of a settler's hut. At every low spot, the rainy season turned the road into a muddy, malarial swamp. As the settlers cleared and farmed the hills, what little soil remained quickly washed away.

Moreover, the resettlement schemes did not serve as a population pressure valve. According to a study by Charles Wood and John Wilson, social scientists at the University of Florida, Gainesville, of the estimated 17 million small farmers and peasants who were forced to leave the farmland in the south in the 1970s, only 766,000 ended up in the Amazon—less than 5 percent of the total. The vast majority wound up in the tin and brick *favelas* that now surround São Paulo, Rio de Janeiro, Curitiba, and other southern cities, magnifying urban problems such as crime, unemployment, and drug abuse. Those few who did head north ended up in a similar setting. Once they abandoned their land, most moved into the cities along the rivers, creating a new galaxy of tropical *favelas* that is still expanding.

Despite the failure of the first two strategies for Amazonian occupation—private investment and internal migration—the planners were not dissuaded from trying one more time. In 1973, dozens of Brazil's wealthiest businessmen were flown to the Amazon by the planning ministry and shown great tracts of undeveloped land that had been made accessible by the new roads. They were wooed with a new package of incentives called Polamazonia, which involved the creation in 1974 of fifteen economic "poles" that would act like magnets to draw industry and people into targeted regions.

One of the biggest poles was the Carajás mining project, which eventually grew to encompass 300,000 square miles, fully a sixth of Brazil's portion of the Amazon basin. This project was centered around a chain of low mountains 340 miles south of the port of Belém. In 1967, a geologist working for U.S. Steel had discovered that this Serra dos Carajás range was rich in iron ore. Later it was shown to be the largest known deposit of iron ore in the world— roughly 18 billion tons of 66 percent pure ore—enough to make Brazil a leading producer for several centuries to come. The mountains also contain copper, manganese, nickel, and gold, among other minerals. The iron mine itself was developed carefully, to minimize environmental damage, but related projects became environmental disasters.

Through the 1970s, Brazil created a $60 billion plan to develop the region, funded by loans from Japan, the United States, Europe, and the World Bank. It included the construction of a 534-mile railway to the coast, a series of hydroelectric dams, ten new cities to house workers, and a network of improved roads to encourage smelters and other industries to move into the area. One destructive offspring of the Carajás mines was pig-iron smelters, plants that extract crude iron from the ore with heat. But their huge furnaces are fueled by charcoal. Eventually, the plan is to make charcoal by burning the wood from plantations of eucalyptus trees, which grow quickly. But right now, the kilns that produce the charcoal are being fed wood that is obtained the cheapest possible way—by cutting down great tracts of rain forest. If the number of smelters grows as fast as projected, the charcoal kilns will consume as much as 900 square miles of forest per year.

Another pole of the Polamazonia project was a series of hydro-electric dams such as Tucurui, a 12-mile arc of concrete built across the Tocantins, one of the largest tributaries of the Amazon. The reservoir that formed behind this dam when its sluices were closed in 1984 has replaced 1,461 square miles of rain forest with a stewing lake full of 50 million tons of rotting timber. The original plan was for the timber to be harvested before the flood. But the firm created by the government to do the job became mired in corruption and the basin was flooded before any wood could be saved. A handful of adventurous entrepreneurs have since taken to harvesting some of the valuable trees submerged in the lake using scuba gear and *hydroserras,* chain saws converted to underwater use.

Normally, hydroelectric power is considered "clean" power, but in this case the rotting vegetation in the reservoir is emitting thousands of tons of methane each year. Like the carbon dioxide that is given off when trees burn, methane is a "greenhouse" gas, one that traps the sun's energy and may contribute to global warming.

Besides flooding a chunk of forest the size of Rhode Island, the reservoir displaced several Indian tribes and six villages. The filmmaker Adrian Cowell was there when the dam began to fill. During the filming, something happened that has haunted him ever since—one of those little incidents in the Amazon that are tiny reflections of a greater tragedy. Cowell had hired an underwater cinematographer to shoot some footage inside a church that was disappearing beneath the rising lake, along with the rest of an abandoned village. All that showed was the roof and the spire. As Cowell recalled it, "The only thing that made it into the film was the floating pews, but during the shoot, the diver saw a cat that had climbed up in the rafters above where the water had already reached. Imagine what it must have been like for that poor cat. The water was steadily rising, higher and higher. There was nowhere to go but up. The cat was starving, hardly more than a skeleton. And then, when they tried to rescue it, imagine what it saw: a man with this mask and oxygen tanks and all. The cat dove into the water and paddled frantically away, then paddled out into the open lake," he said. They lost sight of it on the dappled surface. "Surely it must have drowned."

Just as the biological complexity of the Amazon had confounded generations of biologists, its fragile maze of intertwined causes and effects had confounded Brazil's planners. All of the government's projects resulted in little more than the destruction of great tracts of forest. Few families benefited. Nationwide, long after the military government began its great program to integrate the country geographically and economically, Brazilian society was more divided than ever. Through the period of the junta, Brazil's policies satisfied the goals of the military, industrial, and agricultural elite, with almost no regard for the overwhelming majority of the population. As the economy accelerated, fueled by loans from abroad and incentives for the rich, the plight of the average Brazilian grew dramatically worse. The gulf between rich and poor widened until it could not be crossed.

Before the coup of 1964, the wealthiest 5 percent of the population earned 28 percent of the national income, while the poorest 50 percent earned only 17 percent. Although this imbalance was enormous, the situation twenty-five years later was worse. By 1980, at the height of the military's power, the income of Brazil's richest 5 percent rose to 34 percent of the national total while the income of the poorest half dropped to 12 percent. As a small piece of Brazil vaulted into the First World, the remainder stayed locked in Third World poverty. While skyscrapers soared over the bustling downtowns of Rio and São Paulo, a third of all the homes in the nation still lacked plumbing.

Brazil's grandiose strategy for occupying the Amazon also failed to take into account an important fact: the forest was already occupied. Thousands of Indians, *ribeirinhos,* tappers, Brazil nut gatherers, and other groups had been living and working in the forest for decades, some whose cultures dated back centuries. As the roads chewed farther into the forest, carrying cattle and land-hungry people, the inevitable result was violent conflict. Of all the forest dwellers, the Indians suffered the most. As the military government of the 1960s studied the Amazon, it looked on Indian occupants as nothing more than an inconvenience. "Only when we are sure," explained one general, "that every corner of the Amazon is settled by real Brazilians, and not Indians, will we be able to say that the Amazon belongs to us."

For the Indians, the occupation of the Amazon was simply an acceleration of the wave of murder and disease that had swept the indigenous Brazilians for four and a half centuries. Between 1511 and 1650, most of the Indian population in the region around São Paulo—estimated by some at more than a million—was either slaughtered outright or enslaved to work in the brazilwood trade and on the sugarcane plantations. The colonial economy was so dependent on this labor that when, in 1639, Pope Urban VIII threatened to excommunicate any Brazilian colonist who enslaved an Indian, the Jesuits were run out of town in São Paulo and a riot at the Jesuit college in Rio nearly resulted in the deaths of several priests. In the 1700s, so-called punitive expeditions ventured into the interior with the sole intent of destroying the Indians. They were followed by *bandeirantes,* who fanned out from São Paulo into the hinterlands to take slaves and expand the Portuguese holdings. And this was only the vanguard.

Subsequent waves of miners, slavers, coffee barons, rubber barons, and finally ranchers resulted in a toll that far exceeds even the slaughter in North America. The Indians were considered little more than *bichos do mato,* beasts of the forest. The rubber trade was as devastating to the Indians as any of the other inducements that brought white men into the forest. In some areas, the Indians were forced to tap the rubber trees. The most notorious example was in Peru, where tens of thousands of Indians along the Putumayo River were forced to harvest rubber for a British company and were tortured or killed if they lagged or fled. Skirmishes often erupted between rubber tappers and Indians—with a killing requiring a reprisal and vice versa. (It was only through the efforts of Chico Mendes and the leaders of Brazil's burgeoning Indian rights movement in the late 1980s that the rubber tappers and Indians improved their relations and forged the Alliance of the Peoples of the Forest. They agreed that the new wave of ranchers and miners flooding the Amazon posed a common threat that far outweighed their old animosity.)

Wherever white men went in Brazil, Indians who were not intentionally murdered succumbed. Sometimes the cause was disease; the Indians had no natural immunity to influenza, measles, and other infections carried by the *civilizados,* the white newcomers. And the spread of disease was not always an accident. There are various reports, some from this century, that clothing was taken from smallpox victims and strung along Indian trails as a diabolical gift. At other times, the Indians simply were victims of cultural murder—called ethnocide by anthropologists—as merchants and missionaries ensnared them in the Western net of commerce, religion, and alcohol.

Not until 1910 did the Brazilian republic make its first effort to limit these abuses. The Indian Protection Service was anything but comprehensive; initiated by Colonel Cândido Mariano da Silva Rondon, it was mainly a one-man show. Rondon was born on the edge of the Amazon, in Cuiabá, and led acclaimed expeditions into virgin parts of the territory now named Rondônia in his honor. Rondon insisted that the Indian tribes he contacted along the way be approached slowly and dealt with humanely. His trailblazing teams of *sertanistas* became renowned for their ability to establish relations with reclusive tribes. Their motto was: "Die if necessary, but never kill." Many did die and, until 1930, no Indians were killed.

When Getúlio Vargas came to power that year, Rondon was forced out, and the Indian Protection Service was soon transformed into a tool of the white settlers. By the 1960s, it was widely known that the agency was participating in Indian massacres. In 1968, an investigation into reported atrocities produced testimony alleging that the "protection" service had helped to poison Indian children, infect tribes with diseases, and force Indian women into prostitution.

The Indian Protection Service was abolished and replaced by FUNAI, which was headed by military men; its mandate was to incorporate the Indians into Brazilian society and the economy. But it was run under the Ministry of the Interior, whose motto— "Security and development"—succinctly expressed its antipathy toward the goals of the Indians. FUNAI soon became nearly as corrupt as its predecessor, and Indians who were deemed to be making "unproductive" use of their land were often shifted into villages set up by FUNAI. They were put to work, with their income going to the agency, which supposedly returned the funds to Indian projects. In fact, the money often went to feed FUNAI's own bureaucracy.

Through the twentieth century, the decimation of the Indians continued. As late as 1900, almost half of Brazil's Indians had not yet been exposed to whites. As the southern frontiers expanded and the forests disappeared, dozens of tribes were massacred. The Brazilian anthropologist Alcida Ramos projected that by 1989, only three or four large groups of Indians had not been contacted. Since 1900, it is estimated that eighty-seven Indian groups have become extinct. Out of the five million Indians who were estimated to have inhabited the territory now called Brazil when Cabral landed in 1500, some 213,000 remained as of 1989, with most of them living in the Amazon. Two states now officially record no Indian residents, and the state of Rio de Janeiro, once occupied by many coastal tribes, now is said to have thirty-four Indians. As the anthropologist Claude Lévi-Strauss recounted in *Tristes Tropiques*, "In 1918, the maps of the state of São Paulo, which is as big as France, showed it as being two-thirds 'unknown territory inhabited only by Indians'; by the time I arrived in 1935 there was not a single Indian left, apart from a few families who used to come to the Santos beaches on Sundays to sell so-called curios."

Even as the 1980s ended, pressure on the remaining Indians continued to mount. The army moved ahead with plans for a sweeping 4,000-mile-long military zone along Brazil's northern borders—the so-called Northern Trench—which would entail canceling the demarcation of Indian lands along the border and encouraging "white settlers" to occupy the land. Brazil's unprecedented gold rush, which brought several hundred thousand freelance miners into the Amazon, resulted in the invasion of more than two dozen Indian reserves.

One of the most horrifying recent examples of the abuse of the Indians involves the Ticuna tribe, which has lived along the Solimões River deep in Amazonas since the 1600s. The Ticuna had been the victims of unprovoked attacks by timber crews, who were hired to cut valuable mahogany trees—worth as much as $12,000 each—on Indian territory. On March 28, 1988, about a hundred Ticuna had come into the town of Tabatinga for a meeting. While they were waiting for a FUNAI official to arrive, a gang of timber workers appeared and opened fire. According to Amnesty International, fourteen Indians were killed, including four children under the age of ten. Ten of the victims were shot as they attempted to flee by canoe; their bodies drifted downstream and were never recovered.

For centuries, Brazil's Indians fought such attacks, but as many tribes approached extinction, they began to modify their tactics. Violence sometimes proved effective in the short run, frightening the white settlers or driving them from Indian territory; but inevitably they returned, usually with the government on their side. As small farmers and ranchers moved into Rondônia, for example, the Zoró tribe, considered the best archers in the region, went to war on three fronts, attacking the ranchers who had invaded Indian territory from the east and west and fighting two other Indian tribes that had been pushed into their territory when white settlers advanced from the south.

By the mid-1970s, the Indians had put down their weapons and come under FUNAI's control, moving to a reservation between two rivers. But in August 1985, when they learned that much of their territory was being invaded by still more settlers, they waged one last, brief war. Gilio Brunelli, an anthropologist who was with the tribe at the time, described what happened in the *Cultural*

Survival Quarterly: "On Monday, August 26, 1985, forty Zoró warriors, adorned with red and black dye, macaw and sparrow hawk feather crowns and black necklaces across their breasts, armed themselves with shotguns, bows and arrows, knives and machetes, left the village and disappeared into the bush. They won their first battle, and seized three whites who were brought back to the village to be kept as hostages." They went out again in search of more captives, but three days later returned forlorn, realizing that there were far too many whites already established on their land. They released the prisoners and surrendered to their fate.

More recently, the Indians changed their target. Several times, hundreds of Indians, painted for war and wielding spears, clubs, and the weapon of the 1980s activist—the video camera—took the long bus ride to Brasília to contest government plans that would further reduce their rights and lands. Created in 1979, the Union of Indigenous Nations grew into a powerful lobby with influence in Brazil's Congress. The Indians also flew representatives to the United States, where they were welcomed by American congressmen and in the offices of the World Bank and other international lenders.

The rubber tappers were better off than the Indians with whom they shared the forest; after all, they were white, could resist Western diseases, and spoke Portuguese. But the ranchers had the potential to annihilate their culture and drive them from their land. Just as the Indians found strength in united action, so too did the tappers. As the roads moved north and west, the tappers also began to resist the tide of destruction that threatened to destroy the forest. Along with the Indians, they found allies in the Catholic church and Brazil's free trade union movement, which was expanding as the military loosened its hold slightly on the country. All the tappers wanted was the right to live on the land they had called home for generations and the right to work within the intact, healthy forest. As Jaime da Silva Araújo, a tapper leader from Amazonas, put it, "The roads bring destruction under a mask called progress. Let us put this progress where the land has already been deforested, where it is idle of labor and where we have to find people work. . . . But let us leave those who want to live in the forest, who want to keep it as it is. We have nothing written. I don't have anything that was created in somebody's office. There is no philosophy. It is just the real truth."

The tappers would have to fight to preserve that truth.

Chapter 7
The Fight for the Forest

T HE COLUMN of two dozen rubber tappers came upon the
chain saw crew after hiking through an abandoned *seringal*
for an hour. The area, several miles from Xapuri, used to
be Seringal Nova Esperança, the Rubber Estate New Hope. Now
it was called Fazenda Nova Esperança, the New Hope Ranch.
Earlier, they had passed the disintegrating shack of a rubber tapper
who had long since moved into town, now that a rancher owned
the land. The thatch roof of the shack had come undone, and the
plaited fronds chattered in the wind.

Cumulus clouds were piling up in the afternoon heat, and thunder rumbled across the sky, but the chance of rain was slim. It was
September 1989, well into the dry season; even the low sections of
the trail, once muddy, were now hard, like fired clay. The ground
was pocked with deep hoofprints where cattle had ventured into
the rain forest in search of fodder.

The tappers heard the chain saws first. The whine of the revving
motors carried for quite a distance through the dense, low forest
cover—the secondary growth called *capoeira*. This area had already
been cut once, probably a decade earlier from the look of the wild
tangle of growth that is only seen where the canopy has been ripped
away and there is plenty of sun. The tappers were convinced that
the rancher who had hired the crew, a young *paulista* named Mar-

cos Carvalho Costa Filho, nicknamed Junior, was having them cut
700 acres illegally.

Earlier that same day, Dalmo Rufino, a forestry official, had gone
out to the ranch by boat. A chunky man who did not take well to
exertion, Rufino did not hike into the forest and so concluded that
all was in order. The tappers, therefore, had decided to do his
inspecting for him, and now they had come to *empatar* the cutting
—quite simply, to stop it. They knew that the rancher did not have
a permit; without one he could only cut 120 acres. No one was
surprised by the violation: Junior and his father had developed a
bad reputation among the tappers. In 1981, when the Costas had
offered cash to 127 tappers to leave another *seringal* they had taken
over, the tappers refused to budge. The Costas then sent in the
police, who had the tappers arrested.

Nine months after the murder of Chico Mendes, the *empate*—
the essential element in the struggle to save the Amazon rain forest
—was still alive and well. The *empate* was an instinctive, defensive
reaction of the people who had lived in the forest for generations
to the occupation of their land by outsiders intent on destruction.
To the rubber tappers, it did not matter if the newcomers, these
paulista ranchers, had valid or fraudulent titles. It did not matter if
they were offering cash or brandishing shotguns. What mattered
was that the tappers had a claim to the forest trails that was more
fundamental than any piece of paper, and they were not about to
give it up.

In a way, the *empate* was the ultimate expression of Brazil's
ancient *direito de posse*. Acreanos and *nordestinos* have a very different definition of *empate* from people in the southern, sophisticated part of Brazil—and from Portuguese dictionaries. Indeed,
most press accounts concerning Chico Mendes have misinterpreted
empate, using the standard meaning of standoff or draw, as in a
stalemated chess match. Rubber tappers staging an *empate* have no
intention of settling for a stalemate; their goal is to stop, to prevent,
to drive the ranchers and their workers out.

The column of tappers—both men and women—was led by
the lanky, loping, wolflike form of Raimundo de Barros, Chico

Mendes's cousin and the treasurer of the National Council of Rubber Tappers. Right behind him was the slim, round-headed figure of Júlio Barbosa de Aquino. Barbosa, whose father had taught Euclides Távora how to tap rubber trees, had been voted president of the rubber tappers' council at its first meeting after the death of Chico Mendes. The other tappers had come into Xapuri for a meeting designed to attract new members to the cooperative. One of them had walked through the night for fourteen hours, with only a two-hour break for a nap. Three people on the *empate* were political and union activists from Rio Branco. Also on hand was Gomercindo Rodrigues, a thirty-one-year-old agronomist and firebrand who had worked closely with Mendes since 1986. Rodrigues was the only person from outside the Amazon who was strong enough to outpace a tapper on an all-day hike. His long legs, fast feet, and short goatee were a familiar sight on *seringais* throughout eastern Acre, and his hot temper and combative tone made him a prime target of the ranchers' gunmen.

The trail straggled out of the forest and into a field bristling with lopped-off saplings and bamboo spears that required careful footwork. The field needed to dry out a bit more; then it would be ready for burning. Up ahead were two laborers, each wielding a Stihl 051 AVE chain saw weighing 40 pounds. The saws had an aggressive look, with the hand guard shielding the blade studded with jagged projections designed to grip the tree trunk as it bit in.

The two men balanced the machines on their hips and watched the tappers approach. "You should put down your saws," said Raimundo de Barros to the laborers, who were of the same slim, dark *nordestino* stock as the tappers. Most often, the men who are hired to do the cutting and burning have much more in common with the rubber tappers than with their employers. In fact, many of them were rubber tappers before they were forced off their *seringais* when the land was bought or grabbed by cattle interests. They then moved into the *favelas* around Rio Branco or the shanty communities that sprang up around Xapuri.

With little resistance, the cutters agreed to stop. (Not having a great stake in their work, the cutting gangs almost invariably yield when confronted during an *empate*.) The tappers asked the cutters to show them their camp. The two men heaved the saws onto their shoulders and began the sweaty, half-hour march to their shacks, down where the ranch property met a bend in the Acre River. The camp consisted of three log huts with black plastic tarpaulin for the roofs and flimsy walls of thatched palm fronds. Each was a rough version of the typical forest house, with a kitchen at one end and hammocks strung at the other. One shack belonged to the *gato*, the labor contractor who had hired these men and was overseeing the cutting. He was in town buying some supplies, but his wife was there. Dogs and chickens scooted around, and several children splashed in the silty water that flowed over a white sand beach. Laundry was drying on cords strung between the trees. Two shotguns were propped against a log next to a battered guitar. A tapper cracked open the barrels of the guns; they were loaded.

As was customary in the rain forest, little was said at first. Someone passed around a pack of cigarettes. A few of the tappers politely asked for water, and the *gato*'s wife proffered a shiny cooking oil tin that was used as a water jug. Then the talking began, and they all spoke as if reading a script. De Barros started to lecture the workers about the forest, the ranchers who employed them, and alternatives. "You should understand that when there are trees to cut, Junior pays you, but when the trees are gone, he's going to fire you," he said.

One of the cutters, a man of about twenty, wearing jeans and a tattered, sleeveless T-shirt stained by oil from his saw, said, "We have to work here because we have to take care of our families. We have no other work." He dug the toe of one boot into the instep of the other and drew on his cigarette. "Look," he said, "I knew Chico Mendes. He was my cousin."

De Barros did not like that answer. His big eyes burned and his dark face, framed by muttonchop sideburns, twisted into an angry frown. "If you were close to Chico, I can't understand why you're helping these ranchers, who promoted Chico's murder. With what you're doing, you're saying that the death of Chico is as significant as the death of a dog. You could raise your kids in the forest, so why are you doing this?" He had worked up a head of steam now. "In the forest you can make money not just cutting trees. The forest has many riches. But the big landowners are not interested. They just want to cut and plant pasture. When the *seringalistas* came in the past, they put *seringueiros* against Indians. Now the ranchers are putting their workers against the *seringueiros*. We are actually brothers in this struggle."

Everyone knew what was coming next. After an awkward silence, Barbosa abruptly announced, "There is no permit for the cutting that is going on here. We are going to dismantle your camp. If we don't, you'll be back here tomorrow."

Without another word, the tappers began to lug all of the workers' belongings out of the shacks. They stooped to stay clear of the beams supporting the five-foot-high roof. The wife of the *gato* complained, "You should at least wait until my husband returns!" But no one was listening.

The tappers carried out two brand-new spare chain saws, their opened cartons lying nearby. They carried out the jerry cans of gasoline and all the cooking pots. Many of the implements had been advanced to the work crews on credit, just as the rubber tappers had been advanced the tools of their trade. Once again, the landless poor were working their way into debt.

The tarpaulins were untied from the log framework of each hut. Someone took up a saw and pulled the starter cord; a shrill whine cut the air as the chain sang around the metal tongue. Another saw sputtered to life. "Dismantled" is too gentle a word for what happened next. The *empate* has repeatedly been characterized in the press as a peaceful sit-in, something that Gandhi or Martin Luther King, Jr., might have conceived. But in fact it is frequently an aggressive showdown, a classic Brazilian confrontation in which bluff counts for a lot but must be backed up by a willingness to act.

Barbosa grabbed a *foice,* a hooked machete blade on the end of a long handle, and began to whack at the smaller roof spars. The cutting crew and the women and children stood back, out of the way, watching silently with their hands folded across their chests. Now the chain saws went to work, chewing into the exposed skeleton of the first shack. The tappers wielded them with agility and skill; this time the machines were turned against the invaders instead of the forest. Soon, amid a spray of sawdust, the three huts disintegrated into scrap.

From start to finish, the "dismantling" took three minutes. A soccer ball lay amid the fallen framework of one house. A puppy barked confusedly. The chain saw crew stood silent, slightly dazed. Someone asked a laborer how he felt. "They destroyed everything," he said flatly. "Now we have to leave. We cannot stay. We'll go to Xapuri, where we live. I think we'll stay in Xapuri, out of all this mess."

The tappers left as they had come, marching single file across the stubbly field that had once been a thicket and before that a tall, rich forest. There was a splattering of rain just a few hundred yards away, but it passed them by. A faint sickle of rainbow hung in the drifting drops, almost near enough to touch.

One tapper, José Targino, walked with a new bounce in his step. "It is twelve years now that I've been doing *empates*," he said to a visitor as he marched along. "I never tire of this." Targino had the frame and face of a seasoned featherweight boxer. He was wiry and tough, with a flattened, broken nose that gave his voice a perpetual nasal twang. He had told the cutting crew to take whatever food they could when they left the camp. "After an *empate*, the rancher won't always pay the workers their salary. They have to take what they can get." He said the tappers always talked with the workers first and never took anything, not even a machete—although it was sometimes hard to resist. After all, the ranchers had burned or driven hundreds of tapper families out of their homes. It was especially difficult during the bigger *empates*, Targino said. "When you have one or two hundred people, there are times when someone gets a little hot. Once, a *seringueiro* saw some cattle. He said, 'Let's kill one of these cattle, because we are hungry and need to eat.' But we couldn't do that."

De Barros, who had absorbed some of Chico Mendes's skills at public relations, swooped in when he heard Targino's rambling. He emphasized that tappers never stole or destroyed anything, other than the temporary shacks. The *empate* was defensive, not offensive. "The whole idea for the *empate* is that tappers have the right to defend their homes and their *estradas*," he said. "Tappers and Brazil nut gatherers live from the trees. The only way they found to stop the cutting was to get in a group." As he talked, the column of tappers neared the forest and soon were retracing their steps along an abandoned rubber trail, passing trees whose scarred bark was burled and overgrown.

The tappers returned to where they had parked their truck, piled into the back, and headed down the dirt road toward Xapuri. Here it had rained, and the pasture grass was actually green. The dry season's dust had been pummeled to the earth by raindrops. The sky took on a peculiar glow common in the Amazon—a glow that comes around dusk, when the low rays of the sun catch the high tufts of cloud, and the white light from the glowing mist casts everything in shadowless brilliance. Along the road, they ran into the *gato;* he would have to break the news of the *empate* to Junior. After Barbosa told him what had happened, the *gato* was not a happy man. Barbosa said, "We're not here to play. Your workers cut one whole *estrada* of rubber. Maybe next time you'll learn to do something else besides cut trees." The truck drove on.

"This *empate* went well," Targino said to Aquino. "If that rancher wants to continue cutting, he'll have to hire new people. Those workers aren't coming back."

Although Chico Mendes has frequently been credited with creating the *empate,* this form of protest was really more of a spontaneous reaction from Acre's rubber tapper community—a communal response to a shared threat. Mendes and the other leaders of the rubber tappers, with the help of their new allies from the Catholic church and Brazil's burgeoning union movement, simply took a crude action and honed it into a powerful weapon. *Empates* began in the mid-1970s as an effort to thwart the growing number of ranchers who had run out of room in Rondônia and Pará and had begun acquiring land in eastern Acre—heading north along that notorious road, BR-364. Between then and 1988, Acre's tappers staged more than forty major *empates,* saving some 2 million acres from the saws and fires.

But the activism of Acre's tappers began much earlier. Indeed, the roots of the fight to save the Amazon stem from the early days of the rubber boom, the mid-1800s. As the state's first outsiders, the tappers had fought the Indians for the right to live on the land and harvest its bounty of rubber and nuts. Later, they fought the Bolivians for Acre. A ragtag army of rubber tappers, recruited by a *seringalista* named Plácido de Castro, drove the Bolivian tax collectors from the area. On August 2, 1902, de Castro took over the Bolivian custom house in Xapuri and later made the town the provisional state capital. There are reminders of this conflict throughout Acre. One of the last vestiges of the Bolivian presence, the custom house, stands in a corner of the grid of the old section of Xapuri. The tattered two-story building overlooks the Acre River at a point where it was convenient to stop the boats carrying the rubber downstream.

The rubber tappers' next battle was in the late 1960s, before the ranchers arrived and long before the first *empate.* After a century of exploitation, the tappers started to fight back against the bosses who had used debt bondage to control every aspect of their lives. Ironically, it was the demise of Amazonian rubber as a significant commodity that led to the fall of the powerful *seringalistas* and the independence of the rubber tappers. And it was this newfound independence that sparked the feelings of self-worth and self-determination that motivated the tappers to fight for their livelihood and their forest.

The *seringalistas* were in trouble because the profit margin on rubber had dropped to the point where it simply made no sense to continue the business. The bosses had already shaved their costs by dropping the *mateiros,* the woodsmen who opened the trails between trees, leaving it up to the tappers themselves to do much of the maintenance of the *seringais.* The only reason Amazonian rubber survived at all was that the government taxed imported rubber, which was less than half the price of the native product. The last year Brazil exported any significant quantity of natural rubber was 1947. By 1970, it was *importing* more than 26,000 tons a year of natural and synthetic rubber—more than its own trees produced —to feed its booming industry. In this situation, the *seringalistas* could reap more by selling their land than by harvesting rubber and Brazil nuts. In addition, many *seringalistas* were bankrupt. Their land had to be sold to compensate the government banks that had financed them during World War II. By the late 1960s, Acre's rubber barons were bailing out by the dozen.

During this unstable period, Chico Mendes saw an opportunity to change things. For the first time, he began to use the lessons he had learned from Euclides Távora. Just two years after his death in 1966, when Mendes was twenty-two, he began to agitate for better conditions as he sensed the growing weakness of the rubber bosses. He innocently began to write letters to President (and General) Humberto de Alencar Castelo Branco, describing the suffering of the *seringueiro* and his relationship to the estate boss. The daughter of a family friend showed him how to address the letters. Mendes wrote letter after letter, sometimes one a week, describing how the *seringueiros* were forbidden to have schools and how their illiteracy allowed the bosses to rob their accounts at the end of each month. He listed the inflated prices for soap, sugar, and other goods to show how these charges compared to the real cost. He received some polite but useless replies.

Mendes moved to Seringal Cachoeira after meeting and marrying the daughter of neighbors, a quiet sixteen-year-old girl with dark skin and streaked hair named Maria Eunice Feitosa. They were married on February 7, 1969, at the central clearing of Cachoeira, along with several other couples. (The priest used to make the rounds of the *seringais* and perform several marriages at once.) The couple settled on the shore of a small lake in Cachoeira, but it soon became apparent that this relationship was not destined to last. Mendes had little time to spend at home. When he was not tapping rubber trees, he was walking the rubber trails, trying to organize the tappers. And Eunice was widely perceived as a disappointing choice.

Francisco Mendes did not like her or her family and complained that Chico's house was never clean. Raimundo de Barros told his cousin, "You got married, but she doesn't take care of the house, she doesn't cook. If she was beautiful that would be okay, but she's not even beautiful."

Perhaps it was coincidence, but Mendes's relationships with women came to resemble those of his tutor, Távora. Mendes began the pattern of putting his political career and activism ahead of his personal life. Less than a year after their marriage, Eunice gave birth to a daughter, Angela. But by then the couple was bickering most of the time. After an argument, Mendes and Eunice would often retreat to relatives' houses—she to her parents' and Chico to his aunt Cecilia's.

Mendes stayed away from home, tapping and organizing. His first action on behalf of the tappers was to confront the boss at Cachoeira and demand changes in the exploitative financial relationship that persisted on the *seringal.* He knew that the deteriorating economic conditions in the rubber trade gave him some bargaining power. Accompanied by a burly, older tapper named Mario, Mendes said that the "milk," the latex, was very clean and did not deserve the 10 percent penalty on its weight. He also said that the tappers were no longer willing to pay a rent in rubber for the use of the trails. "There is no more *mateiro* cleaning the trails for us," Mendes said. "So why should we have to pay rent?" Within a year, the estate boss caved in.

At Seringal Santa Fé, Mendes tried to convince a group of tappers to bypass the estate bosses and sell their rubber openly to independent *regatões.* For many years, the tappers had secretly traded a little rubber on the side—small 5- to 20-pound balls of smoked rubber, *principio da borracha,* the beginning of the rubber. These were offered to passing merchants in exchange for needed goods or cash. The problem was that the *regatões* often cheated the tappers just as badly as the estate bosses did. Mendes wanted the tappers to sell their rubber to a merchant *collectively,* thereby reducing the risk of being cheated and getting a better price in the bargain. It was the right idea, but at the wrong time. Most rubber tappers, loners at heart, were reluctant to act as a group.

At around this time, Mendes's marriage finally collapsed. One year after Angela was born, Eunice became pregnant again, hoping that another child might bring Mendes back. But when she was in her seventh month, the couple separated. Eunice went back to her parents' *colocação* for the last time. She could not afford to raise Angela alone, so the child was adopted by her sister. Mendes never saw his second daughter, Roseangela; she died at the age of eleven months. Eunice later remarried and raised a family; she now lives on a small farm outside Xapuri.

In 1971, Mendes left the *seringal* and began to teach adults in a small government school on the road west of Xapuri. This marked an important change in his life. He would never again work full time as a tapper, although the *seringal* served as a haven for him until he was killed. And he always spent any free time as a *meieiro*, harvesting rubber for other tappers to raise some cash.

One of these tappers, at Seringal Santa Fé, was the father of a young, bright-eyed girl named Ilzamar. When Mendes first started working on that *colocação*, he used to take the nine-year-old aside and give her lessons in reading and writing. He taught her how to spell her name and recite the alphabet; a decade later, he would marry her.

Mendes continued to visit *seringais* where he had relatives and persisted in his attempts to effect change. But the military rulers of Brazil were at their strongest and repression was most severe during those years; change was not on their minds. In 1968, President (and General) Artur da Costa e Silva had closed down Congress, and the army began to strike against the smallest signs of leftist activity. Student groups in the cities began to wage sporadic guerrilla warfare. The American ambassador was kidnapped to force the release of political prisoners. In 1970, the junta sent ten thousand troops to southern Pará and Goiás to root out a communist insurgency that later turned out to involve a mere sixty individuals (including Elenira, the sharpshooting guerrilla whose name Mendes later gave

to his second daughter). Mendes had to bide his time until there
was a more pressing reason for the tappers to unite.

He did not have to wait long.

The same year that Mendes moved off the *seringal,* the stretch of
BR-364 connecting Acre to Rondônia was completed. Even though
it remained a dirt track, passable only a few months of the year,
ranchers began making the trip west from Pôrto Velho to examine
this next frontier. Along with the incentives offered by the generals
for investment in the Amazon—Acre was made one of the poles of
the Polamazonia program—there were similar inducements dangled by the governor, Wanderley Dantas, who had been elected in
1970. Dantas saw no future in the rubber and nut harvesting that
were the mainstay of the state's economy (and remain so today).
Although two thirds of Acre's population was involved to some
extent in these activities, the extraction of forest products was hardly
big business. Even with this base, the economy of Acre was by far
the worst in Brazil.

The trade in rubber and nuts had for a century sapped the state,
enslaving its people and leaving little behind. In 1970, Acre had a
lower per-capita income than any other part of Brazil, including
the rest of the Amazon. The state had no infrastructure. Even the
capital, Rio Branco, had few paved roads. Electricity was spotty at
best. Television would not arrive for four more years, even though
the rest of Brazil was already watching soccer matches and soap
operas. No bridge crossed the Acre River where it bisected Rio
Branco. It was only natural for a politician to call for growth.

Dantas had at least learned a lesson from Rondônia's development policies. The last thing he wanted was grand colonization
schemes that would attract poor farmers and peasants from the rest
of Brazil. (The disastrous results were already visible in Rondônia
when he took office, even though the worst was still to come.)
Instead, Dantas wanted big business to come to Acre. He convinced
the state legislature to pass a law encouraging the development of
cattle ranching as the state's "basic economic activity." An intensive
public relations campaign was aimed at the same *paulista* business-

men who were the target of the federal government's Amazon development plans. According to the government radar survey of 1964, RADAM, in contrast to the rest of the Amazon, most of the soil of Acre was relatively fertile—the "filet mignon of the Amazon," according to the promotional literature. One advertisement described the state as "a new Canaan, without the droughts of the Northeast or the frosts of Paraná."

Almost before the graders had finished smoothing the packed-dirt surface of Acre's new link to the south, Dantas was calling for the construction of a new road westward to Peru and on to the Pacific coast. He knew what this would mean for Acre. After all, Rio Branco was just 500 miles from the Peruvian port of Callao. In contrast, it was a winding, 2,000-mile voyage down the Amazon to the Atlantic or an equally long truck ride to the industrial ports of the south. His dream was to make Acre into an agro-industrial center that would ship fresh-frozen beef products to Japan. Dantas's slogan was: "Produce in Acre, Invest in Acre, Export to the Pacific." That call would be echoed by every governor to follow, including Flaviano Melo, who was elected to office in 1986; he approached the Japanese to seek funding for the road, raising the ire of American legislators and environmentalists.

Dantas's efforts paid off. Companies and individual ranchers came by the hundreds, grabbing up both unclaimed land and land with titles held by Acre's rubber barons. When Dantas began his term, 75 percent of Acre was still *terra devoluta,* unclaimed public land. By the time he left office, virtually all of that land had been claimed by investors from the south; and most of what was previously claimed had been sold and then resold, with profits from the sales exceeding any money that might have been made with cattle. In Dantas's term, the prices of land along Acre's roads jumped a hundredfold, in some places rising from 25 cents to $25 an acre.

The rubber barons had all sorts of titles, many dating from when Acre was part of Bolivia. Many were not formal titles, but deeds granting the right to tap trees or harvest nuts. (After all, until the 1970s, it had always been the trees that had worth in the Amazon, not the land itself. Only with the invasion from Brazil's south did the land suddenly assume value.) And many titles were blatant forgeries. The *grileiros,* land grabbers, who had refined the art of fraud in the south and then in Mato Grosso and Pará, had a new frontier to conquer. Despite the weakness of the titles, even the flimsiest documents were grabbed up in the speculative fever that raged in Acre. It was the perfect real estate market. The ranchers were eager buyers, and the rubber barons were eager sellers.

In the center of the state, entire river valleys were acquired by rich businessmen, most from the south. Within a decade of Dantas's inauguration, 28,125 square miles, almost half of the state's territory, was in the hands of ten landowners. Pedro Aparecido Dotto headed the list, with a tract of 9,370 square miles, an area slightly larger than New Hampshire. The smallest of the top ten parcels was owned by a *seringalista* turned federal senator, Altevir Leal; he had to make do with a tract that was slightly smaller than Rhode Island. Much of this land remained undeveloped, for the investors were happy to sit and wait for BR-364 to eat its way across the state, raising property values and providing them with a route to markets for their beef or produce.

The most intensive cutting and burning began along BR-317, the road from Rio Branco to Xapuri, which was gouged out of the forest between 1971 and 1973. The familiar pattern persisted: a road appeared, land values skyrocketed, and, to reinforce flimsy claims, the forests were cut down and cattle put out on the still-smoldering pasture. Most of the *seringais* in this region were sold to small, independent ranchers who wanted to solidify their claims in a hurry. The change was quick indeed. Between 1970 and 1985, the number of head of cattle in the county of Xapuri jumped from 7,000 to 52,000.

It is not surprising, therefore, that the fight for the forest began here. Just as the rubber tappers on these *seringais* were relishing the prospect of freedom from rent and debt and cheating, they were confronted with the new "owners" of their land. The ranchers had no intention of harvesting rubber. And they had no intention of allowing the tappers to stay on the property, no matter what squatter's rights they might have under Brazilian law. In the Amazon, law meant little. As a federal minister in Brasília put it in 1973, "The Amazon is still in the bandit stage. It is only later that the sheriff will be required."

Just as the tappers spoke of "cleaning" their *estradas,* the ranchers now spoke of "cleaning" their land. But where the tappers were talking about cutting vines and undergrowth, the ranchers meant driving out people—by any means necessary. Cattle were ranged right through the fields of the tappers and peasant farmers. Soon their huts were being set on fire along with the surrounding forest. Thousands of people began to flee to *seringais* in Bolivia. Others abandoned the countryside altogether and moved into the growing *favelas* ringing Rio Branco and Xapuri. But some decided to stand and fight.

The handful of rubber tappers who staged the first *empate,* on May 9, 1976, still remember the encounter vividly. The tappers lived on Seringal Carmen, near Brasiléia; the town is on the border with Bolivia, 35 miles southwest of Xapuri on BR-317, the red dirt road that arcs along the southern flank of Acre. A rancher nicknamed Coronel Chicão, who even today is often fingered by tappers as one of the masterminds of the violence against their leaders, had bought Carmen and sent out engineers to survey the land. Acre's rubber tappers by then were angry and restless; word of the ranchers' tactics for "cleaning" land was rapidly spreading. In some cases, tappers and their families were being rounded up at gunpoint, loaded with their belongings onto a boat, and taken downstream. As one rubber tapper recalled it, the gunmen would say, "We are going downriver. When you see a beach you like, we'll drop you there. That will be your new land." The tappers, fearing the worst, would eventually point to the bank and say, "This beach here looks fine."

Chicão's surveying crew walked out of the forest into the clearing at the *colocação* of a young tapper named Emiliano and began marking trees. When Emiliano asked one of the strangers for an explanation, he was told that the new owner planned to convert this forest into pasture. Later that day, Emiliano hiked into Brasiléia to see if the new rural workers' union there could tell him what to do. But the union had been formed just five months earlier. Unions were a novelty in the Amazon, where, traditionally, bosses were always masters and workers were always slaves. The union could not yet help, but Emiliano was warned, "If they start to cut the trees, you're going to lose your rights to the land." A tapper with no title would not have much of a case against a rancher who could show he was putting the land to "productive" use, Amazon style.

Back at the *seringal,* through the dependable links of *radio cipó,* Emiliano learned when the rancher's work crew was going to begin cutting down the trees. The night before, he met with five or six friends, and secretly they set out to stop the rancher. All that night, they covered the maze of forest trails, stopping at each *colocação.* Emiliano and Cicero Gaudino, one of the few tappers with red hair, gave speeches, trying to recruit other tappers to help *empatar* the rancher. "*Companheiro,* wake up," Gaudino said. "If you lose this land you're going to have to move to the town, and then you'll have nothing."

Before dawn, they had gathered twenty-seven men. Armed with shotguns, they marched through the forest to confront the work crew. The tappers moved cautiously. There were some sixty-four men in the cutting crew, and Tonhão, the *gato,* stood six feet six inches tall and usually carried a pistol. The tappers were more accustomed to aiming their weapons at wild pigs and deer than human beings, but they were ready to kill, if need be, to protect the trees. In the half light just before sunrise, they circled Tonhão's hut. Emiliano told the *gato* to come out. "We are all armed," he yelled. "We are only a few people, but if you cross here, somebody is going to get killed." Wanting no trouble, Tonhão and his crew quickly gathered up their things and left the forest.

The tappers staged a brief victory celebration but then worried about revenge. For eight days they camped in the forest, guarding the two paths into Seringal Carmen. But the only people who came were government officials, who wanted to work out a compromise between the tappers, with their squatter's rights, and the rancher, who apparently had a *título quente,* a hot title, one that had some validity. The clearly fraudulent titles held by land-grabbing *grileiros* were considered *título frio,* cold titles, with little value.

Despite the immediate success of the *empate* at Carmen, the results in the end were hardly a compromise. At an eight-hour meeting with the ranch manager and government officials, forty tapper families lost their *colocações,* which averaged 700 acres, and were given new plots of land of 70 acres apiece, much of it already deforested. These families, who for so many years had walked the shaded trails of the rain forest, were forced to adapt to a new livelihood, farming in the full glare of the tropical sun.

Emiliano missed the life in the forest but could not possibly have returned. One year after the spontaneous *empate,* his old *colocação* —which had been called Nova Vida, New Life, and had held more than five hundred rubber trees—was transformed into sun-baked pasture. Even after the tappers were moved to the small plots, their troubles did not end. In 1977, the rancher was using an airplane to sow grass seed, and the hardy, weedy *capim* grass invaded the tappers' fields. Another time, the rancher was deforesting an area near their holdings and used his plane to spray the herbicide Tordon. Emiliano later claimed to have lost thousands of manioc plants to the weedkiller. And the chemical made many of the tappers sick.

The lesson of Carmen was that an isolated *empate* by a few tappers on one *seringal* was only a brief deterrent to the destruction of the rain forest. The power of the ranchers could only be overcome with a much broader, more organized effort. It would take an alliance of three forces—the independent tappers of eastern Acre, the church, and the union movement—to slow the advancing fires.

In Acre's capital, Rio Branco, the way the buildings are placed clearly reflects the balance of power in the Amazon. The center of town sweeps uphill from the Acre River, where lopsided, makeshift shanties cluster on the crumbling banks. The government palace is near the top of the slope, just below the Plaza of the Seringueiro. Flanking the park just downhill from this imposing structure are the gray modern offices of the big banks that have financed much of the recent growth in the region. The Tribunal of Justice, the state supreme court, is tucked on a side street—an accurate portrayal of the minimal role that the courts have played in the Amazon.

Across a plaza from the governor's palace is the castellated, blocks-long fortress of the Military Police—one of the largest structures in the city. That is fitting, because the military still holds most of the power in the Amazon. The building is whitewashed and trimmed in bright blue. The soldiers of this police force, which grew dramatically after the coup of 1964, far outnumber the federal and local police officers. Even now, five years after Brazil's return to civilian rule, when people are asked why a military police presence remains even in the smallest Amazon town, no one has a good answer. That is just the way it is, the way it has always been. Many Brazilians talk of their society as being inherently divided into two cultures: civilian and military.

But there is a counterweight to the military presence. On the other side of the government palace, on the highest knoll in town, is the Cathedral of Nossa Senhora de Nazaré, and it towers over all the rest of the city's buildings. Brazil is overwhelmingly Catholic, a fact that reverberates throughout the society, from its strict laws prohibiting abortion to its innumerable saint's days to Carnaval, the world's most extravagant celebration of the feast before Lent.

Beneath the steep, peaked roof of this cathedral and those of the smaller churches on the town plazas of Xapuri and Brasiléia, the nascent organization of rubber tappers gained much-needed shelter, guidance, and sustenance. In the early 1970s, a large faction in the church began to preach social justice to its minions. That effort was led in eastern Acre by Dom Moacyr Grechi, who was ordained bishop of the prelacy of the Acre and Purus river valleys in 1973. He was perhaps the palest man in Acre, with waxy skin, thin hair that he slicked back, and an accountant's slouch and spectacles; the overall effect was absolutely the opposite of his true nature.

Grechi was one of the Amazon's leading proponents of the "liberation theology" that had swept South America since 1968, when a conference of bishops in Colombia called for the church to devote itself to bettering the lot of the poor. The bishops vowed to return to their dioceses and "awaken in men and in nations a living awareness of justice." For the church of Brazil, which a century earlier had been tightly allied with the elite, it was a dramatic change.

The church soon became a haven for anyone hoping to effect change. It was a social "refugium" of sorts, not unlike the biological refugia to which the many species of the Amazon rain forest retreated when a harsher climate drifted over the region. Virtually all other liberal institutions had been suppressed. Only two political parties were allowed: Arena, the party of the establishment, and MDB, the government-approved "opposition." The press was heavily censored. Student movements were brutally squashed. Unions were tightly controlled by the government, and activists were jailed and tortured.

The church worked on two fronts: the urban slums and the countryside. Outlying regions such as the Amazon, with widely dispersed communities, presented novel challenges to anyone who wanted to organize and instruct the masses. In the early 1970s, the church began setting up "Christian base communities," groups of rural settlers who met weekly for Bible study and political indoctrination that played up the parallels between the struggles of Christ and those faced by the poor in Brazil. In Acre, most of the members were rubber tappers.

As the junta began its policy of *abertura,* opening, that was meant to lead the country back to democratic rule, the church became more aggressive. Its growing involvement with rural conflicts was acknowledged formally in 1975 with the creation of the Pastoral Commission on Land, which has grown into an internationally respected source of information on human rights abuses and violence in the Brazilian countryside. This commission's annual body count of murdered peasants, priests, activist lawyers, and union organizers became a chilling barometer of the intensity of Brazil's land conflicts as the numbers rose steadily through the 1970s and then jumped by a factor of ten in the 1980s.

The base communities were organized by lay workers and a scattering of priests—priests were (and still are) in short supply—who were sturdy enough to withstand the hardships of tropical life and the lengthy hikes through the forest that were usual on the *seringal.* An important objective of the organizers was to identify potential leaders who could be cultivated into self-sustaining monitors for the forest communities. Júlio Barbosa de Aquino, Osmarino Amâncio Rodrigues, and almost all of the other men and women who went on to lead the rubber tappers began their activism as monitors for the church. And Chico Mendes—who by the mid-1970s was so busy building a union that he had no time to participate in the church's work—maintained a close relationship with the priests who organized the base communities around Xapuri and nearby towns.

One of the priests was Otavio Destro, who was raised and ordained in Italy, then moved to the grimy concrete jungle of São Paulo to minister to the poor. In 1975, Father Destro was sent up to the Amazon to help establish Acre's base communities. He was of the same order as Bishop Grechi, the Servos de Maria, an Italian order begun in the thirteenth century by seven wealthy Italian noblemen who gave up their fortunes and worked for the poor. The church had long before given this order the prelacy of the Acre and Purus rivers. Its first goal was to become familiar with the problems of the underclass in the countryside. Destro was based at the cathedral in Rio Branco but spent most of each month wandering the trails and cruising the rivers around eastern Acre, returning to town at the end of the month for a few days to let his feet rest.

Destro often passed through Xapuri, where the current priest, Father Carneiro, resented these newcomers and openly attacked the activist swing of the church. Carneiro was closely allied with the emerging power brokers, the ranchers moving into the region. There were persistent claims that he was an informer for the National Information Service. He was convinced that the base communities were inspired by communists: "religion for people with no faith" was his description of liberation theology. Despite this opposition, Destro and the other new priests were able to create ninety base communities on the *seringais.* One of the movement's central teachings, which probably accounted for its popularity, was that the existing social order—with a few very rich and many very poor—was in no way the will of God. If they acted together, the poor could force a radical change in the system through land reform and justice.

Carneiro tried in vain to continue his traditional ministry, and he continued to attack the activist priests and the growing church and union movement. But increasingly Xapuri's poor—both the tappers and small farmers—chose to be baptized or married within the base communities, not with Carneiro. The tappers were uniting. Eventually, Carneiro simply ran out of work and returned to Rio Branco.

The ranchers were also not happy with the church's new activist stance. Predictably, the new priests started receiving death threats. Destro still had an Italian accent—not a positive attribute now that there was a growing movement to expel foreigners from Xapuri. One day a car pulled up next to him as he was walking down the street; a right-wing candidate for the state legislature was inside. He told Destro to go back to Italy and take his communism with him. Enraged, Destro pulled out his Brazilian identification and yelled that he had just as much a right to be there as his foe.

The priests were perceived as a threat by the government as well. The mayor of Xapuri abruptly canceled the new priests' access to the local radio station. Dozens of letters came in from the community asking that the priests be allowed to give the mass over the radio. When Destro and the other activist priest, Claudio Avelline, met with the mayor to discuss the problem, the politician was carrying a bulky, unfamiliar bag. Avelline said, "I bet you have a tape recorder from the Federal Police in that bag." The stunned mayor admitted it was true. He seemed very depressed and under a lot of pressure, so the priests tried to calm him down, realizing that he was being manipulated by someone else.

The ranchers tried to push the police to crack down on the church. In 1979, a training session for church monitors in Xapuri was broken up when half a dozen heavily armed men from the Military Police broke down the door. They briefly jailed Destro and Avelline. And Avelline was attacked and beaten while walking down the road a few days later. Destro was confronted by one of Xapuri's biggest ranchers and told, "We've had enough of you people here. We're going to assemble two or three thousand people in the town square and demand the return of the other priest." Destro responded, "Okay, call him back. If you're able to do it, bring Father Carneiro back." But the ranchers could not find more than a few dozen supporters. The new teachings were taking hold.

Without the help of the church, it is unlikely that there would now be a rubber tappers movement. The church cultivated leadership and a combative sense of purpose among the isolated forest dwellers. But one other element was required to take them beyond isolated actions such as the first *empate:* unions. The union movement arrived in Acre in 1974, a year after Moacyr Grechi became bishop. Just as the liberation theology movement had its foot soldiers in priests such as Father Destro, the union movement also required someone to spread the word. For Acre, that person was João Maia.

Maia was a field delegate for CONTAG, the Confederation of Agricultural Workers. Born in 1968, CONTAG was dedicated to creating unions in rural Brazil. A tall, thirty-five-year-old man with dark hair and a trim mustache, Maia had previously been a seminary student in Canada and Washington, D.C. His mission now was to spend six months setting up unions in the major towns of eastern Acre. He was used to rural conflict, having spent time organizing the sugarcane workers in the northeast.

He arrived in Rio Branco after an exhausting bus ride from Brasília. The bus had crossed Mato Grosso and then jostled and bumped its way north and west across Rondônia on BR-364. Rio Branco was beginning to grow, but it was basically a dusty, sleepy Amazonian town. Most of the houses were still raised on wooden stilts. The roads were so bad that the trip from the bus station to the center of town—a distance of little more than 2 miles—required a bone-jarring hour in a bus or one of the few cabs. Maia set up shop in a small yellow stucco building near downtown.

The idea of a union in Acre was almost unthinkable. The economic history of the Amazon was built from beginning to end on slavery of one sort or another. The ranchers who were busily moving into the state were hostile. The old Acre families who had made their money in the rubber and nut trades were hostile. Anything smacking of human rights or, worse still, land reform had to be done quietly, underground.

Soon after Maia arrived, the expulsion of the rubber tappers from the *seringais* reached a peak. Maia and a couple of assistants traveled around the eastern half of the state, learning about the rubber tappers' problems and building a network of contacts in various towns. Finally, in early 1975, the first union was established in the isolated town of Sena Madureira, about 130 miles northwest of Rio Branco. But it was the second union, in Brasiléia, that became the seed of the broader movement. This was where Chico Mendes began to find his voice.

Maia moved to Brasiléia in the dry season of 1975 and began giving classes in land rights and union organization to a few rubber tappers. It was extremely difficult to recruit people. Most of the tappers were still locked into the idea that the boss was the boss. And the boss always had the police and the government on his side. No one believed in the potential of organized labor. Maia was frequently attacked by the tappers, who said that union organizing showed a lack of respect. He was also regarded suspiciously as an outsider, having come up from Brasília, a gangly young man with the intellectual air of a college student. But he simply resolved to become an Acreano. He spent three months hiking around the *seringais* and small farms, carrying only what fit in a small pack. He continually gave his pitch, emphasizing a few important points. With the help of the church, Maia printed up a little book for the tappers, explaining how they could defend their land.

First, Brazil's complex mix of laws and statutes gave tappers and small farmers a right to the land beneath their feet, thanks to the old *direito de posse.* Second, if the government upheld a rancher's claim to a tract and insisted on evicting tappers or other legitimate squatters, then the evicted *posseiros* would have to be compensated with money or land. Finally, and most important, *posseiros* had the right to defend their land, using force if necessary. In Brazil's old Civil Code, Article 502 stated, "The landholder has the right to maintain or reinstate his claim through his own force, provided that he does so immediately." In teaching the tappers these basic rights, CONTAG—and Article 502—gave them the legal basis for their fight and justified the *empate*.

The tappers were by now an eager audience, for forest tracts were being incinerated all around eastern Acre. Slowly, they began to trust this outsider. Community leaders, many of them from the church groups established by Grechi's priests, began taking Maia's courses. One of them was Chico Mendes. He had quit his teaching job and moved into Xapuri, where he had taken a job as a clerk for the man who had once been the boss of Seringal Cachoeira, Guilherme Zaire. Zaire had always liked Mendes and had always been impressed by his natural intelligence and honesty.

The union arrived just as Euclides Távora had predicted. He had also foreseen that, initially, the unions would be "yellow"—not independent, but registered and controlled by the government. Távora had told Mendes, "Lenin always said you shouldn't stay out of a union just because it is yellow. You must join it and use it to organize the grass roots, spread your ideas, and strengthen the movement." Mendes moved to a small farm in the county of Brasiléia and registered for the first course with Maia and the other organizers. Thanks to his lessons with Távora, Mendes had a head start on the rest of the class and immediately impressed Maia with his knowledge of union philosophy. Maia also noticed qualities about Mendes that set him apart. For one thing, he could read and write at a much higher level than the others. He also had a natural skill as a politician—not so much in oratory, but in his ability to get people talking and acting.

By the end of 1975, the movement in Brasiléia was sufficiently organized for Maia and the nascent leadership to call an assembly and found the union. Word was sent out to the *seringais* and farms for the tappers and other rural workers to gather in town on December 12. Because it was the height of the rainy season, Maia, Chico Mendes, and the other unionists did not expect much of a turnout. When nearly a thousand people showed up, it was clear to everyone that a fundamental change was about to occur in Acre. In part because of his political training a decade earlier, and in part because he could read and write so well, Mendes was among the leadership elected that day; he was given the title secretary-general. The founding of the first large union was a dramatic moment in the history of the struggle to save the Amazon. No longer would the ranchers be able to push the tappers away so easily. The invaders would have to fight for the forest.

Through 1976, the union went through the formative changes and power struggles typical of newborn movements. That things were still in disarray as the dry season arrived was clear by the union's response to Emiliano when he sought help with Seringal Carmen in May. In 1977, Chico Mendes returned to Xapuri. He had been invited to get into politics by Guilherme Zaire. Zaire was organizing a big push to give the opposition party, MDB, control of the Xapuri town council. Like every other city council around Brazil during the military government, Xapuri's was controlled by the Arena party, which supported the dictatorship. Zaire convinced Mendes and two other employees to run for council seats representing the MDB and paid for their campaigns. At first, the union leaders in Brasiléia balked at the idea, but Mendes convinced them that it would be easier for him to organize a Xapuri branch of the union if he was a councilman. After a brief campaign, Mendes was elected, along with Zaire's other two candidates. Soon after, he founded the new union office. The church gave the union a small shed for its headquarters.

On the town council, the MDB remained in the minority. Arena controlled the group, electing four members. Mendes was never very pragmatic as a politician and always spoke his mind. Often the visitors gallery of the cramped council chambers would empty as he dove into long speeches filled with rhetoric about the rights of tappers. He was ridiculed by the right and even by the other MDB representatives, who opposed his radical ideas. But that did not deter him.

In 1978, the unions of Xapuri, Brasiléia, Sena Madureira, and other towns in Acre formed a statewide association of rural workers' unions, which eventually grew to a membership of thirty thousand.

The unions could now coordinate their efforts and participate in joint actions. After the *empate* at Carmen, the unions began to organize more sophisticated operations, some of them involving one, two, or even three hundred tappers, who would march to the scene of reported deforestation and occupy the region, destroying the cutting crews' shacks and driving them off the land. Often the tappers were forced to leave by the police, who were hired by the ranchers and eagerly beat on the "invaders," as the ranchers called the tappers.

As the land boom in Acre accelerated through the end of the 1970s, the rural workers' unions rose to the task of obstructing the cutting. Soon, the church workers and labor organizers were left behind, and the rubber tappers' movement began to take an independent, more radical course. Indeed, Mendes and the other tapper leaders often fought with Bishop Grechi and Maia, who preferred to make legal challenges and work within the established—albeit impotent—judicial system.

Mendes could often be found now in the forests of his youth, recruiting tappers to join the union and participate in *empates*. To qualify for membership in the Xapuri rural workers' union, he had to do some agricultural work, so when the town council was not in session, he tapped rubber or harvested nuts. The priest Otavio Destro often traveled with him, hiking those same trails to recruit people for the church groups. Despite a difference in tactics, the union movement and the church movement were clearly complementary. At first, Mendes had a hard time convincing people to join the union, because the ranchers had spread rumors that the whole operation was communist-inspired. But the base communities gave Mendes a structure to build on; there he found people who had become aware of their basic rights and of the possibility of determining their own fate.

On these forest hikes, Destro noticed qualities in Mendes that he saw in no one else. The main quality was sheer dogged energy. Mendes displayed the unwavering determination that later pushed him into politics as a socialist candidate in a conservative state— against all odds—and then pushed him to fly to foreign countries and lobby against loans from development banks that were threatening Acre's forests. And it was this same doggedness that pushed him—perhaps too far—to harass the men who were threatening his life and work. Mendes had also retained certain qualities of the *seringueiro* that were crucial to garnering support with the isolated rubber tappers. He had a quiet style that appealed to the tappers— perhaps because they lived in a silent realm, where often the loudest sound was a Brazil nut pod's thud on the forest floor.

When Mendes first arrived in a *seringal,* he would not immediately call a meeting. He would walk up to the house of an individual tapper and sit for a while. After taking a tin cup of water, he would ask the tapper about his life, his situation. Mendes would play with the children as he sat, admiring the construction of the house or the quality of the manioc growing nearby. He would try to learn about that one tapper's problems. Then he would go to another *colocação* and collect more information. Only after he had personally gained the trust of each tapper would he start talking about the union, about organizing, about resistance.

Destro admired Mendes's approach, which was so natural that it was not really an approach at all; it was simply Mendes's nature. This personal style was very different from that of the priests, who would make an announcement over the radio and gather a hundred people or so, then eventually put someone in charge who had the makings of a leader. In this way, Mendes won over the whole of Xapuri.

But Chico Mendes's effectiveness also increasingly made him a target. Although he was quiet, he would freely denounce anyone who posed a threat to the forest. This began to irk Xapuri's ranchers, who swore that Mendes would have to go. But Mendes displayed a remarkable skill for avoiding trouble. As Destro described it, "Chico had the wisdom of the Indian and the guile of the Indian, so it was difficult for a rancher to catch him in the forest." Mendes needed all the wisdom and guile he could muster.

Chapter 8

The Wild West

MANY OF THE RANCHERS who moved into Acre in the 1970s were not bad men. They simply had a different way of measuring the potential of a tract of land from that used by the people who already lived there. A rubber tapper or Indian might take days to survey a patch of forest, checking the springs, counting Brazil nut and rubber trees, *buriti* and *paxiúba* palms, and other useful species. When someone from the new ranching class looked at the same forest, he saw the trees only as a costly impediment that had to be knocked down and burned. The springs could be dammed to make ponds. The giant trees could be sliced into fence posts and siding for houses. Most of the land's value lay in the soil, not in the tangle of wild vegetation that grew on it.

In Brazil, the ranching culture had a certain sense of manifest destiny. The ranchers were the agricultural *bandeirantes,* pioneers, who were leading the country toward its new status as a major exporter of food. They spoke proudly of the natural progression in Brazil as a new region was settled. Cattle always came first because pasture was easy to create on almost any terrain and the product, beef, carried itself to market. After cattle came agriculture, particularly the farming of grains and beans, and after that, industry and services—and the end of the frontier.

These new arrivals had been raised on the rolling grasslands of Rio Grande do Sul or Minas Gerais, the rich uplands of São Paulo state or the deforested plains of Paraná (which five decades earlier had been Brazil's forested agricultural frontier). They had come because they had outgrown their holdings in the south or because land there was now too expensive. Their goal was to raise beef cattle, and cattle needed pasture. Beef was so central to their existence that they even calculated the price of land in terms of pounds of beef; with Brazil's growing inflation, it was best to use some measure that changed with the value of the currency. Twenty-six pounds of beef per acre was a good price in 1975. Because of Acre's reputation for relatively fertile soil, the state was truly perceived as a "new Canaan," just as its governors had described it.

When the ranchers first found that their new possessions were occupied by *seringueiros,* they were puzzled. Many of them had never heard of *seringueiros* before. When they saw how these men lived—scratching tree bark and carving out small clearings, only to abandon them—they scoffed. The tappers were considered a pathetic atavism, unaware of chemical fertilizers and pesticides that would allow them to farm the same plot of land in perpetuity. There was bound to be conflict between this new culture that sought sunny pastureland and the entrenched culture of the rubber tappers, who craved the shade of the canopy. Soon enough, the ranchers' puzzlement and derision gave way to consternation; finally, as more *empates* were staged and cutting crews turned back, consternation gave way to outrage.

Once the land rush of the 1970s accelerated, the tappers and peasant farmers constituted little more than an inconvenience that had to be removed from the land along with the weeds and trees. When a rancher was confronted by a forest full of recalcitrant tappers, he had only a few options. He could negotiate with them, and some did, offering parcels of forested land in return for the right to cut down other tracts. He could use the tricks of the *grileiro,* faking titles, destroying conflicting titles, and the like; some did that also. Or he could use violence, intimidation, and extortion. For many ranchers, this was the most expedient solution.

It was not difficult to have land "cleaned" of tappers or peasant farmers. Plenty of men had come to the region as outlaws, attracted to the anarchy of this tropical frontier just as a previous generation of outlaws had found a haven in the American West. These men were a different sort of Amazon pioneer—people who had fled to the frontier. For them, the Amazon was a "refugium" from the law. It is often possible to tell what is significant to a culture by examining the richness of the vocabulary used to describe a kind of person or object. For instance, it is said that Tahitians have thirty different words for "coconut," and Eskimos have as many different words for "snow." In the Amazon, there is a rich assortment of words for "hired killer," among them *pistoleiro, capanga,* and *jagunço.*

If a rancher—even a relatively civilized one—was having trouble "cleaning" his property, he need only hire a few of these professional thugs and the job would be done for him. Many such killers were imported from southern states such as Mato Grosso. Soon, this renegade breed established a new level of violence in the rain forest. At the height of the rubber boom, there had certainly been some vicious *seringalistas* and bosses, but the merchants could not afford to treat their tappers too badly because there was always a chronic shortage of labor in the forest. The ranchers had no such inhibitions.

One of the earliest documented incidents occurred in 1973, when a rancher named Benedito Tavares do Couto brought in a gang of *pistoleiros* to clear two hundred rubber tappers from Seringal Riozinho. Other *pistoleiros* were hired to intimidate the tappers of Seringal Carmen (where the first *empate* was later staged). In 1974, a *grileiro* who had laid claim to a large forest tract just outside Rio Branco wanted to sell it to ranchers but could get a better price if it was emptied of settlers. He brought in some thugs, but this time there was resistance. A squatter named Raul Veras shot and killed one of the *grileiro*'s employees and wounded another.

By the time Father Destro and João Maia arrived in Acre, it was common to hike into a *seringal* and find that several rubber tappers' homes had been burned to the ground. Sometimes the violence was more spontaneous. Destro was in Brasiléia one day when blood was spilled at the produce market. A rancher had bought a *seringal* and had bought most of the *colocações* from the tappers. But one tapper had refused to sell. When he went to the public market to sell some fruit, the rancher saw him and chased him across the crowded plaza. The two men crashed to the ground, and the rancher split the tapper's scalp with a brick. The same day, swearing revenge, the tapper went out to the rancher's house and started breaking everything in sight. The police were called, and he was arrested and jailed. Destro found the tapper in his cell, lying in his own blood —his head wound was not bandaged. Only after the bishop intervened was he sent to a hospital.

Ironically, the rise in rural violence may well have been prompted by the political liberalization and reform that began in 1975. After five years of the generals' so-called Economic Miracle, from 1968 to 1973, the economy was collapsing, due in part to the worldwide oil crisis. As agitation for an end to military rule was increasing, the generals began their slow policy of *abertura*. In addition to accepting the growing church and union activism, the government legalized opposition political parties, reduced press censorship, and allowed exiled leftists to return.

A series of strikes staged by the metalworkers and other industrial laborers in São Paulo in 1978 led to the creation of the most radical opposition party, the Workers party (PT). It was headed by the burly, bearded, charismatic metalworker Luis Inácio da Silva, known as Lula. Lula soon went out to stump the hinterlands, including the Amazon, to organize the first rural branches of PT. Chico Mendes was among those who helped found the Acre branch of PT. By 1982, PT had become Brazil's fourth largest party, with half a million members. In the cities, PT pushed for higher wages; in the countryside, the issue was land reform.

The new political freedoms encouraged the rubber tappers' unions to increase the intensity of their fight. *Empates* became more frequent. In 1979, the tappers' unions of Acre staged their most dramatic, coordinated action to date. More than three hundred members of all of the unions went by truck north from Rio Branco into the state of Amazonas and to the town of Bôca do Acre (Mouth of the Acre), which sits at the point where the Acre River empties into the Purus. There they marched through the forest to confront a small army of *pistoleiros* who had been hired to drive thirty-six families from a huge tract of land. The gunmen had camped on the land and prevented the squatters from planting crops, threatening them constantly. With only machetes, the tappers surrounded the shacks of the gunmen, who apparently did not want a fight—or did not have enough ammunition—and so abandoned an arsenal of twenty rifles and shotguns as they fled into the forest. The victorious tappers picked up the cache of weapons and posed for a portrait; a copy of it can still be found among the valuables of many rubber tapper households.

The *empates* convinced the ranchers to change their own tactics. Instead of intimidating the peasants and tappers in the forest, they would now combat the movement by gunning for the leadership. From 1964 to 1974, the death toll of peasants, small farmers, rubber tappers, and their advisers and union leaders stayed fairly level— some years only three or five, others fourteen or twenty-two. But starting in 1975, the number of killings in the countryside edged up —thirty-nine in 1975, forty-four in 1976, fifty-one in 1977.

By 1980, the number of deaths had hit three digits, and the targets had been more precisely chosen. Activist priests and lawyers, union presidents, and the most intransigent squatters were singled out, stalked by hired gunmen, and shot dead. It is a chilling tradition in the Amazon—in most of Brazil, for that matter—that the victim is always given notice that his life is scheduled to be taken, as if he were an employee being terminated. An *anúncio,* as such a death notice is called, is not so much a threat as a statement of fact. It is meant to prolong the victim's torment as he waits for the inevitable. The *anúncio* might be a telephone call (if the victim has a telephone), a couple of pistol shots into the side of his house, or a message from a friend of a friend.

Although the Amazon held only 10 percent of Brazil's population, it witnessed half of these killings. The violence followed the advancing fringe of flames wherever it ate into the forest.

In Acre, the union leadership in Brasiléia and Xapuri began to live in constant fear. One of the most important and vulnerable targets was Wilson de Souza Pinheiro, who had been a rubber tapper in Amazonas. He moved to Rondônia and then to Acre, where he was recruited by the church in 1973; two years later, he became one of João Maia's most enthusiastic students of union tactics. Some of the first planning sessions for the Brasiléia union were held in his house. (His daughters recalled peeking around the corner and listening as the tappers and organizers met late into the night.) Pinheiro was elected president of the union in 1977.

He was a lanky man, a head taller than most of his fellow tappers, with a broad smile, long muscular arms, and large hands. He was a powerful speaker and talented organizer, and it was he who first honed the *empate* into a potent defensive weapon. (He had organized the successful *empate* at Bôca do Acre in 1979.) Pinheiro was the first tapper from the region to travel beyond the Amazon. In about 1977, he met with national CONTAG officials in Brasília, where he widened his awareness of politics.

In the early days of the Brasiléia union, Wilson Pinheiro and Chico Mendes became close friends. Sometimes they would retreat together to the rain forest, where they would shed their worries and tease each other and see who could collect more rubber in a given time. Although they were physical opposites—one tall and lean, the other an ectomorph of average height—the two leaders shared qualities that their colleagues saw in no one else: quiet authority and incorruptibility. Moreover, they were the only leaders who developed the crucial ability to convince rubber tappers in one part of Acre to support other tappers wherever they were—in Xapuri or even in another border state, such as Amazonas. Pinheiro and Mendes were able to broaden the perspective of these isolated forest workers, whose concerns had for generations been myopically limited to little more than their own trails.

When Mendes moved back to Xapuri in 1977, much of the

momentum in Brasiléia was sustained only by Pinheiro. In a way, he was too critical a figure; when he was not around, nothing got done. If Pinheiro had a fault, it was that he tried to maintain too much control over the business of the union, making him a vulnerable target.

As Pinheiro organized more and larger *empates,* the tension in the region rose. The tappers kept up the pressure throughout each burning season, knowing that the return of the rains in November would stall any cutting and burning until the following year. Pinheiro made a long list of enemies, one of whom was a ranch manager named Nilo Sérgio de Oliveira. In 1979, de Oliveira had begun to deforest a large tract, rich in rubber trees, on the 500,000-acre New Promise Ranch, once Seringal Sacado. Naturally, he planned to drive out the squatting tappers. Pinheiro organized an *empate* in which ninety-four tappers blocked the cutting crews. When de Oliveira tried, and failed, to get a court order to expel the tappers, he swore that Pinheiro would pay.

In early July 1980, a public meeting was held in Xapuri at which tappers and ranchers from the area vented their differences. At the meeting, which was conducted by government officials in charge of rubber pricing and aired on the radio, the municipal secretary of Xapuri lost control. A former *seringalista,* he had recently sold his *seringais* to some ranchers, and he blurted out what was on many ranchers' minds: "The only way to resolve the land conflicts here is to kill the president of the union, the delegate from CONTAG, and the priests who are instigating the rubber tappers. Soon there will be many widows in Acre." At the time, people shrugged off his outburst as irrational bluster.

All that changed on July 21. As dusk settled over the forests of Acre, Pinheiro was sitting in the tin-roofed union hall on a side street of Brasiléia, watching a detective show on television called *João da Silva* with another member of the union, João Antonio Bronzeado. Pinheiro thought about heading home for dinner, but Bronzeado—in an act that later cast suspicion on him—urged him to stay for the end of the program. At around seven o'clock, two strangers came up the steps and clumped along the creaky veranda to the door. When they asked for the union president, Pinheiro identified himself. The men said they were hoping to find a place to stay for the night—perhaps they could stay there? One was a foreigner, probably from Bolivia or Paraguay by his accent, the other Brazilian. Neither one looked particularly honest.

People were always coming and going in Brasiléia, which had more of a honky-tonk feel than quiet rubber ports like Xapuri. Because it was on the Bolivian border, Brasiléia had a long tradition of trading and smuggling in everything from guns to stolen cars, rustled cattle to illicit drugs. The border was as porous as they come. To cross it, one passed an empty guard shack with a drooping Brazilian flag and a perpetually raised wooden gate, then bumped over a flimsy bridge and passed another unoccupied guard shack and open gate. On the other side, Spanish music blared from the speakers in the electronics shops where Brazilians flocked on weekends to buy imported goods they could not get at home.

It was not surprising, therefore, for strangers to ask for a place to sling a hammock. But this time Pinheiro was nervous. He had recently received an *anúncio*—a letter from some ranchers—which said, "Stay out of the way or you will get yourself killed." It was signed "Mão Branca," White Hand. Then a friend of Pinheiro's had stopped in Rio Branco at a bar and overheard some ranchers talking about hiring a *jagunço* to "work on" the Brasiléia union president. And a few days earlier he had heard a rumor floating around town that a Paraguayan had been contracted to kill him. Studying the two men, Pinheiro decided not to take a chance. He politely told them to leave, saying, "I can't give lodging to someone I don't know." The men asked if they could leave their bags for a few minutes while they got their passports stamped by the Federal Police.

Fifteen minutes later, as Bronzeado and Pinheiro watched the climax of the detective show, the two men apparently returned. But this time they stayed outside. As the television detectives' pistols went off, there was a very real bang, and a .38 slug came through the open door of the union hall toward Pinheiro, who was sitting with his back to the door. That bullet missed, burying itself in a wall beam. At the sound of the shot, Pinheiro jumped up—but too slowly. More shots followed. The second caught him in the left buttock. The third plunged into the left side of his back, near the kidney, and its upward trajectory took it through his chest and out his right breast. Dying, Pinheiro fell to the floor.

When Bronzeado left the union hall long after the doctors and the police had finally arrived, he bumped into Nilo Sérgio de Oliveira. "Oh, so they killed Wilson Pinheiro?" the rancher asked, showing no surprise at the news.

The death of Wilson Pinheiro did at the local level what the murder of Chico Mendes later did globally: it galvanized an intense emotional response to a festering problem. Just a few hours after the murder, tappers stormed the radio station in Brasiléia and began issuing an appeal to everyone on the *seringais* to come into town for the funeral and a demonstration. More than a thousand tappers answered the call. Some walked; others hitched rides on pickup trucks. They came from Xapuri and Assis Brasil and Rio Branco. And word came from as far as Tarauacá—150 miles distant, in the center of the state—that someone had better take action. The head of its rural union said, "If no one from Brasiléia seeks revenge for the death of Wilson, we will come and do it ourselves." The rubber tappers of Acre were now ready to fight, just as they had fought the Bolivians and rubber bosses earlier.

The day after the shooting, João Maia had raced to Rio Branco in the union truck to meet with the governor and the secretary of public security and warn them about the blood lust of the tappers. Then he picked up Pinheiro's oldest daughter, Iamar, at boarding school. Maia looked grim, but at first he told the fifteen-year-old only that there had been an accident. He also picked up Chico Mendes's cousin, Raimundo de Barros, in Rio Branco. De Barros had just quit his job with a government health agency to work for the union movement.

On the way back to Brasiléia, they stopped in Xapuri. Iamar, unaware of her father's death, sat nervously in the truck while Maia and de Barros talked heatedly with people at the union hall. She noticed a revolver in the glove compartment. Then a woman walked by with some cans of paint. When she saw that it was the union truck, she asked Iamar bluntly, "Have you heard that they murdered the president of the union in Brasiléia with three shots?" Iamar screamed and fainted, breaking a tooth as her head hit the door.

Pinheiro's body was laid out for two days so that all of the mourners could file past. Each tapper walked up, took off his hat, and made a little speech, such as: *"Companheiro,* this is the last time we will see each other, but you can be sure that whoever did this will pay for it."

On the second day, the tappers were stunned to see de Oliveira walk up the union hall steps and stop to view the body. *Radio cipó* had been working overtime. Word had got out that the police had heard testimony confirming the rumor that someone had sold a pearl-handled, long-barreled, Smith & Wesson .38 revolver to de Oliveira a year or so earlier. And it was already widely known that this ranch manager had several Paraguayans working for him. Then, chillingly, de Oliveira's fate was sealed. When he walked by the corpse, several people noticed that, for the first time since Pinheiro had died, the corpse started to bleed. In the Amazon, there is a superstition that when the murderer is near the body, the blood drips, asking for revenge.

The tappers used another bit of folklore to ensure that the murderer would not escape. Two days later, as the body was being prepared for burial in a crude cement crypt, a coin was placed under Pinheiro's tongue and the body wrapped in white sheets. It was placed in the coffin upside down—which was said to prevent the murderer from leaving the area.

In urgent meetings, the tappers plotted their response. They said they would give the authorities seven days to find the killers, then they would take over. In the middle of the night, they would surround the houses of de Oliveira and six other ranchers who were thought to have been involved in the murder. The houses would be set afire, and anyone fleeing would be shot dead.

On the day of the deadline, a long-planned union meeting and PT political rally was held in Brasiléia. Chico Mendes, who had been in the western corner of Acre helping to organize a union branch, returned for the meeting only to find his friend in his grave. There were some indications that Mendes's trip may have saved his life. Strangers had been seen around the union hall in Xapuri the same night that Pinheiro was killed. Mendes was stunned. Until now, the violence against the tappers had been somewhat haphazard and, to a certain extent, cautious. Seven months earlier, Mendes had been bundled into a car in Rio Branco by four hooded men and severely beaten, then dumped on a side street. But the men, who could just as easily have killed him, had stopped short. Pinheiro's death was the first real assassination.

Hundreds of tappers and small farmers attended the rally. Lula, the president of PT, and an associate named Jacó Bittar had flown up from São Paulo; they delivered blistering speeches in which they both celebrated the arrival of PT and attacked the violence that had now reached a new level in Acre. The national director of CONTAG, José Francisco da Silva, who had flown up from Brasília, also spoke. Various other speakers then took the microphone and began to whip the crowd into a call for vengeance.

Chico Mendes urged caution. He opposed a violent response to the killing—a stance that he consistently favored throughout the spiral of murder and intimidation that was building. But nothing said that day had any pacifying effect. Blood had to answer blood. If the ranchers had thought that by murdering Pinheiro they would squelch the movement, they were mistaken. Quite the opposite. The workers resolved to protect themselves. They knew that if there was no response, the killing would only get worse.

As it turned out, the tappers' original plan for revenge could not be carried out. Word had leaked to the ranchers, and many had fled to Bolivia or Rio Branco. But de Oliveira stayed. On the day of the rally, he was driving along BR-317 in his Chevrolet pickup, leading a couple of larger trucks taking cattle to the slaughterhouse. He came upon a convoy of several dozen armed tappers who had headed straight to his ranch after the rally. He was a tall, muscular man, and he struggled and tried to put up a brave front as they dragged him from the truck. He probably died from the first shot, but thirty or forty more were pumped into his body for good measure. The tappers made it clear that from now on, a killing would be answered with a killing.

The police, who had been conspicuously lax in investigating the Pinheiro murder, showed an extraordinary level of energy and alacrity as they rounded up more than a hundred rubber tappers and stuffed them in jail, pressing to find out who had killed de Oliveira. Teams of Military Police scoured the *seringais* and confiscated every sort of weapon, from kitchen knives to shotguns used for hunting. Many union members were forced to stand all day in water up to their knees, until their skin cracked and bled. A few had their fingernails yanked out. And some became familiar with a piece of equipment that is still standard issue in almost every police station in rural Brazil, the *pau de arara*. It is a simple device— actually a horizontal wooden pole something like a gymnast's high bar. Its effectiveness for torture only becomes apparent when a man is suspended in an upside-down crouch, with the pole cutting into the backs of his knees and his hands tied to his feet.

Despite the many forms of torture, the investigators got nowhere. Murder charges were filed against twenty-eight people, but the case never went to trial. Within a month, the last tappers were released. But in a separate case, all of the people who had delivered speeches at the PT rally were charged by the military tribunal with fomenting violence and breaking national security laws. Lula, Maia, Mendes, and the two other speakers were all tried in the military court in Manaus. (The case dragged on until March 1984, when the five men were finally absolved. It was the first time that Chico Mendes made national headlines.)

In Acre, the government tried to defuse the tension by taking possession of several large tracts of forested land in Brasiléia and doling out deeds to hundreds of tappers—a tactic that was already well established. From 1976 to 1980, twenty-four *seringais* in Acre had been disappropriated and transformed into "directed settlement projects"—a grid of small plots. But the government land agencies were giving deeds on the order of 120 to 250 acres, whereas a typical *colocação* was 700 acres. The plots did not have enough rubber trees to provide a family's living, so many tappers were forced to sell their holdings and move to the city. In a sad irony, many of these "settlement projects" ultimately became deforested and unusable.

The Pinheiro killing was never actively investigated, and police interest in solving the murder of de Oliveira faded as well. But the two deaths left behind a climate of festering hatred between the tappers and ranchers that still permeates the air of Acre, especially in Brasiléia. Two of the tappers who were charged with de Oliveira's murder were later gunned down; those murders were also never solved.

Pinheiro's death had shocked the community. Before, most of the violence in Acre had occurred face to face; everything came down to a *macho* showdown not unlike the heralded confrontations of the Wild West. As one rubber tapper put it, "There would be a kind of body-to-body fight and one would kill the other, and everyone would know who and how." The climate of fear that lingered after Pinheiro's killing was founded on the realization that now death could come at any time and in any form. The cycle of violence that began in the hot dry days of July 1980 swirled in rising currents around Acre in the months and years ahead.

Of all the *pistoleiros* who had settled in Acre, none was more feared than a family named Alves. Many rubber tappers remarked that the arrival of this family had coincided with a rise in the number of killings and the change from confrontation to ambush.

Four generations of the Alves family lived on several small ranches along BR-317. Ostensibly ranchers, they did not seem to be making much of a living from cattle. Their herds were small, and they had little productive pasture. It was thought that the brothers, Darly and Alvarino, and their many sons and aging father and hired cowboys derived most of their income from doing the dirty work of other ranchers.

The Alveses had had plenty of training for such work. Through three decades of what the authorities once described as "elaborate perversity and cowardice," the family carved a criminal record across the southern states of Minas Gerais and Paraná, then north to the Amazon. The list of laborers and peasants and enemies alleged to have been killed by the Alveses was well into double digits. All rumors aside, even the documented court cases painted a dark picture. As one of their friends described them, "They don't bake anything; they fry everything."

The patriarch of the family was Sebastião Alves da Silva. He was a Mineiro from the rough, tumbling, deforested hill country of Minas Gerais, inland from the Atlantic coast north of Rio de Janeiro. He came from the Vale do Rio Doce, the Sweet River valley. There he and his sons established a pattern that was repeated wherever the family went—a pattern of using violence to resolve the slightest conflict. In February of 1958, Sebastião and three sons—Darly, Alvarino, and another—allegedly waited along a road and ambushed a cattle drover named Manuel Alves Pinto, who had been trying to get the attention of one of Sebastião's women. They left little room for error. Along with a *pistoleiro* nicknamed Mata Quatro (Four Kills), the Alveses obliterated Pinto with sixteen shots. His fifteen-year-old son, Pedro, was killed with six shots. Not even the boy's horse was spared; the animal died screaming.

Typically, five years passed before the murders were investigated. When detectives visited the Alves's hometown of Conselheiro Pena, it was not hard to build a case; the family had openly boasted of the killings. Charges were filed in September 1963, but by then the family had moved on, eventually settling in the state of Paraná. The Alveses lived in a village called New Jerusalem, near the town of Umuarama in a rural corner of the state. Paraná is one of Brazil's richest agricultural regions, a loamy plain that is now covered by vast tracts of soybeans and wheat. The buildings of Umuarama always have a waist-high coat of red dust that has blown in from the fertile fields. The region was once thickly forested with a distinctive type of tall pine, its trunk topped by an awkward knot of branches. (Today, those trees survive only in parks.) The trees began to fall in the 1930s, when Paraná joined the coffee boom that made Brazil the world's leading exporter. Coffee was a labor-intensive crop, so the state developed a vital economy that employed thousands of peasants. When government incentives—and a severe cold snap—pushed the farmers to switch to highly mechanized soybean farming in the 1970s, the peasants were driven off the land; many of them fled to the next frontier—Rondônia, then Acre. With land conflicts all around, this was fertile territory for the Alves family to continue its violent tradition.

In May of 1973, another member of the Alves clan, Isaque, allegedly killed a peasant named Dirceu Dias dos Santos. That June, Darly and three *pistoleiros* invited a neighbor, Acir Urizzi, for a night on the town in the red-light district of Umuarama. Sebastião had lost some land to Urizzi and his father in a court battle. Urizzi never went home.

The police surrounded the Alves ranch in New Jerusalem looking for Darly; it was only a 40-acre spread, a good indication that ranching was not their means of support. The police found Alvarino instead. He had always affected something of an outlaw air, with a taste for large cowboy hats and at various times a long black beard or drooping mustache. He lived up to his looks by greeting them with a blast from a .12-gauge shotgun, wounding one officer. After Alvarino was captured, the police learned that there was an outstanding warrant for him on the double murder that had been committed back in Minas in 1958, so he was sent east to stand trial. The situation had grown too hot for Darly, and he decided to get out of the state. He headed north to the Amazon.

On January 17, 1974, Darly bought Fazenda Paraná, a small ranch of about 10,000 acres at kilometer 132 on the BR-317 highway. The next year he was joined by Alvarino, who had been acquitted for lack of evidence in Minas Gerais. Soon their father followed. Almost immediately the killings continued, starting with two of their ranch workers. And the Alveses were alleged to have been involved in the massacre of nine *posseiros* on the Twelve Apostles Ranch. At last, the family figured, here was a region where the law could not touch them.

Chapter 9
Joining Forces

A S TENSIONS ROSE in Acre, Chico Mendes countered the increased threat by drawing closer to a new circle of friends from the national union movement and PT, mostly people from outside the rain forest. Some, like João Maia, had moved to the Amazon frontier on a mission: to end the exploitation of rural workers. Others had fled to Acre after the military government cracked down on the left in São Paulo and Rio during the darkest days of the military dictatorship. These political fugitives, some of whom were members of Brazil's illegal Communist party, sought refuge on the frontier, just like the region's more violent breed of outlaw. Acre made an excellent hiding place because it was only a short dash to the Bolivian border and safety. The state also attracted increasing attention from young social scientists, who were drawn to the Amazon to study its imperiled Indian and tapper cultures.

Together, the activists and scientists formed a tightly knit group that worked together, drank together, and, in many cases, lived communally in houses in the quickly growing city of Rio Branco. These were the people who would help to transform the isolated battle of Acre's rubber tappers into an Amazon-wide movement.

When Mendes took the bus to Rio Branco on union business, his first stop was almost always the office of a weekly newspaper called *Varadouro*. *"Varadouro"* is the word for the paths rubber tappers cut between adjacent river valleys to connect otherwise isolated communities. The newspaper was founded in 1977 by a pair of liberal journalists who wanted to chronicle the destructive impact of the Acre land rush. Mendes was one of the paper's valued sources, updating the editors on new deforestation and brewing land conflicts; even then, at the very beginning of the movement, Mendes recognized the importance of the media in getting the message across. One of the paper's founders was Elson Martins, who had been born on an Acre *seringal*, went to school in Belém, then became a journalist. Rather than moving to the civilized south, as most university-educated people did, he chose to stay in Acre and report for local papers and one of Brazil's big newspapers, *O Estado do São Paulo*. Martins started *Varadouro* with Silvio Martinello, who had fled from the crackdown on student leaders in São Paulo. Much of the funding and the office space came from the church. Martinello doubled as a stringer for Rio de Janeiro's biggest newspaper, *Jornal do Brasil*, and he and Martins were occasionally able to convince uninterested editors in the south to publish small items about the growing violence on the Amazon frontier.

Varadouro soon became the voice of Acre's rubber tappers and Indians, describing the *empate*, the arrival of the unions, and the spread of violence as the ranchers flooded the state. At its peak around 1980, the paper was selling seven thousand copies a week— an enormous number in a state where the two daily newspapers rarely sold more than three thousand copies of any edition. Each week, when the latest edition was carried out to *seringais* in the forest, dozens of tappers would gather around and listen as someone who could read recited the news. Mendes himself was often enlisted to do such readings. He enjoyed playing town crier, but at the same time he lamented the lack of literacy that persisted in the forest.

Late each day when he was in Rio Branco, Mendes usually stopped by the Hotel Chui, which had the only reasonably respectable bar in town. It was an odd gathering spot, almost a neutral zone where all the warring parties in Acre staked out their tables and drank and chatted just a few yards from each other. At one table there would be young representatives of the Indian agency, FUNAI, and activists such as Elson Martins and João Maia. At another would be some of the rubber barons of Acre's old elite, and down the way would be a table of the newcomers: the wealthy *paulista* ranchers and their gunmen. At the bar, Mendes met with his new friends and made plans for the next step in the movement: bringing schools and economic independence to the *seringais.*

Economic independence would come if the tappers could just break free of the limitation of selling their rubber and nuts only to one or two merchants. What they needed was a cooperative— where the tappers would be their own boss, where they could get a fair price for their rubber, where the profits would be invested in health posts and schools, not drained by some wealthy rubber baron. But it was the prospect of schools that most excited Mendes, who had long ago learned the value of understanding the written word and the manipulation of numbers. The government had still made no effort to make schools accessible to the rubber tappers' children—or adult education to the tappers themselves. A cooperative would not be much good if the tappers could not manage it themselves. Mendes's union in Xapuri had drawn up plans for both schools and a cooperative but lacked the necessary funding.

Among the activists in Rio Branco, one person in particular helped Mendes fulfill these dreams. Mary Helena Allegretti was from a place far from the Amazon, in both distance and culture, but no one more fervently supported Mendes's efforts to improve the tappers' conditions and to protect the forest.

In 1976, Allegretti was an anthropologist who had left her college teaching job in her hometown of Curitiba—the clean, prosperous capital of the southern state of Paraná—and had gone to get a master's degree at the University of Brasília. She was small and energetic, with disarmingly large eyes the color of pale jade. She had tired of the middle-class culture of the south and wanted a change. Allegretti got more of a change than she had ever expected when she met an obsessive anthropologist from Acre. This scrawny, ageless, chain-smoking field scientist, Terri Vale de Aquino, was finishing his thesis on the rubber-tapping Kaxinawá Indian tribe of central Acre.

Aquino, an Acreano, was passionately committed to improving the lot of the Indians in the state. He believed in hands-on anthropology and cultivated that same philosophy in many of his peers. Clearly, if they did not help out the cultures they were studying, there would soon be none left. Aquino had founded the Acre chapter of the Pro-Indian Commission, to push for the establishment of reserves, and since 1975 he had been helping the Kaxinawá set up cooperatives to sell their rubber. These efforts later provided the template for the *seringueiros'* cooperatives and extractive reserves.

Allegretti knew almost nothing of Acre—or the Amazon, for that matter—so Aquino spent many hours telling her about the region and its peoples. When he showed her a map of the state, she commented on the lack of towns. He explained that most of the Amazon's people lived in the forest. Aquino reeled off stories of the Indians' rich forest lore, stories about rubber tapper communities living a century behind the times in their isolated *seringais,* stories about the unspoiled forests of Acre. Then he returned home, predicting that she would soon follow.

Allegretti found Aquino's stories tantalizing. Like most of her peers in academia and the government, she had assumed that the *seringueiro* was extinct—a quaint fossil from the days when the journalist Euclides da Cunha had traveled the rivers of Acre to document the rubber tappers' revolt against Bolivia. Even words such as *seringal* were meaningless. Fascinated, she resolved to head north to see if she could find a thesis topic in all of this.

In February 1978, Allegretti, then twenty-seven years old, flew to Rio Branco, and Aquino introduced her to the activist community, people such as the bishop Moacyr Grechi and the journalist Elson Martins. She quickly became attuned to the tension that was beginning to boil as the forests were being destroyed. Allegretti found *Varadouro* particularly significant. The paper was reporting on the growing crisis facing the forest cultures as events unfolded; she was more accustomed to the detached, unhurried, academic approach to social studies.

Soon Allegretti and Aquino headed out to the Tarauacá River, which cut through the left wing of the butterfly shape of Acre. There she received her indoctrination into rubber tapper life. They boarded a *batelão* and made the slog upriver, with the boat creeping against the current. On the river, Allegretti began to understand the differences between the Amazon and the rest of Brazil. Here, distance was not measured in kilometers or miles, but in beaches. Tappers talked of the next *seringal*'s being four beaches upriver. The sandy, curving beaches formed only at sharp bends in the river and thus made convenient landmarks.

The trip, like any Amazon voyage, was stultifyingly slow. As Allegretti progressed farther upstream, toward the south (in Acre, most of the rivers drain across the state from south to north), she would find the bow of the boat heading at one time east, then south, west, then south, sometimes even swinging north again before curling back around to the south, following the random loops of the channel. Every ten minutes, the wind that had just been blowing pleasantly in her face would become a near flat calm at her back, and that is when the voracious *pium* would pounce. These tiny black flies disperse in the slightest breeze but descend onto human skin like drops of mist whenever the wind stops. Each finds a spot and takes a tiny chunk of flesh, leaving behind a scabbed wound with an itch that is incomparably irritating.

Despite the annoyances, Allegretti was quickly won over. Any trip on an Amazon tributary develops a mesmerizing, intoxicating rhythm. At first, she struggled with the frustration of watching the boat make quick progress through the water but only pass the shore at the speed of a medium-paced walk. Eventually her mind accepted this fact. And as the spectacular world of the rain forest unfolded, the discomforts and concerns about disease faded away.

At each bend in the stream, pink-backed river porpoises, called *boto*, flashed and puffed as they drove schools of fish into the shallows. The branches of half-submerged tree trunks waved steadily back and forth in the current. Larger branches were invariably festooned with puffy gray protuberances that up close became a camouflaged flock of *bapurau,* a relative of the owl. Occasionally, a green flash on the riverbank signaled the departure of a basking lizard. And the daily cycle of weather was unvarying as clouds of water vapor built, then broke, releasing brief torrents and leaving a rainbow dangling in the invigorated air.

Allegretti had a hefty dose of *macho*—a character trait usually reserved for men in Brazil—so she did not admit that any of the hardships bothered her. Despite her small stature and friendly face, she almost never showed weakness. She refused to let Aquino know how scared she was when, five days upstream from the last connection with civilization, the boat pulled over to the shore and deposited her at a *seringal* called Alagoas. Aquino thought Allegretti might be able to conduct her research there without too much trouble because he knew the estate boss. Aquino himself was continuing upstream to the point where the river rose into rapids and a waterfall called Jordão, the pristine country that was the home of the two thousand remaining Kaxinawá. As the boat pulled away from the shore, Aquino waved good-bye and yelled, "I'll be coming back downriver in one month. See you then." He had not told Allegretti until then how long she would be in the forest; she had been expecting something like a ten-day stay. Nervously, she gritted her teeth, smiled, and waved back.

The tappers were very suspicious at first; there had never been a female stranger on that *seringal* before. They questioned her cautiously, probing to see what she was really up to. "Are you sure that you want to stay here?" asked one old man. "What do you really want?" asked another tapper. Allegretti found in them a strange mix of traits: suspicion and submission, aggression and caution. It was in Alagoas that she learned the cardinal rule of Acre: there was no middle ground between the rubber bosses and ranchers on one side and the rubber tappers on the other. Only when she started following them into the jungle did they begin to accept her.

After a month of recording interviews with tappers burdened by debts of as much as two tons of rubber (more than two years' production) and after observing children racked by malarial fevers, Allegretti became consumed with the idea of improving conditions for this isolated, forgotten culture. One of the most pernicious problems was the enforced illiteracy. Allegretti hiked to one remote *colocação* where a tapper eagerly showed her a letter he had received six months earlier. In all that time, he had not seen one person who could read. When she took notes, the tappers would gather around and watch closely, asking, "How do you do this?" She was stunned and distressed. She thought of the privileged students she had taught back in Curitiba, and how their needs could not compare to the glaring problems she had found here, deep in the Amazon rain forest. For Allegretti, the Tarauacá River had become what she later called "a one-way street to activism."

When thirty days had passed and Aquino came back downriver, Allegretti was in a slight state of shock. The month in the jungle felt like ten years. As the boat headed downstream, this time aided by the current, the only thing she was thinking about was a scribbled diary entry she had made back at the *seringal:* "I will come back and build a school."

Before leaving Acre, she wanted to interview a few more people. Elson Martins had told her about the *empates* and the growing rural unions of Acre's eastern fringe. He suggested that she talk to a rubber tapper who came in frequently from Xapuri to update the journalists on the war against the cutting crews; his name was Chico Mendes. Allegretti happened to be at the *Varadouro* office a few days later when a man with dark curly hair, a broad face, and big, friendly eyes walked in. Mendes was slightly amused by this gutsy, earnest young woman, but he gladly sat and told her about conditions in eastern Acre. He was still a town councilman for the MDB, and the Xapuri union was just one year old. They sat and talked for hours, with Allegretti's tape recorder running.

Mendes described the long history of the resistance in eastern Acre to first the bosses and now the ranchers. It presented a strong contrast to the situation she had just left behind in central Acre, where the tappers could not imagine resistance because they had been beaten down for so long. Mendes also talked about the importance of education; as a town councilman, he was pushing for the establishment of schools and health posts in Xapuri. They shook hands and Mendes left. Neither realized that a partnership would later develop that would forever change both of their lives.

Allegretti headed back to Brasília, where she raced to type out her notes, spewing four hundred pages in one month—a stream of descriptions of debt slavery, disease, illiteracy, and profiles of individual tappers that had her thesis advisers scratching their heads. But the thesis had become secondary. The spark that Aquino had fanned was burning. The only thing she wanted now was to get back to the Amazon.

Allegretti returned to Acre late in 1980 and immediately went out to Xapuri to look up Chico Mendes. It had been tense in eastern Acre for months. After the killing of the ranch manager de Oliveira, Mendes had been forced into hiding for two months, moving from house to house to avoid the *jagunços* who were out to avenge the death. He was also dodging the Military and Federal Police, who had begun conducting a surveillance of tapper leaders, including Mendes, and examining possible links to the illegal Communist party of Brazil. (In 1979, Mendes had in fact briefly joined the Communist party. He switched to PT after the support from the communists, most of whom were from Rio Branco or the south, wore thin.) In September 1980, Mendes was hauled in by the Federal Police and interrogated for most of a day about his communist connections.

By the time Allegretti arrived in Xapuri, life had returned to something approaching normalcy, thanks in part to the regular rains, which slowed everything down. Mendes had resumed his routine, albeit cautiously. He, Allegretti, and other outside advisers polished up a proposal for what they called Projeto Seringueiro, incorporating both schools and a cooperative. Mendes's Xapuri union would be in charge.

The theory behind the cooperative was to keep some of the value of the rubber and nuts on the *seringal* by allowing the tappers to be their own middleman. Instead of taking their rubber to the *barracão* of an estate boss or selling it to passing merchants, the tappers would take it to a warehouse owned by the cooperative. There it could be exchanged for goods offered at a fair price, not the inflated prices of the old system. When the rubber was sold in bulk at the end of the season, a share of the profits would be returned to the participating tappers, based on their productivity. The theory behind the schools was simple. For such a cooperative to have long-term viability, it would eventually have to be run by the tappers without the help of advisers. For that to happen, they would have to be literate and numerate.

Another activist from Rio Branco, Tony Gross, brought some good news toward the end of 1980. Gross was a British political scientist who, like Allegretti, had been lured to the Amazon by Aquino. At first glance, no one appeared more out of place in the Amazon than this Briton, with pale skin and a blond pageboy that endlessly threatened to close over his blue eyes like a swaying bead curtain. But Gross was fluent in Portuguese and knew his way around a *seringal,* and he also knew how to get the funding to build the schools and give the cooperative the initial infusion of capital required for it to stock up on goods. In 1980 he had started working for Oxfam, the international relief and human rights agency based in Oxford, England. His good news was a pledge of several thousand dollars from Oxfam for the union's proposal.

Allegretti and a team of educators from CEDI, an organization that supported grass-roots development projects in Brazil, began designing a textbook for the rubber tappers. It incorporated the philosophy of Paulo Freire, who believed in teaching literacy and numeracy to the poor with lessons drawn from daily life. For example, hc had suggested that signs be hung along an *estrada* with the written word for each object placed on that object. The book was called *Poronga*, after the metal headlamp that the tappers used on the rubber trails.

By the time the dry season of 1981 arrived, Projeto Seringueiro was ready to go. For Mendes, it was shaping up to be an important year. He was elected president of the Xapuri rural workers' union, a position he held until his death. For the first time since the dictatorship, unions were organizing at the national level, and Mendes became involved in the establishment of a national federation of workers.

Mendes and the other tappers had decided that the first school should be established on a *seringal* called Nazaré, a two-day hike from the center of Xapuri. It was chosen because its tappers had already been mobilized by Chico Mendes and the Xapuri union and because they were at the heart of the fight against the ranchers. Nazaré had been acquired in the mid-1970s by Geraldo Moacir Bordon, one of the most powerful *paulistas* who had been lured to the Acre land rush. His Bordon meat-packing company in São Paulo exported hundreds of millions of dollars' worth of frozen and canned beef annually—most of it from the stockyards of southern Brazil—to the Middle East, Asia, and Europe. Bordon had acquired a total of 114,000 acres running inland from the banks of the Acre River, including Nazaré. He never intended to harvest rubber. He wanted the land "cleaned" and the tappers gone.

The trouble had started in 1978, when Bordon's manager offered a deal to some of the tappers on his land: he would give each one 135 acres of land in a different part of the forest and the right to tap the rubber trees and collect Brazil nuts on their old *estradas* for two more years. Most of the tappers refused, knowing full well that they could not live on the production from so small a tract. A few accepted, but a year later, Bordon reneged on the deal. Hundreds of rubber and Brazil nut trees were cut in the area that the tappers had been promised would go unscathed. The work crews did nothing with the deforested areas, leading the tappers to conclude that the trees were being felled simply to drive them off the land.

Mendes and his cousin Raimundo de Barros had responded by organizing *empates*. Mendes would take the two-cent ride across the Acre River in Xapuri's one-paddle ferry, then hike to his cousin's house, which was on the way to the Bordon ranch. There, they would relax and listen to overseas broadcasts on a short-wave set— Radio Havana was a favorite—then walk from house to house, gathering tappers to confront the crews.

Now, even as the fight with the rancher continued, Mendes and his cousin, along with Allegretti and other colleagues, began to hike along the trails of Nazaré again, this time to enlist tappers to help build the school and, more important, to recruit them as students. The first classes would be for adults. Soon the simple building was complete—raised in tapper style, with big open windows to let the breeze through and with the first blackboards ever seen in the rain forest. The first teacher was Allegretti herself. She lived on Seringal Nazaré for two months; the classes were then taken over by a woman from the Rio Branco group.

Bordon and many other ranchers charged that the schools were a communist effort to subvert the tappers and destabilize Acre, which, with its long borders, was primed for guerrilla warfare. Their claims were clearly exaggerated, although it was also clear that some of the activists involved were quite radical. Ronaldo de Oliveira, for example, was an earthy intellectual who worked closely with Mendes and Allegretti. One of the most radical people in Acre, he had a deep desire to sow the seeds of a backlands rebellion against the military and landowning classes. Nonetheless, state and federal officials were not eager to stir up the situation in Acre again so soon after the murder of Wilson Pinheiro, and the schools were not opposed.

During this period, Chico Mendes developed a great respect for Allegretti, who had become a tough Amazon veteran, as comfortable in a hammock as a hotel bed. They stayed close friends even after Allegretti left Projeto Seringueiro at the end of 1982 to take a job with an urban planning project for the new mayor of Rio Branco, a young engineer named Flaviano Melo. In the same election that put Melo into office, Mendes had again run for town council in Xapuri. This time, as a PT candidate, he did not have the support of his old friend Guilherme Zaire and never had a chance. Mendes devoted all his time now to his union work.

By 1983, the education project had nearly become self-sustaining. The school at Nazaré had begun to train teachers, and that year, literate women from the *seringais* took over the teaching jobs. Several more schools were built on other *seringais* around Xapuri, and their focus shifted from adults to children. Part of the money generated by the rubber cooperatives paid for school maintenance, lunches, and stipends for the teachers.

Prodded by angry ranchers, in 1983 the military police raided several of the schools, ostensibly searching for evidence of guerrilla activity and subversive literature. (By this time, Allegretti was the subject of an extensive file at the National Information Service; when she had a chance for a higher position in the Rio Branco government, she was rejected as a national security risk.) When nothing objectionable was uncovered, the police left the tappers alone. And one year later, the project gained supporters in the federal government. A branch of the education and culture ministry called Pró Memória, which is dedicated to preserving Brazil's cultural heritage, began funding the schools. Within a year, another six schools had been built around the county of Xapuri. More than two dozen would follow elsewhere in Acre.

The cooperatives established under Projeto Seringueiro did not fare as well. Things went smoothly from 1981 to 1983; studies showed that a rubber tapper and his family could maintain themselves during the tapping season and, when the profits were distributed at the end of the year, could make up to twice the minimum wage set by the government—an excellent income by rural Brazilian standards. But in 1984 the bottom fell out. Just as the cooperatives were being turned over to local control, the national economy began to unravel. After two decades of heavy borrowing by the military government, the foreign debt had ballooned to $102 billion. The International Monetary Fund demanded a draconian reining in of growth. The first years of the 1980s had seen a severe recession; now came inflation, which jumped from 100 percent in 1982 to more than 200 percent a year later. Unemployed workers rioted in São Paulo.

As inflation soared, the value of rubber and Brazil nuts in the Amazon did not keep up with the cost of goods. In 1984 the cooperatives, which had distributed lots of goods but accumulated insufficient stores of rubber, failed. Indeed, all over the Amazon, the rubber tappers were failing to boost their production to keep up with inflation. Twenty years earlier, a tapper who produced 1,200 pounds of rubber in a year would have been considered special; now tappers were harvesting 2,200 pounds a year and not covering their expenses. Undeterred—and buoyed by the success of the schools—Chico Mendes and his friends, both inside and outside the forest, were determined to try again.

Spirits were high despite the economy because Brazil appeared to be on the brink of returning to civilian rule for the first time since 1964. Almost half of the state governors were now from parties that opposed the military dictatorship. In 1984, millions of demonstrators poured into the streets to demand drastic economic reforms and a return to civilian rule. A growing array of opposition parties in Brazil's Congress posed a threat to the dominance of the military's party. Faced with an economy they could not control and a rebellious Congress and population, the aging generals decided to let go.

The left was invigorated by the prospect of an end to political repression. For the first time, there was talk of real agrarian reform and free unions. The national rural workers' organization, CON-TAG, planned a meeting in the capital. It marked an important change for the rubber tappers' fight for the rain forest. From now on, it would take place not only on the front lines—in the forest —but also in a national, and eventually international, arena.

More than four thousand delegates gathered in Brasília, most of them small farmers. Two of the representatives from Acre were Chico Mendes and his cousin Raimundo de Barros; it was Mendes's first trip outside the Amazon. The meeting's goal was to forge a comprehensive proposal for agrarian reform—involving the distribution of undeveloped property to landless farmers and peasants —that would be put before the government.

At the conference, Mendes pushed for a special plan for rain forest regions, where the standard 120- or 250-acre plot established by the land reform agency, INCRA, was too small to support a family. Mendes promoted the creation of a 700-acre "special rural module" for the Amazon. This idea soon became the basis for the extractive reserves through which the tappers hoped to preserve their forest. But at the time Mendes's proposal was rejected as too radical. Once again, he would have to wait.

Later that year, Allegretti was eager to be in a position to influence the new government that would be elected by a special vote in 1985. She moved to Brasília to take a job as an Indian rights specialist for the Institute for Economic and Social Studies, an organization that undertook research to help Congress create legislation. This was one of the first so-called nongovernmental organizations in Brazil, and was loosely based on groups elsewhere in the world, especially in Washington, D.C., where special interests created lobbies to influence legislators. Both the right and the left were now feverishly jockeying for position, hoping to determine the shape of the new democratic government and the new Constitution that would follow.

In January, the presidential vote was taken. The opposition parties built an unlikely coalition and, in a stunning defeat for the entrenched party, their candidate, Tancredo Neves, pulled off a surprise victory. Euphoria swept the country, then turned to shock: one month after the new government took power and before his inauguration, Neves died of an infection after abdominal surgery. His successor was José Sarney, who was closely aligned with the old military guard. Nevertheless, he recognized that without significant political reforms and some kind of land reform, there would soon be an urban and rural explosion. The *favelas* around Brazil's major cities were swelling to the bursting point as the peasants fled from the countryside.

The need for land reform was urgent; the wealthiest 1 percent of landowners now owned 43 percent of the arable land; the bottom 50 percent owned only 3 percent of the land. A survey showed that 395 million acres of fertile but undeveloped land—an area four times the size of California—was being held by a few thousand investors while some 30 million rural residents had no land at all. Every year through the 1980s, another 39 million acres of fertile land, an area larger than Florida, were being snatched up by the major landowners. The government started drawing up a land reform plan as well as new plans for the Amazon.

Allegretti's organization was asked to assess the new scheme for the Amazon. As she studied the policies drafted by the emerging republic, she noticed that there were only scant references to the peoples of the Amazon—and all of them concerned the Indians. Further, all of the plans for the Amazon focused on the proposed free-trade zone in Manaus, building dams and roads.

Thus, the government was giving no hint that it would recognize the existence of the rubber tappers. There was nothing in the new blueprint for society that would help the rubber tappers and Brazil nut gatherers—the tens of thousands of people who were quietly, inconspicuously subsisting in the rain forest. There was no initiative to reach out to these widely dispersed forest dwellers with medical care or education or technical assistance. If anything, the government strategies were designed to get the people out of the forest and onto organized grids of farm plots so that the forests could be knocked down and agricultural and mineral development could proceed. Moreover, there was no indication that the new government planned to do anything for the old *soldados da borracha,* the thousands of veterans of the War for Rubber. Technically, they were owed retirement benefits, including a cash payment and a monthly stipend.

When Allegretti confronted several congressmen from the Amazon and asked them what they were planning to do for the tappers, they responded sheepishly that there had been an oversight. One suggested that she write a couple of paragraphs to be inserted into the plan.

Memories of the month along the Tarauacá River came back to her: people shackled by debt and illiteracy, forgotten. And now they had been forgotten once again. She began to think that perhaps it was time for the tappers to come out from the forest and demand some recognition that was long overdue. Allegretti turned to the one man who could help her the most, Chico Mendes.

She wrote a letter to Mendes, saying: "I'm working here talking to congressmen and advisers to the government and they don't know that you exist." She suggested that together they could organize a meeting of rubber tappers from Acre. The meeting could be in Brasília; that way it would generate publicity and force Congress and the new president to respond. The fight was still simply for recognition, for social justice. Ecology was not yet an issue. She told Mendes to talk over this idea with the tappers in the unions in Xapuri and Brasiléia and to give her an answer.

The answer came back: yes.

But the people of the forest were not the only ones who were closing ranks, seeking alliances, and heading to Brasília to influence the government. The people of the pastures—the ranchers—saw that their interests were being threatened by the increased activity of the left and the rising call for agrarian reform. As far as they were concerned, the prospect of land reform might just as well be a declaration of war. While Mendes and Allegretti planned their assault on the capital, so, too, did the cattle barons.

On the surface, the ranchers' fight was purely rhetorical; it was spearheaded by a new organization that was founded in 1985, the Rural Democratic Union (UDR). Beneath the surface, there were persistent signs that the UDR was a front for organized violence against the leaders of the agrarian reform movement, and it soon became the bane of the rubber tappers, small farmers, and landless peasants throughout rural Brazil.

Initially, the UDR was cast as little more than a club. The organization built a romantic image around the mystique of the Brazilian cowboy and the agricultural pioneer spirit. Some of Brazil's leading country singers, such as Sergio Reis, performed at rallies. At first, the UDR stressed that it was not political; it was simply the manifestation of a mass movement in rural Brazil that sought to promote the holy trinity of "Tradition, Family, and Property." In a way, the UDR used the same tactics to gain the support of the ranchers that the church had used to organize the impoverished masses. Sociologists who have studied the evolution of the ranchers' league say that the UDR's leaders fostered a sense of solidarity, a feeling of being part of something.

But politics soon became a central part of the UDR's strategy, for the ranchers recognized that they needed to influence the policies of the new government. More than anything, the UDR rabidly opposed agrarian reform, claiming that this would put land in the control of uneducated farmers who could not possibly put it to productive use. (In fact, government statistics show that small farmers produce 80 percent of Brazil's food.) As the battle over agrarian reform intensified, and as the drafting of the new Constitution progressed, Brasília's international airport overflowed with the private aircraft of wealthy ranchers, busy pressuring their congressmen for protection.

The UDR was formally inaugurated in August of 1985 with a cattle auction in Goiânia, the capital of Goiás. The event had a festive air, with country music and a huge *churrascada*. The money raised that day from the sale of 1,461 head of donated cattle would ostensibly be used for public relations campaigns and lobbying efforts against land reform. Later, the UDR confirmed that the money was in fact put to a different use: the purchase of 1,636 firearms, to be distributed to members. The guns were to be used to protect the most fundamental of the UDR's values: the value of property. Thus evolved the character of the ranchers' league: harmless on the surface but dangerous down deep.

The agrarian reform plan that was finally enacted by the Sarney government in 1985—after intense lobbying by UDR members and other wealthy landowners, including many of Brazil's leading politicians—was far too weak. But it still scared the ranchers enough to provoke them into an unprecedented frenzy of cutting and burning. They were desperate to secure claims to as much land as possible before the government started redistributing undeveloped tracts.

Ironically, the new land reform act intensified the violence against the forest dwellers. The pace of the destruction put to shame past depradations, such as the winning of the American West.

Back then, there were no chain saws and bulldozers and knock-down herbicides that burn plants from the inside out. Beginning in 1985, the old slogan of Kubitschek, "Fifty Years in Five," took on new meaning.

The violence broke out from Acre in the far west through Rondônia and east to the most dangerous place of all, the Parrot's Beak —a fertile region at the juncture of the Araguaia and Tocantins rivers, where the states of Maranhão, Goiás, and Pará meet. This part of the eastern edge of the Amazon basin had already been thrown into turmoil by the rampant development and deforestation that followed the establishment of the vast Greater Carajás mining project and the Belém-Brasília Highway.

In towns like Marabá and Imperatriz, murder had become a business that was conducted almost casually from storefronts. The Brazilian Bar Association conducted a study in which it alleged that one company, informally known as the Death Syndicate, was operating out of Imperatriz and had a price list for killings. A rural union leader could be murdered for a few hundred dollars. At the top of the list—costing more than $20,000—were judges and bishops. In the Parrot's Beak, press reports linked UDR members to a small firm, called the Solution, that ostensibly provided security for banks and other risky businesses but in reality supplied hired guns to "clean" disputed property.

Despite the efforts of many lawyers working for the Brazilian left, no one was able to link the UDR directly to any of the assassinations of rural leaders that started to become commonplace in 1985. Even so, there were persistent allegations that private planes laden with weapons supplied by the group began touching down in Rio Branco, Imperatriz, and wherever else landowners wanted to stand firm against squatters.

In its message and methods, the UDR bore a striking resemblance to another powerful and dangerous ranching organization that had been established in a frontier territory called Wyoming. In fact, the situation in Wyoming in the latter half of the nineteenth century holds some remarkable parallels to that on the Amazon frontier. With the passage of the Homestead Act in 1862, the American West was put up for grabs. A homesteader could stake out 160 acres and, if he sat on his claim for five years, get the title. The act was intended to lure small, poor farmers west but instead was used by the wealthy, who paid people to stake claims and thus accumulated vast tracts for cattle pasture. Violent clashes broke out between the small homesteaders and the big ranchers as cattle were rustled and land claims overlapped. Soon after Wyoming became a state in 1890, the Wyoming Stock Growers' Association decided to take action. The organization consisted of a hundred of the region's wealthiest cattle barons, including the state's governor and senators. Cattle auctions were held, and the income was used to pay private posses to capture or kill rustlers. One of their goals, which was remarkably close to the goal of the UDR, was to make it safe for a rancher to enjoy the fruits of his labor.

This was the message that the UDR's president, Ronaldo Caiado, spread as he traveled around Brazil. Caiado was a handsome orthopedic surgeon who had studied in Paris and who owned three cattle ranches covering 8,800 acres of hilly grassland in Goiás. A charismatic speaker, he was able to muster thousands of supporters for banner-waving rallies. Especially effective were demonstrations in Brasília, which floats like an island in a sea of Goiás pastureland —one of the ranchers' strongholds. He pushed the idea that Brazil's Civil Code not only gave squatters the right to use force to defend their land, but also gave that right to ranchers. Caiado came on like a slick salesman at first. Depending on the audience, he wore boots and jeans or tailored dark suits. His dark complexion made his fine, white teeth stand out as if they were fluorescent. He started out smoothly, talking in a deep, even voice about the need for agrarian productivity, not agrarian reform. Then he would start to heat up. His neck would redden and teeth would clench. The smoothness would fade, and he would go on the attack against those who stood against progress. In a rousing finale, he would send his audience home to defend the great Brazilian values of tradition, family, and property.

Quickly, the UDR's membership grew to more than 200,000. Soon there would be 350 regional divisions, and Caiado would boast of 156 youth divisions and 146 women's divisions. It became common to see newspaper ads for UDR auctions in rural towns. In one year, there were forty-nine such auctions, in which 35,000 head of cattle were sold, raising some $890,000. There was never any question about how the revenue would be used. Eventually, Salvador Farina, the head of the UDR chapter in Goiás, confirmed the obvious. "Today I think that we can confess that, yes, we bought weapons with the money from the cattle auctions," he said. "Today we have more than seventy thousand, one for every man in the UDR, men who decided to stop being left out of our country's history."

Chapter 10

The Greening
of Chico Mendes

I N 1985, CHICO MENDES BEGAN to make the transition from
grass-roots organizer to national spokesman for the tappers.
The change required great adaptability; he now began to spend
time in skyscrapers as well as on the rubber trails. The same flexible
mind that had allowed him to absorb the ideas of Euclides Távora
was put to work taking in the complex machinations of Brazilian
politics and learning a new vocabulary—that of environmentalism.

In May, the same month that the new president put forth his
proposal for land reform, Mendes flew down to Brasília to try to
raise funds for the national conference of rubber tappers that he
and Mary Allegretti were planning. Allegretti set up an appointment for Mendes with people from Pró Memória, the branch of
the education and culture ministry that had supported the rubber
tapper schools. The contrast between the stark, flat orderliness of
Brasília and the rambling, shabby towns of the Amazon could not
have been more dramatic; but Mendes, on only his second trip to
the capital, was already unfazed by the marble and glass and long
conference tables and starched shirts.

The meeting took place in one of the identical green glass mono-
liths that line the broad plaza leading to the halls of Congress.

There, Mendes described the hidden forest culture that Brazil had for so long chosen to ignore. He focused on the injustice of it all: these soldiers of rubber had risked their lives to help Brazil contribute to the war effort and now suffered untold indignities and illnesses. A conference of rubber tappers in the capital would allow them to prove their existence, display their culture, and demand justice. His original proposal mentioned only a few dozen tappers from the unions of Brasiléia and Xapuri. The Pró Memória officials told Mendes they would help cover the expense of bringing the tappers down from the forest.

Afterward Mendes, Allegretti, and other advisers discussed the details. They decided that the meeting should take place toward the end of the year, to give them enough time to organize and raise more money. Allegretti had contacts at the University of Brasília, which gave them a site for the conference. Tony Gross was now in charge of all three hundred of Oxfam's Amazon projects in the Brazilian Amazon, and he said that Oxfam could also help financially. Mendes was eager to return to Acre to tell Raimundo de Barros and the other leaders of the movement the news. He was also eager to go home because the dry season was beginning and there were *empates* to plan.

After Mendes left, Allegretti and Gross held their own meeting. The subject was money—or the lack of it. Allegretti's Institute for Economic and Social Studies, like most Brazilian nongovernmental organizations, was chronically broke. Oxfam alone did not have sufficient resources to sustain long-term initiatives such as rubber tapping cooperatives. The two activists had long discussed ideas for expanding the bases of support for the nascent Indian, human rights, and environmental lobbies in Brazil. One obvious target was the powerful environmental movement in the United States. What better place to find grants and allies than Washington, D.C., where organizations such as the National Wildlife Federation had annual budgets of half a billion dollars. So in May, after Mendes's visit, Gross convinced Allegretti to go with him to Washington. While there, Allegretti also hoped to find someone who could act as a liaison for her institute, helping it find grants or partnerships that could keep it in business.

This was her first trip outside Brazil, and it provided an intensive education that quickly broadened her perspective on Amazonian issues. Before, she had never really grasped how the rest of the world perceived the Amazon and its troubles. The American public knew little more than the fact that every second, an expanse of rain forest the size of a football field was being leveled by timber companies and land-hungry peasants. Nature magazines and television shows focused on the extravagant lushness of the flora and fauna. Except for a small clique of anthropologists, though, public awareness of the *peoples* of the rain forest was limited to titillating photo essays about vanishing Indian tribes with stretched lips and earlobes and ferocious demeanors. The struggles of the Indians and rubber tappers were largely invisible and insignificant.

Gross told a few contacts in Washington's community of Indian rights specialists that they were coming, and word spread that a potential Brazilian ally was in town. At the Natural Resources Defense Council, an environmental lawyer named Bruce Rich was among those interested in learning more. Since 1983, Rich had been at the center of an effort to influence one of the most powerful engines of Amazonian destruction, the World Bank. He was a prematurely gray, unassuming man with a bookish manner that belied ferocious legal instincts. And veiled ferocity was required of anyone who hoped to take on the World Bank, formally known as the International Bank for Reconstruction and Development. Created to help rebuild Europe after World War II and to promote international commerce, in the 1950s the bank shifted its priorities to promote development in the Third World.

It focused on countries with ample natural resources but little capital with which to exploit those resources. Minerals in the ground, timber in the forests, the hydroelectric potential of river water—all were considered development potential that, once tapped, could raise standards of living and stimulate the world economy. At the same time, they could provide a healthy return on the bank's investment. Even for a country as heavily in debt as Brazil, the banks were happy to lend more. The theory was Reaganomics incarnate: with a little push, countries such as Brazil would grow their way out of debt, just as the United States would (theoretically) grow its way out of the deficit.

More than $20 billion in loans was disbursed each year by the World Bank and three regional counterparts: the Inter-American Development Bank, the Asian Development Bank, and the African Development Bank. (Once a project was approved by one of these institutions, it was considered such a good investment that it quickly attracted two or three times the value of the loan from private lenders—for instance, the Chase Manhattan Bank or the big banks of West Germany.) Potential borrowers would make a proposal that would go through a lengthy approval process as the bank studied its possible impact and fiscal soundness. But to the consternation of people like Bruce Rich, that process rarely took seriously the environmental and social impact of such projects.

The Amazon was a tragic example of how the bank's flawed lending policy could lead to disaster. Most appalling was the situation in Rondônia. In the late 1970s, the Brazilian military government had finally acknowledged that the BR-364 highway and poorly planned settlement schemes had created a monster in Rondônia and northern Mato Grosso. Brazil began to revamp its program for the northwest Amazon in hopes of controlling the flood of peasants who were swarming into the marginally fertile, ecologically fragile region. The new plan, called Polonoroeste, or Northwest Pole, would send settlers only to areas identified as having good soil, would encourage the planting of sustainable tree crops such as cocoa and cashew (which produces both a nut and a fruit), and would build small access roads and pave 930 miles of BR-364, which remained an impassable swamp for half of the year. The paving of the road would ensure that the farmers could transport all these new crops to the markets.

In December 1981 the World Bank—over the objections of its own consultants, who had surveyed the situation—paid Brazil the first installment of a $500 million loan to cover part of the

$1.5 billion cost of Polonoroeste. The terms of the loan required that Brazil guarantee that reserves be set aside for Indians and that environmental safeguards be implemented. But the bank made little effort to check on Brazil's compliance, and the result was chaos.

As soon as the loan was announced, word quickly spread among the misplaced poor of the south that a huge new Amazon project was in the works. The resulting rush dwarfed the previous onslaught of settlers. Between 1981 and 1983, 65,000 settlers arrived yearly. An epidemic of drug-resistant malaria broke out, and the newcomers overwhelmed the shabby infrastructure of the state. Some 80 percent of the colonists failed and had to move on and cut new forest tracts. Many sold their abandoned tracts to cattle ranchers, who completed the process of destruction. After the choking haze of each burning season dispersed, another 5 percent of Rondônia's forests had been incinerated. In 1984, the pace of the destruction quickened as 160,000 settlers arrived. Bus companies brought in extra vehicles and stuffed them full of the hopeful masses, who carried their belongings—if they had any—in cardboard boxes and shreds of cloth. Sometimes thirty busloads of migrants would arrive each night at checkpoints, overwhelming efforts to vaccinate the newcomers for yellow fever. It was said that mayors in the south rounded up drunks and prisoners, filled them with *cachaça,* and sent them north.

The magnitude of the Polonoroeste disaster did not become clear for a few years. By 1985, both the Indians and the rain forests of Rondônia were on the verge of extinction. And Polonoroeste was just worst example among many in which incautious lending by the banks had catastrophic consequences.

In the Ivory Coast, stretches of unique rain forest fell to make room for rubber plantations funded by the banks. In Singrauli, India, the World Bank financed open-pit coal mines and power plants that displaced 300,000 people and covered the surrounding countryside with ash and coal dust. In Indonesia, the bank helped finance the government's Transmigration Program, which moved 2 million people from the crowded islands of Java, Bali, Lombok, and Madura to sparsely inhabited regions of other islands, including Irian Jaya, the Indonesian half of New Guinea. The program destroyed 5 million acres of forest before renegotiated terms substantially reduced the environmental impact.

This negligence on the part of the development banks caused Bruce Rich and an informal network of environmental, Indian rights, and human rights lobbyists to wage war on the banks. The ten-story World Bank headquarters in Washington, covering six blocks, had a monolithic quality, and its six thousand bureaucrats were capable of warding off attacks by some very powerful interest groups. But Rich and his allies came to understand that the key to pressuring the banks—and, in turn, the nations receiving the banks' largesse—was not to assault the monolith at all; the weak spot lay outside the walls. The banks were impotent without the participation—and the funds—of their biggest member nations. And there was no bigger contributor than the United States, which gave the banks $1.2 billion a year, three times as much as the next highest contribution. What was needed were a few well-staged, carefully targeted congressional hearings.

Rich and his allies began the fight in 1983. One of his most valuable supporters was an anthropologist named Stephan Schwartzman. Schwartzman was living in Washington and free-lancing for London's Survival International, which publicized the plight of imperiled indigenous cultures. Because of a lingering case of hepatitis he had picked up in the Amazon, he had taken time off from working on his doctoral dissertation for the University of Chicago. His subject was the Amazon's elusive Krenakore tribe, which was pushed near extinction by road projects and myriad imported diseases. Schwartzman had the slim frame and pasty complexion of someone who had spent years in the tropics and harbored his share of parasites. Although he was an American, his English had acquired the sliding, lilting inflection of Brazilian Portuguese. Because he had seen the impact of big projects on the Indians, he was eager to help Bruce Rich battle the banks.

By the time Allegretti and Gross arrived in Washington, the walls of the World Bank were indeed beginning to crumble. Through

Rich, Schwartzman had heard of the Brazilians' arrival, and he invited them to his small house in the Mount Pleasant neighborhood. They sat in his living room all night, speaking in Portuguese, and each became familiar with the others' frame of reference. Schwartzman told Allegretti about the situation with the banks. Detailed dossiers about the Polonoroeste disaster had been distributed on Capitol Hill. Congressman David R. Obey and Senator Robert W. Kasten, Jr., both of Wisconsin, were among those who had taken up the issue and threatened to cut off funding for the World Bank if assessments of environmental impact did not become an acid test of any proposed project. A hearing had been held in the fall of 1984 at which the Brazilian agronomist José Lutzenberger unleashed a potent attack on Polonoroeste and the global consequences of the decimation of the rain forest. That was something Allegretti already knew about. Lutzenberger's testimony had been televised back in Brazil and resulted in the first national debate there about the Amazon.

As Schwartzman described it, the hearings had no immediate effect on the bank. Late in 1984, forty environmental and anthropological groups from Brazil, Europe, and the United States sent a large package of evidence of problems with the Polonoroeste project to the World Bank's president, A. W. Clausen. A month later, a curt response had come back from a low-level functionary: the bank would recommend that Brazil make modifications of the project "if and when needed." In desperation, Rich, Schwartzman, and their friends had approached Senator Kasten. He was a conservative, and the environmentalists were not sure what to expect. But Kasten was outraged. He sent a blistering letter to Clausen, saying that the coalition "had raised a number of legitimate concerns and suggested some reasonable approaches to alleviate those concerns. The response from the World Bank was at best a brush-off, but frankly more correctly described as an insult." As chairman of the Senate Foreign Operations Appropriations Subcommittee, Kasten was in a position to do more than just chair hearings. He could easily cancel the annual billion-dollar contribution to the bank from the United States.

Kasten demanded that the bank review the Rondônia project. On April 8, 1985, shortly after Brazil had returned to civilian rule, the bank announced that it had halted all funding for the road project until a detailed review of the situation could be completed. To qualify for the support, the Brazilian government eventually agreed to implement environmental protection programs and establish a 4.4-million-acre reserve for Rondônia's besieged Uru-Eu-Wau-Wau Indians.

This was the first victory in the long battle to force the multilateral banks to create internal environmental sections and invite environmentalists to their meetings. In the meantime, Bruce Rich and other lawyers were drafting legislation that Kasten and Obey would later push through Congress. Schwartzman explained to Allegretti and Gross that the legislation could change the way the banks administered loans and would require the U.S. Agency for International Development to devise an "early warning system" to eliminate bad projects.

Allegretti was overwhelmed by what she heard that night. She found it astonishing that a few environmentalists could successfully force policy changes in an institution the size of the World Bank. The tactics of these North American activists were completely foreign to her. In Brazil, political action was always fighting *against* something—nothing more. Two opponents could meet for several days and in the end come away with nothing. She was electrified by the concrete results possible in the United States.

Allegretti then told Schwartzman about the national meeting of rubber tappers and how they had devised a strategy for saving the forest. She talked about Chico Mendes's union and the schools and the *empates*. But she had to backtrack. Despite his years of experience with the Amazonian Indians, Schwartzman hardly knew what a rubber tapper was, let alone that tens of thousands of them were still living in the Amazon. Allegretti described the debt slavery and brutality, the long history of the tappers' struggle, and the tragic irony of the *soldados da borracha*, many of whom had died trying to produce rubber for the war effort under a program backed by the United States.

As she spoke, Schwartzman grasped the significance of what she was telling him. During the campaign against the banks, he had come to appreciate the power of the press, having fed reams of information to reporters such as Jack Anderson. The soldiers of rubber were a natural for the American media, Schwartzman thought. American dollars had been put up for a pension for these rubber soldiers, and Brazil had never given it to them. Moreover, the existence of these tappers would strengthen the American environmentalists' hand by giving them people to fight for—not just birds and trees.

As he listened to this conversation, Tony Gross saw a dramatic turning point developing in the fight for the forest, a meshing of disparate experiences and tactics—each complementing the other. The Washington lobbyists were fighting the destructive lending policies of the big banks but lacked an alternate development policy that would do a better job of preserving the environment. The rubber tappers and their *empates,* schools, and cooperatives might be able to provide that crucial *sustainable* alternative, but they lacked support. If the two initiatives could be linked, each would gain strength. Not only were the tappers an effective defense against deforestation, but, if their cooperatives could be made to work, they could provide an alternative to the old-fashioned, from-the-top-down development of the Amazon.

As the evening wore on, they recognized that common ground was shared by the big Washington environmental lobbies, budding environmental organizations in Brazil, the trade union movement in the Amazon, and development agencies such as Oxfam: they all wanted to preserve the Amazon in a sustainable way for the people who lived there. As the Briton, the American, and the Brazilian talked, disparate threads of motivation and meaning were woven into a unified course of action.

Schwartzman told the others that this meeting had come about at the ideal time. The Washington environmentalists were particularly interested in getting the help of Allegretti and Acre's rubber tappers because of the threat posed by a new road project that had just been announced by the World Bank's smaller sister, the Inter-

American Development Bank (IDB). The road was once again BR-364, but this time the plan was to complete the stretch connecting Rondônia to Acre. Just as the World Bank was getting its environmental programs in order, the IDB was announcing a $58.5 million loan to Brazil to pave the 310 miles between Pôrto Velho and Rio Branco. But once again, insufficient attention was being paid to the environmental consequences of the *asfaltamento,* which had already laid waste the heart of Rondônia.

Allegretti guaranteed Schwartzman that she and the tappers would help him and his allies force the bank to add environmental safeguards or cancel the loan. (That promise was later fulfilled. Under pressure from the Brazilian contingent, the American lobbies, and the U.S. Congress, the bank agreed to add a $10 million package of programs to protect the Indians, rubber tappers, and their homes.) In return, Allegretti asked Schwartzman to be the Washington contact for the Institute for Economical and Social Analysis; he immediately agreed.

When the meeting finally ended, it was clear that an alliance had been created between the battlefronts of Washington and the western Amazon. This alliance brought new significance to the forthcoming national meeting of rubber tappers. As Allegretti flew back to Brazil with Gross, they began to refine their plans for the meeting: if the tappers broadened their goals to include the fight for the environment, the movement could gain enormous strength. There was just one nagging concern in the minds of these two social scientists, based on one of the old taboos of anthropology: when scientists lose the distance between themselves and their subjects, they risk affecting their subjects' behavior. Allegretti and Gross agreed that there would be unpredictable consequences for the rubber tappers if they were exposed so abruptly to the outside world. At the same time, they knew that if the tappers did not come out of the forest, they might soon have no forest and no culture left.

No one thought it would be easy to sustain this new bond between the rural unionists and the environmentalists. After all, the environmental organizations outside Brazil would have to acknowledge that people lived in the pristine forests. And the hard-line labor groups in Brazil would have to recognize that environmental questions were not just superficial issues for the idle middle class; Brazilian labor unions and political parties such as PT had usually spurned environmental causes for that very reason. It would take the resilient mind and determination of Chico Mendes to make that alliance stick.

The grassy campus of the University of Brasília meanders along the shores of Lake Paranoá, just below the east wing of the capital. The lake was created by damming a river in an effort to add a little humidity to the dry, hot air of the high plains around the city. The lake is pretty to look at but too polluted for swimming. The residents of Brasília swim in a vast outdoor pool in a public park. The pool, a concession to the bureaucrats who once could enjoy the beaches of the old capital of Rio de Janeiro, has artificial surf created by heavy paddles, the only surf for 600 miles. There is a persistent feeling of resentment among most people forced by their careers to live here. The only people who seem to like Brasília are the *candangos*, the people who created the city and have now raised the first generation born there. They feel uncomfortable in any other Brazilian city. As one young native put it, "Here things are clean and organized. Other cities are chaotic and filthy."

Between October 11 and 17, 1985, one hundred and twenty rubber tappers gathered at the University of Brasília for the National Meeting of the Rubber Tappers of Amazonia. Many of them had never before been more than a one-day hike or boat ride from their *seringais*. But they had happily spent days traveling by bus caravan down from Rio Branco and Pôrto Velho and Manaus to the edge of the Amazon and beyond. The buses left the forests behind and passed the scorched, abandoned plots and tin-shack towns of Rondônia. As the miles went by, the fine orange dust that always hung over BR-364 and the other Amazonian roads permeated the travelers' every piece of clothing and every pore. The buses climbed into the dry highlands of Mato Grosso and then across the *planalto*, the windswept plateau of Goiás.

The tappers passed the time by chattering and smoking and

singing songs; many had brought battered guitars or leaky ac-
cordions. They shared a sense of excitement and destiny that some
of the oldest among them had not felt since their ships left the
coast of the northeast, bound for the Amazon to fight the Nazis by
harvesting rubber. They sang the old ballads from the glory days
of the War for Rubber:

> Let's go to bring glory to *seringueiros*, let's go to
>   bring glory to this nation.
> Together with the efforts of the people who make
>   car tires and tires for airplanes. . . .

When the tappers finally arrived in the capital—a clamorous collection of people with *nordestino* looks and ill-fitting shoes and
trousers—they were regarded with curiosity and some amusement
by the conservative citizens of the capital. Clearly, they belonged in
the slums on the outskirts of town, not in the sleek auditorium of
the Technology Department of one of the best universities in the
country. After all, the slums were filled mostly with people of the
same stock—*nordestinos* who had been enticed to Brasília to build
the shining city, then abandoned once the job was done.

But there was something in the way these visitors held themselves, something in their simple speech and straightforward style,
that lured hundreds of politicians and students to a series of lectures and discussions and cultural events throughout that week.
Some were fascinated by the diagonal slashes, the "flag" cuts, that
a tapper made in a decorative tree on the lawn—one of the few
trees in the city—to demonstrate how latex was coaxed from the
rubber trees. Others were drawn by the lilting sound of Hélio
Melo's fiddle. This rubber tapper from Rio Branco was something
of a Renaissance man. He was a skilled musician and talented
painter whose whimsical, often surrealistic canvases depicted such
things as a hybrid between a rubber tree and a cow, with a tapper
collecting his milk from this "second mother" (as tappers often
referred to the trees). Melo, who displayed dozens of paintings at
the meeting, explained that he had learned to love drawing out
on the *seringal* when his mother once drew a mermaid who had

a body that looked like a guitar. Melo had started to experiment, smearing green leaves and flowers on paper to create colors.

And then there were the stories, told by people who had never left the forest and who loved nothing better than to tell stories: about the horselike being that occasionally came out of the Juruá River in the moonlight; about porpoises who took on human form and made love to women. One old soldier of rubber from Rondônia recounted to anthropologists his memories of the day the news came that the war was over. "I woke up in my boss's hut," he said. "I heard a shoot-out. I thought the Germans were in the *seringais.* Then someone said the radio was broadcasting news of peace. People were shooting their guns in the sky. We were so anxious for peace, for the opportunity to see our families again. I cried from happiness. We spent the rest of the evening drinking and singing and celebrating." Of course, he never did get back to his home in the northeast—his debts to the estate boss prevented his leaving.

But the purpose of this meeting was not simply to provide a showcase for a quaint, reclusive rural culture. When Mary Allegretti had returned from Washington in May, she immediately scrapped the original plan for the meeting—simply a narrow forum at which the rubber tappers could prove their existence and demand social justice. In discussions with Chico Mendes, she had described the looming problem posed by the paving of BR-364 and the new allies she had found in Washington. Until now, the struggle of the tappers had always been cast as one of justice and free labor and land rights. These talks marked the first time that Mendes understood that the environment itself—the extraordinary biological splendor of the Amazon—could help them win support and save their way of life. He recognized the possibility that with the environmental issue on their side, the rubber tappers might well be able to have a voice in the national debate over the Amazon.

Allegretti had modified the project outline, changing the wording in a way that added enormously to the significance of the event: "The only way to launch a broader movement to defend the Amazon and its inhabitants and to show Brazilian society the conditions of slavery under which rubber tappers continue to live and work is to bring them from the forest to speak out in the political center of the country." Allegretti had confronted Mendes with the question that had plagued her and Tony Gross, the question about the impact of bringing the tappers out of the forest. Mendes never hesitated; he made the final decision to go ahead with the meeting.

Mendes and Allegretti had then spent five feverish months organizing the meeting on two fronts. Mendes's union became the official sponsor. Allegretti canvassed more than twenty organizations and raised several thousand dollars to cover bus fares and a few plane tickets. Then she, Mendes, Raimundo de Barros, and some other members of the Xapuri union held planning sessions around Acre to recruit participants and explain the added significance of the tappers' struggle. Allegretti told the other tappers that there were people as far away as Washington, D.C., who were concerned with the fate of the Amazon.

At first, only tappers from Acre were going to attend. But word of the meeting spread around the Amazon through the union and church networks. When calls came into Xapuri from as far away as Manaus, Mendes and Allegretti decided that the meeting should involve all of the Amazon. They got calls from Amazonas, from tappers who were working with the church to establish schools. From Rondônia, they got a call from an association of soldiers of rubber, war veterans of sorts. Mendes traveled from state to state to coordinate plans.

Finally, the tappers were actually at the meeting. Each day, the tappers and advisers, technocrats, and politicians filed into a brick and wood auditorium and participated in panel discussions. The sessions often began with the singing of ballads from the rubber war or hymns such as "Asa Branca" ("White Wing"), one of the most popular songs from the northeast. The topics ranged from the government pricing system for rubber to the road paving project that was flooding Rondônia with poor settlers. Tappers from eastern Acre complained about the ranchers who were toppling their Brazil nut and rubber trees. Tappers from the Juruá, in western Acre, spoke of the continuing conditions of debt slavery under which they labored and died.

Government officials from environmental agencies promised that the new plan to pave BR-364 would be accompanied by environmental programs designed to mitigate the impact of the flow of settlers that was sure to follow. The tappers were not convinced, however, especially those from Rondônia, most of whom had long since been run off their land by the paving of the southern stretch of BR-364 and the settlers who followed. They railed at the officials for not consulting the people who lived in the forest before designing policies to develop the region.

For two decades, the development of the Amazon had been planned and implemented from the top down. The basic premise had all the subtlety of an ax: first build a road, then find people to settle along it, even if you have to fly them in by jumbo jet. Now, at this meeting, these people claimed that their experience with the unique qualities of their environment justified their having a say in its fate. As one Acre tapper explained, "When we say we're against deforestation, people say we're against the development of Brazil. We're not against development, but we are against the devastation of Amazonia. We want development that doesn't only benefit the big companies and the powerful, but the people who work on the land." For Brazil, this was a novel concept. Public hearings and the "not in my back yard" syndrome so common in America were not yet a part of its culture.

Chico Mendes was not able to attend the first few days of the meeting. He had been politicking back in Acre in the weeks before the November elections, where he was waging a losing battle for the mayoralty of Xapuri. (He insisted on running as a representative of PT, even though it had little support in the conservative state, where even union members feared that PT could do nothing for them. Allegretti had discouraged him from running, saying that he could accomplish more by focusing on the union and the growing tappers' movement, but Mendes stubbornly persisted.) In his absence, Osmarino Amâncio Rodrigues, a fiery, radical leader from Wilson Pinheiro's town, was the most prominent representative from Acre. Acre had by far the largest bloc at the meeting: sixty tappers from Xapuri and Brasiléia. But even Rodrigues was up-

200 THE BURNING SEASON

staged by a wiry, almond-eyed loner from the tiny town of Novo
Aripuanã, deep in Amazonas, who became the master of ceremonies
and the first national voice of the tappers—Jaime da Silva Araújo.

Araújo was a surprise to everyone. He had heard about the
meeting at the last minute through an activist priest in his region
and was barely able to round up another tapper to take advantage
of two plane tickets that had been sent by the conference organizers. He took control of the meeting through sheer force of person-
ality. A natural poet, he sang songs about the mother of the forest,
who punished those who harvested the forest bounty too heavily.
His tales had audiences rapt.

When Mendes finally arrived, he avoided the spotlight, although
as one of the primary organizers of the meeting he could have easily expected it. He did take the chair for one day at the end of the
conference, but he did not give any impassioned speeches. Mendes recognized that his strong suit was not poetry or statesmanship.
He was a politician and an activist in the most literal sense. His
strength was in organizing and quiet diplomacy. He was the person
who could round people up and get them talking; more important,
he could get them to act. Everyone who worked with him said over
and over that Mendes was not doing what he did for power, glory,
or money—which some others among the leadership of the tapper
movement were sometimes accused of—but simply because he felt
so strongly that it had to be done.

Allegretti and Mendes had arranged several levels of activities.
Along with the public seminars and cultural events, there were
closed-door meetings with advisers at which the tappers were urged
to shift the focus of their strategy. Many still thought that their
most significant bargaining chip was rubber. They had been raised
to believe wholeheartedly that Brazil would someday laud them as
long-lost heroes who harvested a valuable strategic material and
who, during World War II, had saved the free world from Nazi
domination. Thus they still sang the tired patriotic ballads. One
anthropologist, Mauro Almeida, who had done a lot of work in the
isolated Juruá River valley, discovered how difficult it was for some

of the tappers to understand that Asian plantation rubber and synthetic rubber now dominated the market. One elderly soldier of rubber broke down and cried when he learned about synthetic rubber for the first time. Almeida, Allegretti, and the other advisers agreed that the tappers needed a sort of cold shower. Almeida had to sit with them and say, "Look, people just couldn't care less about your rubber now. Forget about it." The older tappers were stunned.

As the importance of rubber was downplayed, the importance of the tappers' role as defenders of the environment was emphasized. Allegretti and the others stressed that the future of the rain forest did not have to be bound to rubber. Mendes, who was already a convert to the new approach, helped convey this idea to the other tappers. One goal of the movement thus became the promotion of research into other forest products, ranging from oils and nuts to crops such as cocoa, which grows naturally in the shade of the canopy. And Allegretti constantly reiterated the importance of the *empates* and how effective they had been at saving trees. After their initial shock, the tappers seemed to accept the situation and turned immediately to the new strategy—the idea that they could be the defenders of the forest. Said one, "If this is why people will support our struggle, this is how we will fight."

One of the most important results of the meeting was a call for the creation of a national organization of rubber tappers. This need arose after the tappers were spurned by the National Council on Rubber, a government agency that helped determine the price for Amazon rubber. The tappers had asked to meet with the bureaucrats but had been turned down. As a result, it was decided—with some intended irony—to create a national council of rubber tappers, the Conselho Nacional dos Seringueiros. The council would work to promote health, education, and cooperatives for the tappers and push for land rights that would allow them to live and work in the forest without fear of expulsion or deforestation. The other justification for such a council was that the existing unions represented all rural agricultural workers; the tappers wanted an organization that was theirs alone.

Allegretti and Mendes had never intended that the meeting would produce a permanent entity. There had been no long-term plans. They had not even called it the first national meeting. But soon the National Council flourished and became the international voice of the movement that had begun, a decade earlier, on a few *seringais* in the forests of eastern Acre.

The most significant proposal to emerge from the conference was the tappers' call for a special system of agrarian reform to be established for the Amazon basin that would create areas reserved for "extractive" activities such as rubber and nut harvesting—extractive reserves.

The term had been coined at one of the regional planning sessions before the national conference. The session brought together tappers from the forests around Ariquemes, a town in the heart of the destruction in Rondônia. These tappers had had a longstanding conflict with the Indians over the demarcation of an Indian reserve, so an anthropologist named Carlos Teixeira cited the Indian reserves as an example of what the tappers should ask for themselves. Mary Allegretti was at the meeting. As she recalled it, a tapper said, "Yes, but we are not Indians, we are extractivists," whereupon Teixeira came up with "extractive reserve." It took more than two years before Allegretti and other advisers could forge a detailed plan for extractive reserves that would fit the complexities of Brazilian law. But the basic meaning—and the importance—of the concept was clear to everyone. It was the same idea that Chico Mendes had proposed a year earlier when he talked of "special rural modules."

The national meeting succeeded in publicizing the plight of the rubber tappers, whose situation until then had been discussed only in the past tense. The newspapers in São Paulo and Rio ran articles about these *desbravadores,* tamers, of the rain forest. Rubber tappers went on talk shows. The rector of the university, an old friend of Allegretti's, invited two tappers to teach a course there for six months. The Brazilian establishment had assumed that the *aviamento* system of debt slavery and the rubber battalions of World War II were already dusty history. And few people outside the

Amazon and the activist community had been aware of the violent conflicts between the tappers and the encroaching ranchers. Suddenly, in the auditorium filled with people from the forest, federal congressmen and senators from Acre appeared and made strident speeches calling for benefits for the rubber veterans.

Before the meeting adjourned, Mendes, Araújo, Rodrigues, and the other leaders drew up a sixty-two-point manifesto demanding, in part, that the peoples of the Amazon be given a say in its development, that they be provided with health care, education, fair pricing for rubber, and retirement benefits for the soldiers of rubber.

The manifesto concluded with a simple demand that hinted at the dramatic change in their orientation: "We demand to be recognized as [the] genuine defenders of the forest." Although the tappers continued to voice their old calls for social justice, workers' rights, and agrarian reform—standard issues of the political left— at the urging of Chico Mendes and Mary Allegretti, they modified their message in a subtle but important way. For the first time, they made a simple, uncluttered call for the preservation of Amazonia —not only for the sake of its peoples, but for its own sake as well.

The Brazilian government was clearly beginning to wake up to the need to change its policies in the Amazon. In Belém, just as the tappers were preparing to leave for their homes, the minister of the interior addressed a meeting on the Amazon and said, "The predatory use of Amazonia must be forgone. The wealth of the region must be used, but in a selective and intelligent way." At a closing session of the meeting, Ulysses Guimarães, the president of the Congress, shook hands with the tapper leaders and accepted a copy of their manifesto, which he promised to give to President Sarney.

Over the next few months, as small follow-up meetings were held, the environment became a more prominent fixture in the tappers' argument for forest preservation. This was the moment when a new term entered the lexicon of the *seringueiro.* Along with *seringal, colocação,* and *borracha* could now be heard *ecologia*— ecology.

The national meeting brought together for the first time four people with remarkable and complementary abilities: Chico Mendes, Mary Allegretti, Stephan Schwartzman, and the filmmaker Adrian Cowell. Over the next three years, each played a key role in the fight to save the Amazon.

While Mendes and Allegretti had been planning the meeting, Cowell had been frantically filming the raging destruction in Rondônia. He had first met Allegretti on a visit to the capital earlier in the year; over lunch, he heard a bit about the situation in Acre, where he had never filmed. She had mentioned the upcoming meeting, but only briefly. Just one week before the meeting, Cowell returned to Rondônia from an editing session in London. He called Allegretti and asked if she thought the meeting was important and whether he should come down to film it. She told him about the tappers' coming from four Amazon states and their plan to propose extractive reserves.

Cowell immediately decided to attend. He was halfway into his *Decade of Destruction* epic, filming a segment called "Banking on Disaster," which reported on the destructive effects of the World Bank's loan for Polonoroeste. Hoping to find something positive amid all the ashes and blood, he thought the tappers and their movement might be just the thing. He later recalled how he and his cameraman, Vicente Rios, had had to scramble to get to the capital in time. They had a pickup truck full of gear, so had no alternative but to drive from Rondônia—at the peak of the burning season. As Cowell recalled, "Everything was burning. A road had been cut all the way through to the Guapore Valley"—a pristine forested region— "and the result was appalling. We passed through this gauntlet of fire and smoke. We had to drive for three days without stopping."

Cowell filmed most of the meeting, even though he knew that the rather bland footage would not make it into his film. He felt it was nevertheless important to document what was happening for history's sake. Especially impressive to Cowell was the tappers' decision to create a national council. In the past, he had seen too many individual Indian tribes fight for their small tract of forest, to no end. He had been aware of the developments in Acre and had been encouraged to see the tappers fighting, defending their land. But only when they decided to become a national movement did Cowell drop everything else and give them top priority. He was convinced that his instincts had been right and that these rubber tappers, along with their advisers, had come up with a proposal that truly had the potential to preserve large tracts of the rain forest.

Stephan Schwartzman, too, had heard about the meeting from Mary Allegretti. He had managed to fly down to Brazil for the meeting and a fact-finding trip up the Amazon. After the meeting had officially ended, the tappers and their advisers gathered at the national headquarters of CONTAG to discuss their next move. Schwartzman was introduced to Chico Mendes and some of the other leaders. He addressed the tappers and tried to explain in more detail the connection between their battles against the ranchers and rubber bosses and his work in Washington. He felt that his audience only partially understood what he was saying, and at that time, he did not understand everything about what the tappers were doing. More important, however, was that he could see now that the tappers would indeed constitute a valuable ally in the fight against the banks.

The same kind of pragmatic acceptance typified some of the rubber tappers' reactions to the environmentalists. One of the more politically minded tappers, Osmarino Rodrigues, initially saw the environmental issue as a bit bourgeois, something of a luxury. Even after he became convinced that this strategy would help the tappers, his persistent impression was that the alliance "joined the *útil* and the *agradável*"—the useful and the pleasant. On both sides, the motives did not matter; what mattered was that each partner strengthened the other.

Just as the tappers were about to head home, Cowell heard that the United Nations World Commission on Environment and Development was going to São Paulo on October 25 for several days of hearings. Headed by the Norwegian prime minister, Gro Harlem Brundtland, the commission was preparing a book-length report on prospects for promoting economic growth that did not harm the environment. (The Brazilian government had tried to keep news of the visit from spreading to environmental groups.) Cowell rounded up a couple of plane tickets and arranged for Allegretti, Jaime da Silva Araújo, and another tapper to fly south. Chico Mendes could not go; because of the pending elections, he had already returned to Xapuri to finish his campaign.

The Amazon contingent at the São Paulo hearings also included a delegation of Indians headed by Ailton Krenak, a leader of the Union of Indigenous Nations. In his speech, Krenak made the first public reference to the plan for an alliance of the forest peoples— Indians and rubber tappers together. And when Araújo spoke, he was in finest form, explaining in dramatic terms the new proposal for extractive reserves. His speech was a clear articulation of the new approach that had been promoted by Allegretti and Mendes. "I am a *seringueiro*," Araújo said. "My people live from the forest that some want to destroy. We want to take advantage of this opportunity to meet so many people gathered together with the same goal—to defend the environment, to defend the conservation of tropical forests. We *seringueiros* call for this struggle to be intensified, for pressure to be applied to the banks that send foreign money to Brazil to destroy our forests. . . . In the region where I live, for example, we extract some fourteen or fifteen different native products. This should be preserved, because it is not only with cattle, not only with grass, not only with roads that we bring about the development of Amazonia."

Araújo was elected the first president of the National Council of Rubber Tappers a few months later, but he eventually withdrew from the movement. His failure was partly due to his isolation in Amazonas, where he had only a handful of supporters. (Araújo tried to have the National Council set up a branch office in Manaus, but there was no money for such a venture; the only office was in Rio Branco, where the movement's strength lay.) At the same time, he came under intense pressure from local political enemies. His house was set on fire one night when the anthropologist Mauro Almeida was visiting, and several attempts were made on his life. Ultimately, the pressure was too intense. Araújo disappeared from sight and only turned up again in 1989. But he never returned to the movement.

In the meantime, Cowell had turned his attention to the one man among the tappers who seemed to be smart enough, cool enough, and honest enough to take the tappers' message out of the forest and straight to the boardrooms of the banks and the halls of Congress, both in and out of Brazil. That man was Chico Mendes. Cowell had quietly observed all the leaders at the Brasília meeting, and Mendes seemed by far the quickest at grasping new concepts. He was not just quick at absorbing the new environmental approach, but quick at making it a fundamental part of his mental and emotional framework. Mendes equated ecology with his life-long love for the forests in which he had grown up; he was inherently an environmentalist. His other important quality was that he was not affected by all of the change that was taking place; he stayed himself. Cowell never liked to think that he was meddling in things. He did not want to transform the movement, only to give it a louder voice.

After the hearing in São Paulo, Cowell decided to follow Chico Mendes back to Acre. For the next three years, Cowell and his camera became near constant companions of the union leader. Cowell had spent two decades making impassioned films about environmental and social crises around the world, and his instinct for communication told him that Mendes had the perfect voice with which to communicate the plight of the forest.

Chapter *11*

An Innocent Abroad

W HEN CHICO MENDES RETURNED to Acre from the
meeting in Brasília, he threw all his energy into the final
battle for mayor of Xapuri. And, as everyone expected,
he lost badly to the candidate from the ranchers' party. This loss
took a lot out of him. He was already under great strain, as the sense
of danger in Xapuri rose with the frequency of conflicts between
the ranchers and the tappers.

To put the election behind him, Mendes quickly resumed the
activities he did best: tramping the rubber trails of Xapuri and other
counties to organize *empates,* recruit more union members, build
schools, and spread the word about extractive reserves and this new
phenomenon called *ecologia.* The character of the *empates* had recently become more refined, and women and children had begun
to come along. They effectively intimidated both hired gunmen
and the Military Police. And with Adrian Cowell's camera rolling
and several journalists regularly filing stories about the *empates* for
the big newspapers of São Paulo and Rio, the women and children
also were good for public relations.

Although the media later reported that Mendes had conceived
of this as a Gandhian kind of strategy, many women from Xapuri's
seringais insist that they had to fight to go along. One of these
women was Mariazinha, the wife of Raimundo de Barros. She was

one of the first proponents on the rubber estates of the nascent women's movement, which had begun to gain strength throughout Brazil in the early 1980s. She said that Mendes and her husband were particularly opposed to having women participate for fear they might get hurt. In the end, the women won them over, becoming a powerful addition to the front lines.

And the tappers needed all the help they could get. In the dry season of 1986, the tension between the tappers and the ranchers rose to a dangerous pitch. In May, Geraldo Bordon, the owner of Seringal Nazaré, received a permit from the forestry office to cut down 1,730 acres of rain forest. The tappers were outraged; the area harbored 1,500 rubber trees and 600 Brazil nut trees—each one a vital natural factory producing valuable products. Bordon's permit was in direct violation of the Forestry Code, which prohibited the cutting of these two tree species as well as deforestation along the banks of rivers or streams. Even so, Bordon was able to enlist the help of the Military Police, who sent eight officers to the ranch, ostensibly to protect the cutting crews.

In June, Mendes rounded up two hundred tappers for a march to the federal forestry office in Xapuri. There, they staged a sit-in but were quickly evicted by the Military Police. Soon thereafter, Mendes and Raimundo de Barros organized several *empates* against Bordon. Whenever they and their column of tappers came upon a cutting crew slashing through the underbrush, they were almost always able to talk the men into dropping their machetes and saws and leaving. Faced with the steady, relentless opposition fielded by Mendes, Bordon finally gave up and sold his land in Acre.

Another powerful *paulista* was also driven out by the *empates*. Rubens Andrade de Carvalho, the King of Cattle, had sprawling ranches in southern Brazil as well as the United States, and he had bought Seringal Filipinas, where de Barros had grown up. But Mendes and de Barros and their *companheiros* simply made the business of deforestation too difficult, and the so-called king was forced to give up in Acre.

Victories such as these fueled the ranchers' hatred of Mendes, who by now had become the most prominent representative of the tappers' movement. Lately, on Friday nights, as rough ranch workers drove into town to drink and chase women, it was not uncommon for them to cruise slowly by the union hall, taunting and threatening Mendes, sometimes brandishing pistols. Since 1983, Mendes had been licensed to carry a revolver because of the threats against him, and he had avoided two ambushes over the previous couple of years. In November 1984, three men with revolvers were waiting for him in the shadows of the bus station in Xapuri. A woman sitting nearby overheard them whispering about their plan to shoot Mendes. She ran to the Military Police barracks, just 50 yards from the bus station, and when the soldiers appeared the gunmen fled. During the dry season of 1986, a *tocaia*, an ambush site, was found in the bushes along a river where Mendes was scheduled to pass to join an *empate* at the Bordon ranch.

Despite the power of the ranchers, late in 1986 Mendes decided to run for office one last time as a PT candidate, this time for a seat in the Acre state legislature. He must have known deep down that it was a futile effort—his opponents were heavily funded by the ranchers—but he never let such doubts show. By 1986, it was clear that Mendes had no real gift for conventional politics. He had last held elective office in 1979, when the forced resignation of the president of the Xapuri town council had given Mendes the leadership, if only briefly. And once he switched to the Workers party, PT, he never again won a political race. In 1982, he had lost a bid for state representative, and then came the failed mayoral race. Politics was in his blood, but he refused to do what all politicians must do to win—bend his principles to suit the electorate.

Even within PT he was constantly battling for support; his Marxist leanings made him unpalatable to the leftist mainstream. The national leadership—which focused on the big cities—always kept him at arm's length and gave little backing to his campaigns far away in Acre. Compounding Mendes's problems was the fact that only a fourth of the eligible voters in Acre were registered. In Brazil, substantial documentation is required for registration, and most of the rural poor either lack the papers or do not know how to get them. (On one *seringal* a three-day hike from Xapuri, a recent survey showed that of 106 adults active in the tappers' movement, only 3 had documents that would permit them to vote.)

Failed politician or not, Mendes doggedly insisted on launching his new campaign. As the dry season of 1986 ended and the burning season approached, he tried out a new strategy. This time he tied his platform directly to the environmental message of the tappers' struggle: he would lead the "defense of Amazonia." His supporters drove through town in a jeep with megaphones on top that blared, "Chico Mendes, in defense of the Amazon forest. For the creation of extractive reserves!"

As the campaign began, Mendes's problems went beyond his political difficulties. Once again, Mendes had no money. (In fact, he may have chosen to run because he needed the job.) His union position brought in negligible income, and he spent much of his time working to promote the National Council of Rubber Tappers. Whereas before he had always supplemented his income with occasional work in the forest, now he had no time.

His three-year-old marriage was suffering too. In April 1983, Mendes had married a woman he had known since 1970. Ilzamar Gadelha Bezerra was just a girl then, and he was the man from the government school who used to hike to her father's *seringal* to help harvest rubber and teach her how to read. In 1978, when Ilzamar was fifteen, they had become lovers. Finally, when Ilzamar was twenty and he thirty-nine, they were married in a civil ceremony in Brasiléia. But lately their relationship had become sporadic and stormy, with allegations on both sides of affairs and neglect. They had separated for a time after Mendes claimed to have caught Ilzamar having an affair with a male nurse at the Xapuri clinic. Mendes was in such a rage that he told friends he was going to shoot her. Only with the help of friends were they able to get back together.

By 1986, Mendes was traveling nearly constantly. For months, he had hardly spent any time with Ilzamar and their two-year-old daughter, Elenira. They had no house of their own, and Ilzamar was living with her parents on Seringal Santa Fé. Mendes often slept at the church or the union hall in Xapuri or the houses of friends.

And when Ilzamar became pregnant in mid-1986, Mendes was never around to help out. With no rancor, Ilzamar later told one reporter, "Chico never should have had a family. . . . He used to say that although he'd like to give his family more, his heart was with the *seringueiros.*"

Mendes's personal problems came to a head in the early hours of August 2. Ilzamar had gone into labor and delivered twins just before dawn. But one of the twins died in childbirth. The surviving twin was Sandino, who as he grew took on a remarkable resemblance to his father. Ilzamar remained hospitalized for several weeks. When Mendes had no money to pay for the hospital bill, Adrian Cowell paid it for him. Cowell and Mendes shared a lot of sorrow at that time; Cowell's own son died shortly thereafter in a boating accident in Europe. Despite the pressures on him, Mendes remained stoical. Cowell was often amazed by his controlled nature.

As the election drew near, Mary Allegretti flew up to Acre and joined Cowell. (They were in the middle of a three-year relationship.) While Mendes had continued his grass-roots work, Allegretti had returned to Curitiba to create her own nongovernmental organization, which she called the Institute for Amazonian Studies. Its focus was the rubber tappers' effort to establish extractive reserves, and its primary goal was to get the government to create a legal definition for this novel system of agrarian reform. To keep the budget low, Allegretti ran the institute out of her two-story stucco house on a suburban side street.

Allegretti and Cowell were both deeply concerned now about that road project funded by the Inter-American Development Bank the previous year. By 1986, the asphalt was progressing steadily along BR-364 toward Acre. But the environmental programs that Brazil had pledged to create were lagging far behind.

Allegretti had stayed in close touch with Stephan Schwartzman, who had returned to Washington and written a report that became influential in bringing further attention to the rubber tappers. In the paper, his zeal was evident: "The potential importance of a grass-roots movement in Amazonia calling for forest conservation can hardly be overestimated," he wrote. Here was a movement by a productively employed local population that had a vested interest in keeping the rain forests as they were. The existence of Chico Mendes and his tappers' union meant that Brazil could no longer make nationalistic claims that the fight to save the Amazon was merely a case of foreign ecologists meddling in Brazilian affairs.

After discussing the road project, Allegretti and Schwartzman agreed that the time was right to make the conceptual alliance between the American environmentalists and the Amazonian rubber tappers a reality. Schwartzman, who now worked for the Environmental Defense Fund with Bruce Rich, said that the lobbies were ready to assault the bank again, but they needed that all-important voice from the forest—proof that the road was going to harm someone—to justify their attack. Through Cowell, Allegretti knew that Mendes had included attacks on the road paving in his campaign speeches; it was an unpopular stance in Acre, where an all-weather road was seen as vital to the development of the state. Meeting in Rio Branco, Allegretti and Cowell concluded that Mendes would be much more effective if he left local politics behind, came out of the forest once again, and directed his criticisms directly at the bank.

They left Rio Branco and caught up with Mendes on the campaign trail. He was with Raimundo de Barros and Gomercindo Rodrigues, the agronomist and PT firebrand who had moved to Acre and was helping the tappers organize. He was also serving as Mendes's campaign manager–bodyguard. They all met up in the tawdry border town of Plácido de Castro, which sat on a sand embankment 40 feet above the Abunã River. On the opposite bank was the Bolivian village of San Luis, which looked like a mock-up of Main Street in a Hollywood Western. There was nothing beyond the two rows of unpainted two-story wooden buildings except forest. Each housed a duty-free store stuffed with electronic toys and watches, perfumed pens, and Johnnie Walker at half the Brazilian price. Andean music blared, and a steady trickle of Brazilians paid two cents to be paddled across the slow, murky river.

Mendes had come to Plácido de Castro to give a speech along

with the local candidates from PT. Cowell decided to film the speech, but it had been dark all day, so he had to set up some floodlights. Soon a crowd gathered. The first speakers urged the workers to get out the vote. Then two Indians spoke, supporting Mendes's call for the defense of the forest. Finally it was Mendes's turn. Cowell turned on the floodlights and rolled the film. Instantly, the streetlights dimmed, then everything went black. It seemed typical of Mendes's luck in politics: they had shorted out the entire town.

In the darkness, Mendes, de Barros, and Rodrigues retreated to a small bar with Cowell and Allegretti. They all drank some beer by candlelight and talked of what lay ahead. In the ensuing conversation, Mendes made a commitment that would take his life down two dramatically different tracks. One Chico Mendes would become something of an international celebrity, the subject of profiles in leading newspapers around the world, the recipient of prestigious environmental awards; the other would remain a man of Xapuri and face a growing number of death threats, political attacks, and domestic troubles.

During the discussion that night, Cowell and Allegretti raised the prospect of Mendes's flying to the United States to deliver his message directly to the Inter-American Development Bank and the U.S. Congress. They spelled out why this action would be useful: the American environmentalists could effectively campaign against the road only if the rubber tappers themselves formally said they did not want it. The environmentalists needed to campaign on behalf of someone.

Allegretti well knew what it meant to take the fight overseas. In May 1986, while Mendes was staging *empates* against the Bordon ranch, she had made her second trip to Washington. She and Schwartzman had testified about the situation in the Amazon at a Senate hearing, chaired by Senator Kasten, on the environmental problems created by multilateral bank loans. Back in Brazil, Allegretti had been attacked by both politicians and the press as a front for American interests who wanted to control the Amazon's riches. She was the *papagaio da pirata*—the parrot of the pirate. The

National Confederation of Agriculture, the most conservative ranchers' lobby, issued a white paper denouncing her.

Once the proposal was laid out, de Barros said quite flatly, "I can't understand any of this." Mendes was quiet and seemed distracted. He may have been thinking about his probable loss in the upcoming election and trying to chart his future. Finally, putting his trust in the strengthening—if improbable—friendships he had forged with these people, Mendes said he would go.

The thicket of beer bottles on the table grew denser, and talk turned to other ramifications of the decision. The group debated whether this step would increase the risk of Mendes's being killed. Several times recently, people had been seen following him or hanging around the union hall at night. Rodrigues and Mendes both said that going abroad certainly could not make things worse than they already were—and might make them better. If Mendes had a higher profile, people might be less apt to try to kill him. There was no turning back, Mendes said. But first he had to finish his campaign.

His prospects remained bleak. The gubernatorial candidate for the conservative PMDB, Rio Branco's mayor Flaviano Melo, had received enormous contributions from the ranchers and businessmen and was certain to carry most of the state deputy seats on his coattails. Melo was a dynamic young man who had craftily designed a campaign that blared progress but recognized the growing environmental issue. He promised that Acre would be developed with respect for the forest, but at the same time he took up the old call of Wanderley Dantas: to build a road to the Pacific, to make Acre Brazil's gateway to the economic boom in Asia. (He later dubbed Acre "the Green State with New Ideas.")

However, despite the odds, Mendes never gave up hope as he doggedly stumped the *seringais* and small farms. His waistline began to grow despite all the exercise; he was obliged to sit and politely eat a meal at every stop. Cowell took him aside several times during the campaign to film interviews. Cowell would ask, "Chico, there's so much strength on the government side. Do you think you can win?" Chico would respond stubbornly, "Yes, yes, I've never had so much support. I think the country is ready to change."

During the campaign, Mendes claimed that a private plane had landed at the Xapuri airport full of cash to buy votes for PMDB. Cowell's documentary later confirmed that rampant vote selling had taken place. It showed a boy on election day sidling up to Mendes as he crossed the plaza in Xapuri. The boy said, "*Oi chefe,* give me a thousand. At least you could be sure of my mother's vote." Votes were being traded for kitchen implements, such as a pressure cooker. A family with many voters could be bought with a small chain saw. In addition, the return of civilian government in Brazil had resurrected old-fashioned patronage. In 1982, Acre had 7,800 government employees. By 1986, the bureaucracy had grown to 20,000. It was estimated that 70 percent of the workers in Xapuri were employed by the local, state, or federal government.

Clearly, Mendes did not have a chance. First, he was almost compulsively honest, a trait that was evident in Cowell's footage of election day. Early that morning, as Cowell filmed from a distance, Mendes stopped at the tiny blue stall of his friend Dona Maria to get his daily breakfast of a glass of thick espresso. A woman asked him to buy her something to drink and he said, "Look, it's prohibited for me [as a candidate] to give money." Further, Mendes's poverty meant that he could not have bought a vote even if he had wanted to. At this stage, he was desperately broke, often lacking money even for bus fare. Financial support from PT was minimal. He hitched rides and ate meals with Cowell whenever he could.

When the ballots were tallied, Mendes and PT had indeed lost. Nationally, Melo's party, PMDB, won 96 percent of the governors' seats and 55 percent of the Congress. In Acre, the PT candidates got only 3 percent of the vote. Even though Mendes's union had 2,000 members, he received only 800 votes—half of the 1,500 he needed to win. Once again, although he was highly regarded within the union and liked by almost everyone except the ranchers, Mendes had come up empty as a politician. His chronic lack of support may have stemmed from fears that his staunch opposition to many policies of the federal government would ensure his inability to get money for programs in the state—and 87 percent of Acre's budget was paid by federal largesse.

In public, Mendes rarely allowed himself to show any emotions except happiness and hopefulness. But this night he was despondent. Cowell took him out for a drink and tried to cheer him up, but there was no breaking his black mood. His eyes looked tired; he looked almost broken. But by the next day he had bounced back so strongly that Cowell was startled. He seemed to have gone through a catharsis, perhaps finally washing politics out of his system. As he had planned with Allegretti and Cowell, it was time to take this fight out of the forest and north of the equator, to the one place that had the power to stanch the smoke and flames. It was time to go to the United States.

Mendes began preparing for his new career in international relations with the help of Cowell, who enticed some people from the United Nations to visit Xapuri. Among them was Robert Lamb, another Briton who had become curious about the rubber tappers' movement. Lamb worked at Central Independent Television, the London network that financed Cowell's documentaries, and also did public relations work for the head of the United Nations Environment Program (UNEP) in Kenya.

Mendes took Lamb into the rain forest to attend a two-day meeting of several hundred rubber tappers. From Xapuri, they drove for two hours, then cut off the road and hiked for what seemed like what Brazilians call *toda vida,* all of your life. As they walked beneath the arching green canopy, which partially shielded them from the steady rain of the wet season, Mendes stopped every few minutes to pick up some nut or fruit or scrap of wood and explain what it was used for. When they finally reached the clearing of a *seringal,* Lamb came to understand the significance of having people living in the forest. Here he had walked for a day through what appeared to be pristine jungle, and suddenly he was face to face with two hundred people who were happily living in the depths of the untrammeled ecosystem. Nothing could go on there without someone's knowing about it; at the same time, the people were not harming the forest.

Mendes explained to the gathering how the designation of extractive reserves would mean that the land would be held by the government or communal title and protected from the fires. Lamb was struck by Mendes's magnetism, which had drawn so many people to the meeting. He returned to London determined to bring Mendes to the attention of UNEP.

Adrian Cowell and Mary Allegretti realized that before Mendes went abroad, he had to be seen as a leader of the tappers by officials in Brasília; after all, he had had little exposure during the 1985 meeting. In December 1986, Allegretti, Cowell, Mendes, and the other tapper leaders met in Acre to complete plans for a new series of meetings in the capital. Cowell gave Mendes a dramatic photograph, taken by an American weather satellite, that showed the fishbone pattern of devastation that had eroded as much as a fourth of the forest in Rondônia. Cowell had gotten the image from NASA scientists who, with some Brazilian colleagues, were for the first time turning their sensitive probes on the burning in the Amazon. Mendes could use the pictures to illustrate what they were fighting.

In January, Mendes and Osmarino Rodrigues met in Brasília with officials from the Ministry of Commerce and outlined the extractive reserve idea. For the first time, the head of the agrarian reform ministry supported the concept, as did Brazil's chief environmental official.

While visiting the capital, the tappers were joined by a delegation of Indians; together they made the rounds of the ministries as the first joint committee of Indians and tappers. In meetings with Ailton Krenak, the head of the Union of Indigenous Nations, Mendes had led the effort to develop an Alliance of the Peoples of the Forest. As Mendes later recalled to Miranda Smith, a filmmaker, "People became amazed at the time, saying, 'Indians and rubber tappers together? Didn't you fight before? Weren't you enemies?' . . . And we responded, 'We understand today that our fight is the same one. The struggle of the Indian should be the same as that of the rubber tappers. . . . We should be together today to fight to

defend our Amazonia.'" This new alliance presented the first prospect of an end to a century of animosity and violence between the
two groups.

With the involvement of Allegretti and Cowell, Stephan
Schwartzman had been working out a plan for Mendes's trip to the
United States. He had spent the previous year laying the groundwork: spreading the word about the rubber tappers, writing articles
for American, British, and Brazilian magazines, and pushing reporters to cover the story. With a grant from the World Wildlife Fund,
Schwartzman and Allegretti did a study comparing the economic
potential of extractive reserves with that of other land uses, such as
ranching. They calculated that, in twenty years, an acre of land in
Acre would produce only $15.05 if converted to cattle pasture, but
would produce $72.79 if kept as standing forest for extraction of
rubber, Brazil nuts, and other forest products. (And, of course, the
cattle pasture would be useless after the first ten years, while the
forest would continue to be productive.) Mendes needed hard
numbers such as these to fortify his assault on the banks.

Meanwhile, more agronomists and forest ecologists from Brazil
and abroad were making the trip to Acre and other parts of the
Amazon to study the tappers and the economic potential of the
standing forest. One study showed that a rubber tapper family—
in areas where the tappers were free of rent and other obligations
to the rubber bosses—earned more than $1,250 in cash in an
average year from the sale of rubber and nuts, and that did not
include the value they gleaned from the forest by hunting, raising
manioc and other crops, gathering fruits and building materials,
and the like. The total income was estimated at $2,400, more than
double what a family in the slums of Rio Branco scraped together.
And the quality of life among free tappers was uniformly considered far superior to the life of those who moved into town. If research were undertaken to boost the rubber harvest and develop
markets for other tropical products, the extractive reserve could
prove to be a positive component in the Brazilian economy.

Plans for Mendes's trip were finally set. The annual meeting of
the Inter-American Development Bank was scheduled for March

23–25, 1987, in Miami. Representatives from the ministries of finance or treasury departments of the forty-four member nations would be there—borrowers and lenders alike. Mendes's target was the contingent of lenders; many, including the United States, were ready to pull out of the IDB, considering it the worst of the multilaterals. The borrowing member nations had too much power and could often give themselves money at will, with few controls on how it was spent. The Latin-American borrowers, led by Brazil, constantly battled with the Northern Hemisphere lenders, led by the United States. The U.S. Treasury Department under the Reagan administration considered the IDB little more than a Third World pork barrel operation and was looking for "a bludgeon with which to beat the bank," as Schwartzman put it. The environmental issue could be the perfect weapon.

Schwartzman flew out to Acre to brief Mendes before his journey. Mendes began to memorize facts about the BR-364 project, facts about the economic value of the standing forest and how it could outproduce cattle pasture. Allegretti and Schwartzman quizzed him and helped him polish his delivery. And they gave him his itinerary: Mendes would fly alone and be met in Miami by Schwartzman, a couple of other lobbyists, and Cowell, who planned to film the entire visit.

As Mendes went around Xapuri and Rio Branco before the trip, he tried to stay calm, but this time he could not hide his anxiety and excitement. He often stopped to visit one of his closest friends, Sister Zelia, a quiet nun who was a nurse at the Xapuri hospital. They would sit in the garden behind the house she shared with two other nuns, down the street from the public market. Mendes had girded himself mentally for the trip, but as he sat talking with Zelia one night, he panicked about something simple, his wardrobe. He had nothing to wear—and no money with which to buy something. Zelia had an idea. One of the other nuns had received a shipment of donated clothing from Italy. They went over to the church and fished around until they found a gray suit. It was a little small, but Mendes did not care.

Just a week before the meeting, Allegretti finally rounded up the money for Mendes's ticket from friends in the Brazilian Ministry of Culture. (If other branches of the Sarney government had known of it, heads would have rolled in Brasília.) Mendes took the interminable, multistop flight out of the Amazon, gliding over the dark green canopy, the brown swathes of pasture, orange ribbons of muddy roads, and the sediment-laden rivers of the rainy season. Then he boarded a jumbo jet and left his country for the first time.

Schwartzman and Cowell met him as planned and took him to the Intercontinental Hotel, one of those sprawling, soaring, postmodern complexes that have sprouted throughout the United States. Mendes was astounded by the indoor world of the hotel: there were enough attractions inside that conventioneers never need step outside and face the gritty reality of the street. A forest of flags greeted the arriving officials, who pulled up in a fleet of Cadillacs. Now the only problem the environmentalists faced was getting Mendes inside. He was not a government official, and the only people allowed at the meeting were government representatives, their guests, and the press. Cowell managed to spirit him in the back door by getting him a press pass.

Once inside, Schwartzman worked the hall feverishly, introducing Mendes to just about anyone who did not look busy. Cowell and his camera trailed behind. At a series of elegant cocktail receptions, ministers in their chalk-stripe suits found themselves confronted at every turn by a tieless, tousled man who quickly rattled off his spiel. "We are not against the road," Mendes would quickly say, with Schwartzman translating when necessary. "We are against the devastation caused by the bad planning that has taken place without the participation of the people living in the Amazon." Cowell, as he often did during his filming, took Mendes aside and asked him to tell the camera how the Amazon could benefit from his visit to Miami. "Cattle ranching . . . has economically brought nothing to the region," Mendes said, staring into the lens. "The only thing it's been good for is concentrating land in a few hands. My hope is that the governments of the people who give money to the Inter-American Development Bank will listen to the *seringueiros'* complaints. Otherwise, the forest will certainly be destroyed."

Some officials were taken aback by the sight of this motley crew, described later by Schwartzman as "several foaming environmentalists and a *seringueiro*." Particularly nonplused were the Japanese representative and a World Bank representative from Brazil, who were introduced to Mendes at a lavish reception for more than a thousand guests. Japan was already on the environmentalists' blacklist for buying up and destroying vast tracts of the Asian rain forest. The Brazilian official just barely maintained his decorum as this earnest rubber tapper reeled off his demands.

But Mendes made a favorable impression where it counted most — on the delegation from the United States. One of those attending was Jim Bond, Senator Kasten's specialist on multilateral banks. Bond later recalled, "Here we were at one of these classic meetings where everyone is saying, 'Let's have fresh raspberries, sip champagne, and talk about the poor.' And here was Chico Mendes." Bond felt uncomfortable because Mendes seemed so out of place, but he was also impressed with this man's straightforward approach. Bond discussed with Schwartzman the idea of flying Mendes to Washington. Richard Collins, who was representing Senator Daniel K. Inouye, also met Mendes and immediately saw a new and potent weapon. And it was the right moment for a new weapon. On February 20, Brazil had unilaterally announced that it was suspending interest payments on its commercial bank loans, and the United States and other creditors were outraged.

After the meeting, Mendes, Schwartzman, and Cowell flew up to Washington. March 27 was one of those sunny, early spring days when most Washingtonians brave the breeze without overcoats. Still wearing his ill-fitting suit, Mendes pulled his arms in tight to keep warm as he walked over to one of the Senate office buildings. He was led into an office and sat with Schwartzman on one side of a broad walnut table as Kasten rushed in from a meeting of his Subcommittee on Foreign Appropriations. With Schwartzman translating, Mendes explained his hopes for extractive reserves and his fears about the impact of the paving of BR-364 without environmental safeguards. He nervously fumbled with a stack of papers as Kasten thanked him for his help. "I can promise you that our subcommittee is going to continue to put pressure on the [Inter-American Development Bank] to withhold funds—to cut off all funds, possibly—if they are not more cooperative," he said. Before he returned to his meeting, Kasten shook Mendes's hand, sealing the unlikeliest of alliances—between a staunch conservative from a state of rolling, treeless pasture that based its economy on cows and a Marxist forest dweller whose worst enemies were cattlemen.

A few days later, Kasten and the subcommittee's chairman, Inouye, sent a threatening letter to the president of the bank, Antonia Ortiz Mena. It said: "The Senate Foreign Operations Subcommittee insists that the environmental components of the loan be implemented before further work on road construction is allowed. . . . We cannot allow a repeat of the devastation which occurred in Rondônia." According to Bond, that letter was a direct result of the meeting between Mendes and Kasten. By setting these powerful senators in motion, Mendes had accomplished as much in a few days in the United States as he had in years back in the Amazon.

Mendes flew back to Acre and took the dusty, four-hour bus ride to Xapuri. Just a week after nibbling on shrimp in paneled reception rooms at a luxury hotel, he found himself again living from handouts and under other people's roofs. And he still found himself under siege. A reporter for the *Gazeta Mercantil,* the Brazilian equivalent of the *Wall Street Journal,* had filed a small story from Miami about Mendes's visit. The article caused a minor explosion back in Acre. Its state legislators and representatives in Brasília lashed out at this presumptuous activist who threatened Brazil's future by opposing the bank loans. (The story was by the same journalist who produced the same homecoming greeting for Mary Allegretti after her Washington trip in 1986.)

João Tezza, a state legislator and a lawyer who often represented the ranchers in actions against the rubber tappers, gave a speech in which he charged that Mendes was much too naive and poorly educated to comprehend such things as international development loans; he was obviously being used by Americans who wanted to gain control of mineral rights in the Amazon. In Xapuri, the conservative mayor and town councilors also blasted Mendes; if the paving of the road were delayed, it would put a damper on the land boom and building spree that were enriching the local elite.

Once again, Mendes heard rumors that he would be killed. He became increasingly cautious, never returning by the same trail when he hiked into the forest. He knew his concern was not misplaced. All around the Amazon and other parts of rural Brazil, the violence against the poor and those trying to help them was reaching a peak. Between January 1985 and June 1987, 458 peasants, rural workers, union presidents, and activist priests and lawyers were killed. The government was fully aware of the spate of murders but did little to stanch the flow of blood. In 1987, the Brazilian ministry of agrarian reform issued a report confirming the organized nature of the killings. It estimated, for example, that 114 of the 298 murders of such victims in 1986 were committed by hired *pistoleiros*. The murders were contracted by land speculators, mineral companies, ranchers, and real estate firms. According to the report, "The means of violence and coercion traditionally maintained by large landowners is undergoing a rapid and fundamental transformation. We are witnessing in rural violence a gangster-like activity which has replaced traditional forms of coercion."

For Mendes, the only haven was the forest where he had come of age; only there could he relax. One of the first places he visited after returning from Washington was Seringal Cachoeira. He spent a long evening telling his aunt Cecília, his cousin Sebastião, and other relatives about the big cars and odd language of America— and about his meetings with some of the world's most powerful men. His friends later recalled that they never saw Mendes as happy as he was after that first trip abroad. It was not that the trip had gone to his head—at least not in a material sense. Indeed, he hardly seemed affected by the fancy hotels and marble monuments, and he still disliked "meat from the cow," preferring armadillo or monkey. His happiness seemed to spring from a perception that the prospects of the rubber tappers' movement were greatly improved. Despite the renewed attacks from the opposition, he was convinced that the people of the forest were now poised to win their battle.

The trip also proved that Mendes did in fact have the qualities that Adrian Cowell had believed lay within him. Though he had initially been a little shellshocked in Miami, he had quickly learned how to handle himself with the bankers just as easily as he had learned to handle himself on the rubber trails.

In the course of a year, Mendes, Cowell, Allegretti, and Schwartzman had become an effective quartet of lobbyists. Indeed, the trip was so successful that Cowell and the others immediately began thinking of where else Mendes should visit. But the rubber tapper still had no real credentials, and posing as a member of the press would not always get him an audience with influential people. The solution, Cowell decided, was an environmental award. Mendes could use it as a legitimate calling card to gain access to the circles of power. It also might bring him some much-needed income so that he could feed his family back home. Cowell wrote nomination letters for two awards: the Global 500 Award, given annually by UNEP to leaders in conservation and environmental action around the world, and the Better World Society Protection of the Environment Medal. The Better World Society was the creation of the media magnate Ted Turner; its mandate was to use television programming to broaden people's awareness of global problems that threatened life on Earth. With both Robert Lamb at the United Nations and José Lutzenberger of the Gaia Foundation on his side, Mendes came away with both awards.

In July of 1987, Mendes flew to England to receive the Global 500 Award. He was taken to the working-class city of Birmingham, where Cowell's network was filming a debate on the development-environment dilemma. The panel included Mostafa K. Tolba, the executive director of UNEP, and in a small ceremony, Tolba presented Mendes with the award.

Mendes was received warmly in England. His message, emphasized as always with a waving right fist, hit home, even though this mosaic of deforested hills and grimy industrial cities outwardly had little in common with the vast green wilderness of the Amazon. The link was labor. To the English, Mendes was the incarnation of a typical British trade union leader of the 1920s, when the unions were first fighting for power. As Cowell put it, "Chico was the person—there always was somebody—who cemented the brothers together. Chico was the cement. If you'd said he was a rubber tapper that didn't matter." The *Guardian,* the *Observer,* and other papers were quick to pick up on the story.

That same month, Senator Kasten began preparing new legislation to promote the preservation of tropical rain forests by debt-for-nature swaps. This new strategy was developed by Thomas Lovejoy, a leading tropical biologist now at the Smithsonian Institution. Lovejoy had long been decrying the destruction of rain forests and the mass extinction of species that accompanied the cutting and burning, but he recognized the inability of indebted nations to deal with the problem. He came up with a surprising solution. Environmental groups should raise funds to purchase some of the international debt of forested Third World nations from banks that were eager to dump the bad loans. Then the indebted nation would "pay back" the debt to the new, environmentalist creditors by issuing bonds in its own currency. The interest from the bonds would finance the purchase of endangered forest tracts or the creation of local environmental projects. Such exchanges would solve two difficult problems at once: they would ease the debt crisis in the Third World and preserve the forests. Lovejoy's approach was already being tested: earlier that year, conservationists had arranged small swaps with Ecuador, Bolivia, and Costa Rica.

Also in July, Kasten and Inouye's subcommittee held hearings on the multilateral banks and learned that Brazil had done little to satisfy the IDB's demands for environmental reforms on its Amazon road project. After the hearing, Kasten issued a stern threat: the United States would significantly reduce its contribution to the IDB if nothing was done to improve the situation in Rondônia and Acre. The bank responded by passing on the threat, warning Brazil that it would cancel its support for the road unless Brazil complied with the environmental provisions in its contract within sixty days.

As Brazil began to endure more criticism, so too did Mendes. When he returned to Acre, he was depicted by his political opponents as anti-Brazilian, antiprogress—even a tool of the CIA. Wanderley Viana, a Xapuri town councilman (and soon to be mayor), derided the laurel bestowed on the union leader. On the radio, he said, "That was not a medal. That was a rattle to put on a donkey's neck." The awards and international attention thus cut both ways: they gave Mendes greater influence but inflamed the animosity toward him. And as the dry season of 1987 came to an end and the burnings began, the physical threat against Mendes increased. Late one night in August, as he was sleeping at the union hall next to the church in Xapuri, a man tried to clamber up the side of the building and jimmy one of the wooden shutters. He slipped on a loose board and then ran when the noise awakened Mendes and some of the other tappers inside. One of the tappers got a glimpse of the intruder and thought he saw a gun.

Mendes again traveled abroad. In late September, he flew to New York City to receive the Better World Society award. At a dinner in the Grand Ballroom of the Waldorf-Astoria Hotel, Mendes rubbed shoulders with a strange assortment of power brokers, celebrities, politicians, and potentates, among them Ted Turner, Bella Abzug, and Prince Sadruddin Aga Khan. That Mendes had now achieved a certain celebrity was clear; other award recipients that night included the United Nations peacekeeping force and Phil Donahue. The next day, Mendes flew down to Washington, where Schwartzman had arranged for another meeting with officials of the IDB. Mendes was joined by Marco Antonio Mendes, a reporter for *Gazeta do Acre*. Reluctantly, the state government had begun to acknowledge Mendes's growing power.

This time, with two awards to his credit and a reporter at his side, Mendes walked in the front door of the bank. He and Marco Antonio met with the environmental management committee. Under pressure from Kasten and environmentalists, the bank was now seriously considering canceling its support for the road project. But that was exactly what Mendes and Schwartzman did *not* want. If the loan were cut off altogether, Brazil would undoubtedly seek other sources of funding, such as Japan, and the tappers and environmentalists would lose all their hard-won influence. So Mendes repeated his refrain: "We are not opposed to the road. We just want a road that benefits the *seringueiros* and other people who live in the forest."

Mendes was in Washington just as the World Bank was convening its annual meeting. This event was so important that it was always accompanied by a galaxy of meetings of the smaller multilateral banks as well as meetings of environmental and Indian rights groups eager to lobby for changes. Representatives of twenty-eight such groups from nine nations assembled for a strategy session and issued a report called "Financing Ecological Destruction: The World Bank and the International Monetary Fund." Just two weeks earlier, Adrian Cowell had held a screening of the latest installment in his *Decade of Destruction* series. Journalists and congressmen watched the segment, "Banking on Disaster," which featured Chico Mendes prominently. He was squinting in the orange dust clouds out on BR-364, explaining how the road imperiled the people of the forest, as heavy road-building equipment growled by in the background.

On this trip to Washington, Mendes finally hit the jackpot coveted by all who want to influence policy: he made it into the *New York Times,* Section A, photograph and all. The article described the latest death threats against this union organizer and the tappers' proposal for preserving the forest. The story gave Mendes's case a new legitimacy; it also did more to get him noticed back in Brazil than nearly anything he had accomplished to date.

When Mendes returned home, he was a changed man. He had begun the year as an obscure rural union leader and failed politician. Now, it was only October, and he was flying back from a foreign country for the third time. The National Council of Rubber Tappers and Mary Allegretti's institute had received grants from the

Ford Foundation, which was eager to foster sustainable development in Brazil. There was the prospect of a small stipend from the Gaia Foundation, which might allow Mendes to move his wife and children back to Xapuri so that he could see them more than once a month. He had been featured in some of the world's leading newspapers; he had met with bankers and lawyers and political leaders. And, on the long flight across the Atlantic, his newest award, encased in polished tropical wood and velvet, was carefully stashed in his bag. Mendes would later say he felt that the awards were like a shield that would protect him from the dangers in the forest.

But storm clouds were gathering over the Amazon. And they were not the usual cumulonimbus towers that rise and tumble each day in the moist tropical heat. They were clouds of smoke, millions of tons of combusted trees and insects and lizards and orchids, all oxidized by fire and converted into that basic chemical constituent, carbon, and into the gases of combustion—carbon dioxide, methane, carbon monoxide, and more. In what was becoming a mesmerizing, relentless rhythm, the burning season had returned. It was a rhythm not unlike that of Maurice Ravel's *Bolero,* which took a simple Moorish dance theme and built it to a diabolical crescendo that sent ladies screaming for the exits at its Paris premiere.

Throughout the 1970s and 1980s, the cycle of the Amazon's seasons had remained the same—the wet, the dry, the burnings, the wet, the dry, the burnings—but with each repetition the flames had grown more intense. Now a swathe of fire cut across the Amazon from southwest to northeast, an arc big enough to run from Canada to Florida; it was this cataclysmic landscape that greeted Mendes. After the eight-hour intercontinental flight, he boarded one of the Varig 737s that hopscotch their way around the Amazon on all-day, five-stop, four-meal flights. Through most of the dry season, the pilots of such flights could count dozens of smoke plumes rising from the carpet below. But in the burning season of 1987, the individual plumes had coalesced into a choking pall the size of India that wore out engine parts, scorched throats and lungs, and reduced visibility to 200 yards in places, closing airports for weeks at a time.

After landing in Rio Branco, Mendes quickly walked through the terminal, a favorite hangout of Acre's ranchers; they would often fly in from their barren tracts, park their private planes, have a beer, and do a little business. He never lingered there. The same men who derided him in the state legislature and threatened him on the street would sit and glare as he walked past.

Mendes took a cab to the bus station. Clutching the bag holding his award, he stepped onto the bus that would take him home to Xapuri.

Chapter 12

Into the Fire

SOME 990 MILES above the earth, a pair of weather satellites operated by the U.S. National Oceanic and Atmospheric Administration orbit from pole to pole, following paths like string being wound into a ball. Each one, NOAA-9 and NOAA-10, has sensors that gather data from a 1,700-mile-wide strip of the earth's surface as it sweeps around the planet. The sensors detect not only visible light but also infrared radiation — the heat you feel when you hold your hand over a glowing stove element. When the data are transmitted to a ground station and digested by a computer, they can be converted into a mosaiclike picture of the heat emanating from the earth. The data can be used to distinguish features, such as variations in plant cover, which reflect different patterns of light and heat. The data can also be used to check for fires. Any fire occupying an area larger than a football field shows up as a bright white spot.

On September 9, 1987 — two weeks before Chico Mendes went to New York City — NOAA-9 passed over the Amazon. The resulting image was a lazy crescent of dense white dots on a black background. Without the labels and the superimposed map, it could have passed for one of those grand pictures of the Milky Way. But the dots were fires, not stars: 2,500 dots in the tortured state of Rondônia, and 7,603 in all — 7,603 fires burning on that one day.

The person who had the patience to count them was Alberto Setzer, an environmental scientist for Brazil's National Institute for Space Research. Setzer worked at a sprawling complex in São José dos Campos, a city in the heart of Brazil's version of Silicon Valley, ninety minutes by bus from São Paulo. This area was very much the First World part of Brazil—the part that was the fifth-leading arms merchant in the world, the part that produced advanced jet fighters and personal computers and microelectronics. For two years, Setzer and several colleagues had been monitoring the spreading fires in the Amazon through the electronic eyes of American satellites. They had never seen a day quite like September 9—which turned out to set the record for a single day in the burning season of 1987.

To make sure there was no mistake, the scientists compared the September 9 image with others taken by different satellite sensors that detected smoke clouds instead of flames. When the two images were superimposed, long, wind-driven plumes of smoke could be seen spreading to the southeast from each bright spot. This was no computer glitch: hundreds of smoke plumes were coalescing into a single massive cloud.

Once the burning season ended, Setzer created a view graph in which he combined the data for forty-eight days in the heart of the season, from mid-August through October, to produce a cumulative picture of the burning. And a chilling picture it was. In the central corridor of Rondônia, along BR-364, it was no longer possible to pick out individual dots. The entire region was white, graphically showing where the settlers and ranchers were scorching the earth. Mato Grosso and eastern Bolivia looked more as though someone had spilled salt on a piece of black paper: the dots were everywhere, but not as concentrated. The line where BR-364 ran north and then west toward Acre glowed as if illuminated by streetlights—all fires set where squatters had followed the paving crews and cut into the forest to stake their claims along the road. Setzer estimated that 170,000 fires had burned in the Amazon that year. And that was an extremely conservative estimate; the raw data showed 350,000 hot spots.

Alarmed, Setzer examined data from different years and found that the area burned had almost doubled just since 1985. There was little consolation in the fact that only 40 percent or so of the burning was of newly felled rain forest (60 percent was the regular burning of brush or secondary forest that was invading existing pasture). This still meant that in 1987, some 48,000 square miles of virgin forest, an area the size of New York State, had gone up in smoke. All in all, the satellite images showed that the Amazon was now disappearing twice as fast as previous studies had estimated.

Setzer's work confirmed that an extraordinary acceleration of the cutting and burning had begun in 1975 and skyrocketed exponentially in the 1980s. Translated into a graph, the estimated deforestation rates in the Amazon through the twentieth century produced a slowly ascending curve that, in 1985, suddenly became a soaring, almost vertical line. All of the cutting in the decades before 1975 was estimated at a mere 14,880 square miles. By 1978, the cut area had grown to 47,740 square miles, and by 1980, some 77,500 square miles. By 1988, 370,760 square miles had been transformed from forest to fields—an area more than twice the size of California.

Before the space institute's study, no one had been able to provide solid proof that deforestation in the Amazon was out of control. A few researchers had long guessed that the rain forests were in trouble; the first scientific assessment of the issue appeared in 1971 when William Denevan, a geographer at the University of Wisconsin, presented a paper entitled "Development and the Imminent Demise of the Amazon Rain Forest." In 1975 Robert Goodland and Harold Irwin went into more detail in their book *Amazon Jungle: Green Hell to Red Desert?* The Brazilian edition of the book was chopped up by military censors and attacked by ranchers, but environmentalists in Brazil fought back, circulating a translation of the expurgated sections. Still, the charges of Goodland, Denevan, and like-minded researchers did not have much impact because no one could back them up with hard data.

The idea of using satellites to examine the situation in the Amazon and other ecologically fragile regions first arose in the early 1980s. People such as Tebaldi Tardin at the Brazilian space center,

Compton Tucker at NASA's Goddard Space Flight Center, and
George Woodwell, in Woods Hole, Massachusetts, had been re-
fining ways to use the reams of data collected by American Land-
sat and NOAA satellites to assess changes in vegetation. Their pictures revealed the fishbone pattern of deforestation that showed
where new roads had lured settlers into the forest.

But using the satellites to record fires was an innovation devised
by Setzer. The idea sprung serendipitously from an unrelated project. In 1985, Setzer and Tucker began planning a study of the
interaction between living forests and the atmosphere—the inter-
change of carbon dioxide, oxygen, and other gases—which was to
be a joint project of the Brazilian space agency and NASA. It was
part of a long-term global study of the lower atmosphere that
included scientists from around the world. Other teams, for instance, were studying the connections between the oceans and the
atmosphere.

Setzer and Tucker needed to find a relatively unpolluted region
in which to collect data. They assumed that the Amazon had clean
air and so, using the Brazilian space institute's Bandeirante twin-
engine aircraft, began collecting gas samples between Belém and
Manaus. When they examined the samples, however, they found
all sorts of contaminants. In some places, the air was as smoggy as
that of Setzer's home base, São José dos Campos, where a perpetual
sooty pall hangs over the highways. But the Amazon had no traffic
jams, and there was no heavy industry to speak of for hundreds of
miles. So the men started looking at the satellite images taken on
the days they had collected the samples, hoping to uncover some
sign of the source of the pollutants. They found it: the images
showed clouds of smoke emanating from big fires burning in southern Pará, hundreds of miles away, and drifting to the test area.

Setzer was startled by how much smoke was evident over the
Amazon basin. The satellite data seemed to confirm anecdotal accounts of the raging fires in Rondônia and the rest of the southern
rim of the rain forest. He decided to spend all of his time working
out a system for using satellites and computers to detect fires in the
Amazon. He received funding for a collaborative study with Brazil's

forestry agency and soon was regularly producing images such as the one taken on September 9, 1987. The results would not be published until February 1988, but in the meantime, Setzer showed the graphs and images to Fabio Feldmann, a São Paulo congressman who was the first Brazilian politician to build a career around the new environmental issue.

Feldmann presented Setzer's data to the Brazilian Congress, charging that the big landowners of the Amazon were burning the forest at a frenzied pace because they feared that Brazil's new Constitution, scheduled for ratification in 1988, would limit their ability to burn in the future. The landowners also feared that the financial incentives that had for so long encouraged deforestation were going to be suspended. The thinking was: burn now or lose your land.

Brazil's agricultural elite was outraged by the study. Setzer, who had received his doctorate at Purdue University, was attacked variously as a stooge of the Brazilian communists or the American capitalists. Many critics simply dismissed the data as fiction. As one leading Amazonian businessman said, "The numbers are not real, and I will prove this to President Sarney. I state and I will prove to the National Security Council that the pictures are fake." Another lumped Setzer with the environmentalist Green party, reviving the age-old argument employed by Brazil's generals and businessmen: that those interested in preserving the Amazon must be after something else—either political advantage or selling the Amazon to foreign interests. The team at Brazil's space center soon found their already meager budget under siege, forcing them to eliminate several important projects.

Undeterred by the attacks, Setzer and his colleagues continued to assess the data. They found that the Amazon fires were releasing a host of substances each year that could disrupt the chemistry of the atmosphere and cause human health problems: 44 million tons of carbon monoxide, 6 million tons of soot and other particles, 5 million tons of methane, and millions of tons of nitrogen oxides and ozone. (Ozone is only beneficial at very high altitudes, where it forms a shield against harmful radiation; down near the earth's surface it is a component of smog and harms plant growth.) In addition, satellite photographs showed that the winds that swept southeast over the Amazon during the burning season were transporting much of this noxious cloud across São Paulo and the South Atlantic and on over the fragile Antarctic. An atom of carbon that had been locked up in a tree trunk for perhaps a century, once liberated as pure carbon soot, took just ten days to travel from the tropics to the South Pole. The impact of this material on the atmospheric chemistry there—including such phenomena as the hole in the ozone layer that had been only recently discovered over the pole—had yet to be measured.

Finally, the scientists had the proof they needed to capture the world's attention. The burning of the Amazon was no longer a regional but a global problem. Even for those who doubted the value of preserving a great reservoir of genetic wealth, there was something startling about fires so vast that they emitted more pollutants than the industrial complexes of West Germany and Poland combined. Setzer had another way of putting it: "El Chichón, a huge volcano in Mexico, emitted only twice as much as this. So it was as if we had found a volcano in Brazil that was not known before. The only difference is that it doesn't erupt in one or two days. It takes a couple of months. But it erupts every year."

Setzer saw the ensuing reaction as the result of an instinctive fascination. As he said many times, "Fire has a strange effect on people's minds. It attracts their attention." And the world did take notice. The satellite photographs and the disturbing data galvanized environmentalists and the media. Drawn by the flames, the international press made one of its rare forays south of the equator and focused on the rain forest. In 1988, reporters began to fly out to the Amazon from the United States and Europe—even from the distant cities of Brazil itself, which had ignored the wilderness for so long—to catch film footage and photographs of the conflagration. And this in turn helped bring more attention to the fight waged by the rubber tappers.

Chico Mendes liked to tell stories to his visitors. He would take them for a walk along an *estrada* and point to the flanks of the rubber trees and the scars from cuts that he had made two decades earlier. He would name the birds that cooed and whistled high above in the mottled light of the canopy and point out the bulbous termite nests that could be boiled into a tea for a cough. Then he would chip a bit of the bark off a *copaíba* tree. When he ignited it, the bark sputtered and flared because of its kerosene-like sap. He once told Mary Allegretti a story he had heard as a child, about a *seringueiro* who hears the trees talking and talks back to them. When you are alone and quiet, Mendes said, that is when all the mysteries of the forest come to you. The trees will speak to you of forces that protect men who treat the forest well, and other forces that threaten those who are careless or greedy.

One of his favorite stories was about how Xapuri got its name. He said that *xapuri* was an Indian word that meant "before the storm." Indian legend had it that the Xapuri River was created in a single night when an earthquake split the ground and water flowed forth. Perhaps the story held a germ of truth, since Acre is in fact the most seismically active region in Brazil. And, as 1988 began, it quickly became evident that the town's name was eerily appropriate.

First came the floods. Just a few months after the most intense burning season in the history of the Amazon, Acre was hit with one of the rainiest wet seasons in memory. In late January, much of the eastern part of the state was submerged as the Acre and Purus rivers and their tributaries overflowed their banks and kept on rising. A third of the state's crops was destroyed. When relief supplies were airlifted to Rio Branco, 100 tons of food ended up being stashed in a warehouse by corrupt officials—to be handed out in return for votes in the next election.

In Xapuri, many of the natives attributed the flood to a battle that had been waged in 1987 over the statue of São Sebastião in the little park along the river where the *batelões* unloaded their cargo of rubber. The statue—painted in lifelike flesh tones, dripping in blood where arrows pierced the torso—stood with its back to the river. Surrounded by neatly trimmed grass and blue picket fences, the patron saint of Xapuri stood on a pedestal stained by clumps of melted wax where votive candles had been burned. When it had been installed decades earlier, the statue had faced the river. The hope was that it would ward off floods and bless the steady boat traffic that had been Xapuri's only lifeline to markets.

Early in 1987, an activist priest and the mayor, a right-wing friend of the ranchers', fought over who was going to sponsor the upcoming São Sebastião festival that took place every January 20. (It was one of those typical disputes in which the underlying clash of egos was far more important than the surface quarrel.) The new mayor believed that since the river no longer represented the future of Xapuri, the statue should face the road and bless the passing trucks. One day, he sent out a work crew to rotate the statue; immediately thereafter, the heavens opened and the river rose. Perhaps it was coincidence—but no one in Xapuri believed in coincidence.

From then on, tensions in the town mounted steadily. Whatever protection the martyred saint had offered seemed to evaporate. Across Acre, tempers were short and were stretched further because the loan for the paving of BR-364 had just been suspended by the IDB; Senator Kasten had finally convinced the Subcommittee on Foreign Appropriations to cut U.S. support for the bank by $200 million, thereby forcing the bank's hand.

The governor of Acre, Flaviano Melo, was eager to satisfy the conditions imposed by the IDB for the resumption of the loan. Having recently visited Japan, he felt more strongly than ever that the future of Acre lay to the west. As usual in the rainy season, BR-364 was already a swamp of mud. In February, Melo's team of forestry engineers and land rights specialists began meeting with federal officials, with Chico Mendes and other tappers, and with consultants who had been hired by the tappers—thanks to small grants from the Ford Foundation—to help firm up plans for the first extractive reserves. Officials from the bank had decided that such reserves would help protect Acre's forests.

After a week of rancorous debate, the governor announced that the first such reserve would be at Seringal São Luis de Remanso, a two-hour hike from the road linking Rio Branco and Xapuri. But

São Luis de Remanso was already on government land, so it was not an area of contention between the ranchers and rubber tappers. Mendes and the other unionized tappers were frustrated because the officials had conveniently ignored other *seringais* where there was imminent danger of deforestation and violence in the coming dry season.

One of them was Seringal Cachoeira, where Mendes had grown up. By this time, Cachoeira was one of the last large tracts of virgin rain forest left in the county of Xapuri. It was surrounded by ranches or partly deforested *seringais* on three sides; the fourth side was the Xipamanu River, the border with Bolivia. The tappers of Cachoeira knew they were in for trouble: they had heard that Darly Alves da Silva, the violent owner of the Paraná ranch, had made a deal with the four São Paulo businessmen who owned the *seringal*. The owners were apparently frustrated that the tappers were impeding their efforts to develop the land. Late in 1987, Júlio Maia, one of the owners, had sent in workers to cut some timber, but tappers had gathered at the ravine where the road ended and forced the crew to turn back. The *fofoca*, gossip, around Xapuri was that the *paulistas* had agreed to sell Darly 14,000 acres of the 60,000-acre tract at a bargain rate. In return, Darly would do what he did best: "clean" the area, using guile or firepower.

There was little doubt that Darly could handle the task. The Paraná ranch had developed a reputation as a den of perversity and *pistoleiros*. More than ten families lived there in a cluster of pink ranch houses and outbuildings. There were far more wives than husbands, and Darly's teenage children were having children of their own. The Federal Police in Rio Branco considered the ranch a probable way station for cocaine shipments from Bolivia to the south and thence on to American and European markets. One officer estimated that a third of the cocaine being smuggled into Brazil from the Andean nations to the west was being funneled down BR-364, which the police had already nicknamed the "Trans-coca highway," a reference to the failed Transamazon highway. When the bodies of two young Bolivians were found near the entrance to the Paraná ranch later in the year—and when witnesses later testified that the men had been carrying bags of white powder —few in Xapuri were surprised.

Darly had passed on his penchant for violence to his many sons. Oloci and Darci were especially known for their hot tempers. Oloci was twenty-one, with smooth olive skin and tight curly hair, and often carried a revolver in his belt. He was one of the five children of Natalina, who was Darly's only legal wife. Oloci was the most trusted of the children and managed the ranch when his father was away. Darci was also twenty-one, but he had never finished primary school and generally did manual labor around the ranch, building fences, cutting trees, working with the cattle. He had loosely curled dark hair, a strong brow that shaded his piercing eyes, and a small, tightly muscled frame. He hated it when people joked about his *boiadeiro* legs—which looked as if he had spent a lifetime in the saddle. The cowboy image was reinforced by his taste for pointed boots and tight black jeans. The one thing that did not fit was his small, shy voice, which was a lot like his father's. And his quiet air only reinforced the sense that, like his father, he was someone to handle carefully.

Many of the ten ranch employees were from the same mold. The two most feared were Amadeus and Sérgio Pereira, who had moved to the ranch from Minas Gerais with their mother, who was related to Darly. The brothers, called the Mineirinhos after their home state, were rumored to have killed more than half a dozen people, some over trifles, in their four years at the Paraná ranch. (Late in the year, a third Mineirinho, Jardeir, joined them.) A teenager at the ranch, Genézio Barbosa da Silva, later testified about a string of killings purportedly committed by Darci, Oloci, Sérgio, and Amadeus. Genézio, whose sister was Oloci's lover, said that the four young men often boasted openly of their kills. He alleged that they had killed one ranch worker, Celso, because he had tried to steal some horses from a neighbor. Darly had ordered the killing, the boy testified, simply because "this was not the kind of man they wanted at the ranch." When a friend of Celso's, Edilson, swore revenge, "Darly offered a cow each to Sérgio and Amadeus and asked them together with Darci and Oloci to kill Edilson." One prosecutor later observed: "The Alves da Silvas are not a common family. For them, violence is their emblem. They kill for nothing. They are responsible for a rosary of crimes"—so many that they were like beads on a string.

Darly's purchase of the portion of Cachoeira was completed in early 1988. But when Alvarino heard about the deal, he said, "Brother, you have bought yourself a problem." There were a dozen rubber tapper families on this property, and the tappers of Cachoeira, many of whom had already been displaced from other *seringais*, were not going to be moved easily.

To solve his problem, Darly first tried persuasion. He offered to give each family 500 acres and build them a chapel on land that he would not touch; he knew they were devout Catholics, he said. The valuable hardwood on the remaining 8,000 acres would fetch enough money to pay for the land. Then he would hire a couple of rubber tappers to harvest latex and Brazil nuts from the trees that were left standing. The tappers refused to make a deal. Said one, "We were not stupid. We knew that Darly only wanted to live along the Xipamanu River and had no plans for a church—only plans to kill us."

Then Darly tried intimidation. Early in the morning of March 18, 1988, he and a small group of workers and *pistoleiros* headed out along the rough road to the *seringal*. The road was awash at this time of year, and progress was slow. When the men finally reached the *seringal,* they faced forty rubber tappers, who refused to let them through. One of them, Manduca Custódio da Silva, had heard about Darly's plans in Xapuri the day before. Chico Mendes happened to be away, so Custódio had rushed back to Cachoeira and hastily organized an *empate.* Wearing his thick glasses and carrying two pistols in his belt, Darly cut an odd figure—something akin to Groucho Marx playing Long John Silver. As he stood there in the mud face to face with the tappers, Darly burned with anger. But he got no farther that day.

Next he tried guile. Rather than confronting the union head-on, he would come in through the back door. One tapper, José Britto, was eager to sell his *colocação*, which was toward the back of the *seringal.* He had been having a running fight with a neighbor, Agripino; the police had been called more than once to settle the dispute. Britto wanted out. He was not tapping anymore and needed money. Besides, he concluded, what better way to avenge himself on his neighbor than to let Darly in. With his added tract, Darly could build a new access road into Cachoeira that avoided the main entrance, which the tappers controlled. Although Britto had previously agreed to sell his holding to the union, without telling anyone he sold it to Darly for the equivalent of about $100 (not an unusual price).

The tappers of Cachoeira organized a meeting; when they found out what Britto had done, they were shocked: he had been a good man. Mendes had always stressed how important it was that no tapper sell his holding to anyone except another tapper. Britto had broken an essential trust. Some of the tappers wanted to kill him. But Mendes, who had returned to find Cachoeira in turmoil, settled them down.

Darly hired two lawyers to help him strengthen his hold on Cachoeira. One was João Tezza, the rancher and state legislator who had so sharply attacked Mendes after his trips abroad. A judge confirmed Darly's title and issued a court order allowing Darly to pass through to his property. So empowered, Darly sent two of his workers out to Cachoeira, this time accompanied by the police and a court-appointed official. The workers had hammocks, chickens, pigs, and everything else they would need to set up camp. But the tappers had had plenty of warning. Mendes had gathered more than seventy men, and they quickly convinced the would-be settlers to leave.

But Mendes knew they would return. He was convinced that Darly was trying to provoke a confrontation with the help of other ranchers and the ranchers' league, the UDR. Its president, Ronaldo Caiado, had just flown up to Rio Branco for the first time earlier in March, delivering a planeload of flood-relief supplies. The tappers claimed that the UDR planes were ferrying weapons into the state just as the organization was about to open a headquarters for its Acre chapter.

To Mendes, this attempt to take Cachoeira—the source of his strongest support—was a direct assault on his personal heritage and the core of the movement. Mendes spent days hiking from house to house in the *seringais* around Xapuri, mobilizing several hundred people to converge on Cachoeira. The plan was to camp there indefinitely—or as long as it took to get Darly to give up. At a meeting in the central clearing, the tappers voted that they would refuse to let anyone pass, no matter what any judge or police officer said. Some were tired of nonviolent tactics and demanded that an armed militia be formed; a number of the tappers had brought firearms with them. Mendes disagreed, saying that they would risk losing political support and would surely give the Military Police an excuse to crack down. Another vote was held, and more than three quarters of the tappers sided with Mendes.

Everyone settled in for a long stay, slinging hammocks in nearby homes and in the schoolhouse. Mendes's aunt Cecília, whose house was at the entrance to the *seringal,* cooked around the clock, keeping big aluminum pots brimming with rice and beans. Mendes used a pickup truck, which had been given to the union by the Canadian Embassy, to bring in supplies—milk, butter, crackers, rice, beans, meat, eggs, tobacco, and lighters. As Cecília recalled, "He didn't need guns. Food was his ammunition." Despite the downpours that continued through March and into April, the tappers remained at Cachoeira. When Darly's workers tried coming in from the far side of the *seringal,* they were rebuffed once again.

At the same time, Mendes started to make things difficult for Darly. He began feeding stories to his contacts at the Acre newspapers, including allegations about the murders at the Paraná ranch. The stories said that the local police did not try to solve the crimes because Darly had a brother working in the Xapuri police station and was a good friend of the sheriff's. Exasperated, Darly went to the Military Police, but a major told him that it was useless to try to expel the tappers from Cachoeira—with or without a court order. They were too firmly entrenched. There would be deaths on both sides, and Darly could be held responsible.

Fed up with all the trouble, Darly met with officials from the federal agrarian reform office, INCRA, who tried to work out an agreement acceptable to both sides. At a meeting in the courthouse, Darly tried to make a deal with Mendes directly and even extended his hand. But Mendes refused, saying he would never shake a dishonest hand. Eventually, INCRA and Darly agreed that the government would disappropriate the land and compensate him. Mendes charged that INCRA should not compensate Darly because he had never had a legitimate right to the land. But the governor and land reform officials were anxious to ease the tense situation, so the plans for the disappropriation went ahead. In April the papers were signed, and Darly never returned to Cachoeira.

In public, Darly called the fight even. "It was a good deal for everybody," he said. And one day, when he met up with Mendes in Xapuri, Darly told him, "Chico, what you wanted was done, and what I wanted also I managed to get. I sold the *seringal* for a good value. And you will have your extractive reserve." In private, however, Darly was still furious.

As more land was disappropriated by the government, Acre's ranchers began to worry that the extractive reserves might pose a risk to their investment. Tappers and squatters throughout the eastern part of the state were now refusing to budge from the forested parts of ranches, demanding compensation, at the very least, or disappropriation of the land. More and more, Mendes found himself invited to sit down at a table with a few ranchers. They would have a quiet *cafezinho*, the thick black espresso of Brazil, then get down to business. The persistent characteristic of Mendes that set him apart from his peers was this willingness to talk with everyone—even the devil himself.

But these ranchers did not want to negotiate; they wanted to buy Mendes off. He was offered money, cattle—he could even pick the finest animals himself—if he would tone down his union's actions. He would not be the first union president to become a *pelego*. (A *pelego* is a blanket or sheepskin placed on a saddle. In Brazil, it refers to union leaders who are bought off by the local power brokers and no longer represent the interests of the workers; they exist only to cushion someone else's rear end.) But Mendes refused. The ranchers said, "We have all the money and all the guns. Your movement is like mosquitoes against a jaguar." Mendes responded, "But you don't have the people."

Finally, after the longest, wettest rainy season in decades, the western Amazon began to dry out. Tendrils of thick mist rose from the dank green canopy. Wasps swarmed in the brightening sun. Butterflies lapped at the last moist stains where puddles had evaporated along the rubber trails. And around Xapuri, there was a remarkable silence. The chain saws had nearly all been stopped. The relentless pressure from Mendes and his union had forced the ranchers to go elsewhere. Cachoeira had served as an effective warning that the ranchers would have a hard time finding pasture in Xapuri. (At the end of the year, it was estimated that only 125 acres of forest had been cut in Xapuri in 1988.) Mendes had won the battle, but he knew very well that the war was just beginning.

The situation at Cachoeira seemed stable now that the government was going to pay Darly for his land. But in Xapuri, quiet did not mean safe. Here, you worried when your enemies *left* town. They were usually off to find a convenient alibi while their hired guns did the dirty work. Even though the heat of the dry season was settling onto the forest, Mendes and the other tapper leaders began to sleep with the wooden shutters of their houses closed and latched.

One night, weeks after the tappers at Cachoeira had disbanded and returned to their homes, Mendes sat with his aunt Cecília on her veranda, looked out over the small clearing that he had known for four decades, and talked of the future. In many ways, Cecília had become the mother Mendes had lost back in 1962. "Now everyone is calm," he told her. "Everyone is in his own *colocação*, thank God. But there is one thing I know. The Cachoeira *empate* is going to cost blood."

The dry season of 1988 brought a mixture of good and bad tidings. The good tidings included the prospect of more financial support for the tappers from the Canadian Embassy and the Ford Foundation. The Gaia Foundation grant that José Lutzenberger had arranged for Mendes had come through, allowing him to move his wife and children into Xapuri. They rented the small cottage on Dr. Batista de Moraes Street, and when it looked as if the owner wanted the house back, Mary Allegretti and Adrian Cowell chipped in a total of about $1,000 and bought it outright for Mendes. His marriage improved somewhat, although Ilzamar still felt neglected.

More good news came in late April, with the arrival of a delegation from the IDB, which was finally getting serious about enforcing the environmental and Indian rights provisions of its loan to Brazil. The team sent up to Acre planned to do something unprecedented: they would include rubber tappers and Indians in their negotiations over the new design for the BR-364 paving project. Mendes went to Rio Branco, along with Indian representatives and advisers such as Allegretti. Also present were officials from the military, which still played a leading role when it came to developing the Amazon; almost a third of the region was considered under military control. The old officers were barely able to tolerate the presence of the tappers and their liberal allies. When Allegretti introduced herself, one colonel snorted, stood up, and left the room. Ever since military intelligence had put together a dossier on her, she had been considered a traitorous rebel by many in the establishment.

At this meeting, Mendes proved that the alliance he had begun to forge between the Indians and the tappers was not mere show. The government was eager to separate the discussion about Indian reserves from that over extractive reserves. Officials figured that if they satisfied the tappers' demands, no one would worry about the Indians; after all, the tappers were getting all the press. But Mendes knew that the government wanted to shift the Indians to planned colonies—the small farm plots that would effectively erase their culture and cultivation methods—and he would have none of it.

Mendes demanded a private session with the two chief bank officials to discuss the Indian issue. He met with them by the pool at the Pineiro Palace, the only hotel with a pool in Rio Branco. There, Mendes displayed the straightforward style that had taken him so far so fast. He looked Gerard Johnson, the environmental officer, in the eye and asked, "Will the bank play ball with Brazil even if Brazil cheats the Indians?" Johnson knew that what Mendes suspected was true—the bank was planning to reactivate the loan even if the Indians were not given their reserves—and told Mendes as much. At that, Mendes stood up and left the hotel. The bank officials knew that without the tappers' support, the negotiations for resuming the loan would fall apart. In the end, the bank and Brazil were forced to give the Indians the right to reject unacceptable projects.

While the fight for the forest progressed on the international front, it became clear that the struggle at the local level was not so simple. As the Xapuri tappers' union prepared to celebrate May Day, they could sense that the dry months would be dangerous. In April, the UDR had officially opened its Acre chapter, with a lawyer and rancher named João Branco as the provisional president and one hundred and twenty active members. April was also the month that things heated up. One night, during a large meeting at a *seringal* near Xapuri, a tapper noticed an unfamiliar face in the crowd. He turned out to be one Ronilson Martins Nogueira, a *pistoleiro* for Darly Alves. When confronted, he said he had just run away from the Paraná ranch because he did not want to obey Darly's order for him to meet two other gunmen, go to Cachoeira, and shoot Chico Mendes. He had learned that many employees of Darly's had been murdered, and he wanted none of it.

In the early morning darkness of April 29, one of the tappers staying at Mendes's house—there were always a few men there now as bodyguards—got up to relieve himself and heard some noise in the back yard. Mendes had risen as well, and he started to open the shutters on the back window. One of his friends pulled him away from the window and began to yell: "We have guns! You'd better get lost!" Crashing in the underbrush followed. On May Day itself, leaflets were found at the union hall and elsewhere in town, threatening Mendes, Gomercindo Rodrigues, Raimundo de Barros, and the other union leaders and their friends.

Just as the threats were increasing, Mendes gained a new and influential ally. Lucélia Santos, one of Brazil's most popular soap opera stars, had flown to Acre for the May Day celebration and the First Meeting of Women of the Seringais—the first organized effort to imbue the women of the Amazon with a sense of their rights. Santos was almost as well known for her sizzling left-wing political activities as she was for her steamy screen roles. She had recently become a leading voice of Brazil's young Green party, which promoted a respect for ecology and human rights. Her T-shirts never lacked a slogan, and her garish horn-rimmed glasses studded with rhinestones could not hide the beauty of her face. When she heard about the threats against Mendes and the ambush attempt, she demanded—and got—an audience with Governor Melo. And she convinced him, aided by the bevy of journalists accompanying her, to provide two police guards for Mendes.

But the guards were only temporary, and soon the threats were replaced by action. Groups of *pistoleiros* from the Paraná ranch began to parade openly through Xapuri, resting their palms on the butts of the revolvers stuck in their belts. They taunted the tappers and playfully pulled out their weapons, aping gunfighters from the Old West. And in what the tappers claimed was a case of harassment, the owner of Seringal Equador applied in May for a permit to cut down 125 acres of forest near the entrance to Cachoeira, an area rich in Brazil nut trees. Mendes charged that the ranchers really planned to deforest almost six times as much acreage. Despite the prohibition on cutting Brazil nut and rubber trees, the permit was issued.

Mendes quickly arranged an *empate* to block the chain saws one more time, marshaling several hundred men, women, and children. But the owner had called in the Military Police, and one hundred soldiers were deployed to protect the crews as they revved up their machines and attacked the trees. Mendes confronted the sergeant in charge of the police units. "All we want is peace," he said. "We are only here to stop the deforestation. We want to make this *empate* without a fight." But orders were orders. This time, the tappers could only stand and watch as the green tops of the trees shivered and then slowly toppled, ripping through the canopy and sending up clouds of insects and dust as the trunks crashed to the ground.

Mendes led some eighty tappers to the Xapuri office of the forestry service—a small house with a shingle roof and a wrap-around veranda near the central plaza. Their plan was to occupy the office peacefully until the permit was revoked. Mendes also telephoned his friends at the Green party office in Rio de Janeiro, and they staged a simultaneous sit-in at Rio's forestry service office, 2,000 miles away.

On the second night of the sit-in in Xapuri, several dozen tappers were camped out at the office. Most of them were inside, but nine people were curled up under a black plastic tarpaulin on the veranda. Everyone was on edge. Several times that evening, Darci Alves and a cousin had buzzed by on Oloci's Honda 250 motorcycle, trying to provoke a fight. On one pass, they knocked down a woman who had come in from a *seringal* to participate in the protest. Although the tappers called the police, no one appeared. At 2:00 A.M., a motorcycle buzzed by once more. This time, it stopped briefly. A passenger jumped off and ran around the side of the office. Then he and the driver both opened fire. One shot a 7.65-mm pistol, emptying the clip at the forms huddled under the tarp (pistols of this caliber are banned in Brazil for all but military use). Seven of the bullets hit a fifteen-year-old boy from Cachoeira. The other gunman wounded a seventeen-year-old tapper with two slugs from a .38. The assailants roared away into the night.

Remarkably, both boys survived. But the attack seriously damaged the rubber tappers' movement as fear and rage drove a wedge through the community, with violence demanding more violence. The next day, one hundred and fifty tappers met in the church, and many called for vengeance. Everyone knew who had been on that motorcycle. Mendes refused to give in to violence and instead threatened to begin a hunger strike. Faced with mounting pressure and publicity, both in Acre and Rio, the government finally can-

celed the permit to cut on Seringal Equador. Some 700 acres of
forest were saved from the saws. Mendes's allies far to the south
now put intense pressure on Governor Melo and the federal officials to investigate the incident.

In early June, Mendes briefly escaped the tension that had enveloped Acre. Lucélia Santos helped him arrange a trip to Rio de
Janeiro for a series of speaking engagements, dinners, radio talk
shows, and other interviews with the media. Largely ignored when
he won the awards overseas in 1987, now Mendes was featured in
some of Brazil's leading newspapers. Other tappers, too, began to
gain recognition. On June 6, Raimundo de Barros became the
second rubber tapper from Acre to venture overseas when he was
invited to West Germany to address a meeting of environmental
organizations. In his suitcase were the bloodstained clothes of the
two teenage victims of the shooting at the forestry office—a graph-
ic visual aid.

But the attention was coming too late. Matters in Xapuri were
following a course independent of the perceptions of the outside
world. Even as reporters converged on the town to tell the story of
the tappers' fight to save the Amazon and consultants for the Ford
Foundation wrote checks to support the movement, Darly Alves's
pistoleiros began a reign of terror. The Alveses may have been
spurred on by other ranchers, or even paid by the UDR, but it is
likely that their thirst for the blood of Mendes and his allies would
have driven them to act with or without encouragement. Sometimes fifteen or twenty gunmen at a time wandered the streets of
Xapuri, looking for trouble, pulling out revolvers and pointing
them at Mendes, his wife, his brother, or other tappers. Tappers
sleeping in the union hall heard someone prying at the shutters on
two different nights and the next morning found footprints outside
the windows. On June 11, Darci had an unlicensed revolver confiscated by the Military Police after he pulled it and began shooting
during an argument in Boate Eldorado, a bar on the waterfront.
But there were plenty of other weapons back at the ranch.

Upon his return from Germany, de Barros met in Rio Branco
with Genesio de Natividade, a young lawyer who had been hired

by Mary Allegretti to help the union, and they drafted a letter to Governor Melo, the state secretary for public safety, and the newspapers. The letter was signed by representatives of six human rights and union groups (Mendes was still traveling in the south and so could not sign the letter). It described the recent escalation of violence and the brazen display of weaponry by Darly's gunmen and lamented the lack of a serious investigation of the forestry office shooting. In conclusion, it placed the full responsibility for any further violence directly in the lap of the governor.

The letter was printed in the June 18 edition of the *Gazeta do Acre,* but seven hours before the first stack of newspapers arrived in Xapuri on the midday bus from Rio Branco, fresh blood had already been spilled.

This time the victim was Ivair Higino de Almeida, a twenty-six-year-old church monitor, union director, and PT candidate for the town council. He lived on one of the small planned farms along the road to Brasiléia, not far from the Paraná ranch. Ranchers in town later recalled that Oloci and the Mineirinhos had said that they were tired of Higino's harassing them and that Higino was *puxa-saco,* holding the "sack," of Chico Mendes—too close to the union president. Higino was also loathed by a competing candidate from the conservative PMDB. At five-thirty on that Saturday morning, Higino left his house to get some milk from a neighbor's cow for his month-old son. As he passed his father's farm, a blast from a .12-gauge shotgun shattered one of his arms and knocked him to the ground. A second blast hit him in the torso. He crawled along the road, desperately trying to escape, leaving a trail of blood in the orange dust. Now a revolver rang out, and his body was hit five times. Finally, someone walked up, stood over him, and delivered what Brazilians call the *tiro de misericórdia,* the shot of mercy.

Mendes had returned home from his trip. Ironically, his last stop had been a visit to the Ministry of Justice in Brasília, where he warned federal officials about the volatile situation in Acre. In Xapuri, Mendes joined more than a hundred people who gathered on Saturday afternoon to view Higino's body, which was set on a table in the church annex, still wearing the shredded, blood-sodden clothing in which he had died. The crowd was angry, and cries for revenge again reverberated under the tin roof of the church. Again Mendes pleaded for restraint, and again the rubber tappers refrained from striking back.

The Alveses became even more brazen. That night, Darci and three gunmen from the ranch, after hanging around outside the union hall and the church, paraded into the church to view the corpse that most of Xapuri was convinced had been their handiwork. Darci walked up to the body, which was by now surrounded by candles and covered with a white sheet. He said, "Hey, someone pull back the sheet so I can see who this is." When no one complied, he began to reach for the revolver stuck in his belt but stopped. He and his friends strutted back outside, laughing all the way.

The tappers' restraint paid off. The murder of Higino finally got the attention of the federal government. The following Monday, Jáder Barbalho, the Brazilian minister of agrarian reform, was dispatched to Rio Branco in a Lear jet; he was met at the airport by Governor Melo and a crowd of protesters. At a meeting with Chico Mendes and Higino's widow and parents, Barbalho signed a decree declaring that Seringal Cachoeira, São Luis de Remanso, and two other *seringais* in Acre would become Brazil's first extractive reserves. Acknowledging that the decision was motivated by concern about the violence, Melo said, "With the disappropriation of Cachoeira and the advent of extractive reserves, the tension in Xapuri has to diminish."

The tragedy of Higino's death was also mitigated somewhat when, on June 30, the tappers of Xapuri inaugurated a new rubber tappers' cooperative. This cooperative rose from the ashes of the cooperatives that had been nurtured by Mary Allegretti and Oxfam seven years earlier but that had failed because of inflation and lack of training. This time, the cooperative started out with a capital reserve, detailed plans, educated tappers, and expert advice.

At last the tappers' calls for change were being heard, but given the price in blood, the celebratory mood was muted, at best. And the victory was still incomplete: much had to be done before the tappers could be sure that their lands were protected from further destruction. Moreover, Darci, Oloci, the Mineirinhos, and the rest of Darly's *pistoleiros* were still prowling the lanes of Xapuri.

Mendes never walked alone now. His small house had a nest of hammocks slung from every rafter. Along with his wife and children, Mendes's brothers, Zuza and Assis, were standing guard with three other tappers. The threats continued—and were very real. One reporter who visited Mendes during this time was Malu Maranhão, a seasoned correspondent for *Folha de Londrina,* a paper from Paraná, the home state of Darly Alves and Mary Allegretti. Maranhão knew about tension, having previously filed stories from Nicaragua, where she had watched as a Sandinista soldier next to her was cut in two by a bazooka round. She later said that the feeling in eastern Acre was the same as it had been in Nicaragua—you never knew where the next shot would come from. Maranhão later recalled one night in particular, when she had stayed in the house of Osmarino Rodrigues in Brasiléia, just before the union elections were held there. At around three o'clock in the morning, three bullets had split the thin siding of his shanty. Maranhão was also a guest at Mendes's when, late one night, she and the others were roused by a voice hissing at the front door: "Chico, Chico, we need your help." Ilzamar peered through a crack and saw someone standing with a hand behind his back. As five pairs of heavy feet hit the floorboards, the figure melted into the darkness and vanished.

At a rally in Rio Branco on July 1 to commemorate the slaying of Ivair Higino de Almeida, the PT candidates spoke mostly about themselves and focused on the upcoming election. Mendes spoke last. He was irritated that the other speakers were using the demonstration to promote their own interests. In contrast, he waved his fist and said that the tappers must fill the vacuum created by the lack of police protection and justice. "Our struggle has always been peaceful," he said, but now he was ready to discard his strategy of nonviolence, and he called for the creation of a people's militia. It was time for the tappers to defend themselves.

As the burning season of 1988 began, and the fields and felled forests around Acre blossomed in flames and threw brown clouds into the sky, Mendes resumed his hikes from *seringal* to *seringal,* bringing more tappers into the union and speaking out about the violence. Gomercindo Rodrigues, the young agronomist who had worked closely with Mendes since 1986, became his shadow. Both men carried revolvers. They marched quietly along the *estradas,* leading pack animals laden with food and supplies, listening for any change in the rhythm of bird calls and insect trills, a change that might signal the presence of an ambush. At each *seringal,* Mendes gathered as many people as he could and made a speech. "We're in immediate danger," he said. "We're seeing people killed. The gunmen of the Paraná ranch are terrorizing the whole popu-lation of Xapuri to strike at me. There are a dozen names on their *lista negra.*" This was the black list of people who had a price on their heads; it was said to include Mendes, Raimundo de Barros, Gomercindo Rodrigues, and Osmarino Rodrigues.

Mendes said that the tappers had to be united so that the death of one person would not kill the momentum of their fight. "After death we're useless," he said. "Living people achieve things— corpses, nothing."

Chapter 13
The Dying Season

I N 1988, AS IN 1987, the best vantage point from which to grasp
the immensity of the environmental crisis in the Amazon was
outer space. But this time the eyes looking down on the flaming
forests were human. On September 29, the space shuttle *Discovery*
was launched from Cape Canaveral, marking the long-awaited resumption of shuttle flights, which had been halted by the explosion
of *Challenger* two and a half years earlier. Circling the earth every
ninety minutes at an altitude of 200 miles, *Discovery* flew with its
belly toward outer space and its windows toward the ground, giving
the astronauts an unobstructed view of their planet.

On this flight, like most, the shuttle circled the earth parallel to
the equator above the tropics. One of the crew, George "Pinky"
Nelson, later recalled that although there were few clouds over the
center of South America that first day, he could not see the Amazon
basin. He knew where it should have been because the Andes range
was clearly visible, a lumpy chain of mountains straggling along the
continent's west coast, with the blue Pacific spreading beyond. But
to the east of the mountains, everything was obscured by a dense
pall of smoke. Here and there, the thick carpet roiled and bubbled
where the core of one of the vast conflagrations hidden by the
smoke threw so much heat and water vapor into the atmosphere
that it generated a huge thunderstorm.

Round and round the shuttle flew, and as South America slid into the planet's shadow, the scene below changed, as if someone had turned down the house lights in a theater. Now, with each sweep over the Americas, Nelson *could* see the Amazon. And it was burning, glowing with fire. Long arcs and ringlets of glimmering light were visible where the advancing brushfires and forest fires were burning brightest. Small twinkling spots, like stars, showed the locations of smaller fires. As the shuttle swept through day and night for five days, the Dantean scene in the Amazon basin did not change.

Nelson retired after this, his third shuttle flight, and gave lectures across the country before settling into a teaching job at the University of Washington. In his speeches, he often showed the pictures he took of the Amazon smoke on that flight, and he talked about the planet's atmosphere, "this thin blue ribbon around the earth." Having risen through it and flown above it, he was now especially attuned to the fragility of the thin veneer of nitrogen, oxygen, carbon dioxide, and other gases that for so long had shielded, warmed, and nurtured life on Earth. From the surface, this gaseous envelope was easy to take for granted, but from space it had all the substance and strength of tissue paper.

Like those before it, the burning season of 1988 assaulted the atmosphere with a monstrous amount of pollution. The day with the most fires, September 21, broke the record set the previous year as 8,438 pixels in the satellite image flared white. Overall, though, the deforestation estimated for 1988 turned out to be 40 percent less than the peak year of 1987, thanks mostly to those same rains that had flooded Acre. Even so, the issue had developed unstoppable momentum in the press and the public consciousness; more than ever before, eyes were attracted to the advancing flames.

One reason the Amazon attracted so much interest was that in 1988 it seemed that the whole planet was ablaze. It had all begun with heat—the great, unrelenting blanket of heat that settled over the continental United States, parts of Europe, and central China. As Yellowstone National Park and vast tracts of France's forests burned like tinder, a drought withered crops across the Northern

Hemisphere. In the American Midwest, farmers began making comparisons to the Dust Bowl days of the Great Depression.

The extreme weather patterns revived concerns about the greenhouse effect, the tendency of carbon dioxide, methane, and other gases produced by combustion to act as a window for sunlight but a blanket for heat—just as the panes of a greenhouse roof make it possible to grow tomatoes in the dead of winter. The greenhouse effect was first described in 1896, when the Swedish chemist Svante Arrhenius postulated that the massive amounts of these gases emitted by human industry might disrupt the globe's naturally stable thermostat. Through the years, no one disputed the basic chemistry and physics of the idea.

And there were convenient natural experiments elsewhere in the solar system that confirmed the theory. Venus, with an atmosphere that is 96 percent carbon dioxide, has a scorching surface temperature, hot enough to melt lead. Mars, with a thin atmosphere devoid of carbon dioxide, is in a perpetual deep freeze. In between lies Earth, with just the right trace of carbon dioxide and water vapor (which also traps heat) to maintain its mean temperature at 59 degrees Fahrenheit. Take away that trace of carbon dioxide—which has hovered at a few hundred parts per million for hundreds of thousands of years—and Earth would have a surface temperature of zero degrees. Increase that trace by even a little, and Earth's mean temperature would rise significantly.

Now scientists were becoming convinced that Arrhenius was right. In 1957, instruments that measured carbon dioxide were installed on the slope of Hawaii's Mauna Loa volcano. Year after year, the concentration was inexorably rising. As the world's industrial output increased fortyfold from World War II to 1988, so too did the output of carbon dioxide. In the 1960s, the new environmental movement concerned itself primarily with pollutants that were overtly noxious—cancer-causing compounds, sulfur dioxide, and the like. But each year, millions of tons of invisible carbon dioxide were being pumped into the atmosphere by coal-fired power plants and factories and automobiles. By 1980, the carbon dioxide levels were 25 percent higher than they had been in 1860.

Some scientists projected that the concentration would double in only thirty or forty years. By 1988, industry and automobiles were pumping some 16.5 billion tons of carbon dioxide into the atmosphere each year.

And that did not include the carbon dioxide from manmade fires, such as those consuming the Amazon. In fact, no one had made a solid estimate of just how much carbon dioxide was being emitted by those fires until 1988, when Alberto Setzer, at Brazil's space agency, published a new study. His team had found that the Amazon fires of 1987 had added 3 billion tons of carbon dioxide to the atmosphere. This put Brazil in the ranks of the greatest polluters in the world. And the burning of the rain forest was doubly disastrous because trees are one of the planet's most important "sinks" for carbon dioxide. Through photosynthesis, plants remove enormous amounts of carbon dioxide from the air, break it into its component parts—one carbon and two oxygen atoms—release the oxygen atoms, and lock up the carbon. The carbon then becomes the backbone of compounds such as cellulose, which makes up the mass of a tree. There it can stay for a century or more, until that tree is burned or dies and decays. Because of the Amazon burning, only the United States, the Soviet Union, and China—in descending order—produced more carbon dioxide than Brazil. Without the contribution from the burning forests, Brazil would not even be in the top fifteen polluters.

Worldwide, the growth in carbon dioxide levels seemed unstoppable. And levels of other greenhouse gases, such as methane, nitrous oxide, and chlorofluorocarbons (CFCs have the honor of being both a potent greenhouse gas and a long-lived destroyer of the ozone layer) were rising even faster than the level of carbon dioxide. Even if the industrialized nations slowed their growth, the emissions of these gases would still increase as developing nations rushed at full tilt to exploit their oil and coal and to develop their industries. China planned to double its coal use in fifteen years. When scientists put doubled carbon dioxide levels into computer models of the atmosphere, the globe's temperature, simulated in the model, rose as much as nine degrees, enough so that the equable climate that had nurtured human civilization for ten thousand years would be terribly disrupted. Droughts and heat waves would wither crops; the Antarctic ice sheet might collapse and raise sea levels enough to flood Manhattan and Bangladesh and extinguish entire island nations.

Interest in the ailing atmosphere reached a new peak on June 23, 1988. James Hansen, a climate specialist from the Goddard Institute for Space Studies in New York City, flew to Washington that day and testified at a congressional hearing that he had calculated with "ninety-nine percent" certainty that "the greenhouse effect has been detected and is changing our climate now." His evidence was not tied to the current heat wave; instead, he pointed out that of the first seven years of the 1980s, five had global mean temperatures that were hotter than any other year on record. And 1988 was well on its way to being another record year (as it turned out, 1988 tied for the record). Any one heat wave was a random event, Hansen said, but the odds of so many record warm years occurring so close together were minuscule.

Hansen's statements were criticized by many of his peers; they agreed that warming was on the way but thought it premature to conclude that it was happening now. Hansen's timing was impeccable, however. On the day he testified, thermometers in forty-five American cities topped 100 degrees. (Washington reached a mere 97.) Suddenly, the warming atmosphere was front-page news; both *Newsweek* and *Time* ran cover stories on the issue. The environment as a whole became a lead story as rising thermometers and carbon dioxide levels were joined by beaches littered with medical waste, the growing hole in the ozone layer, and massive die-offs of fish and seals in Europe. The broiling, noxious summer of 1988 was the first time that the average person really seemed to look around and wonder just what it was that humanity was doing to the home planet.

At about the same time that Ivair Higino de Almeida was gunned down in Xapuri, Chico Mendes's friend José Lutzenberger flew up to Toronto to address an international conference on the changing atmosphere and the greenhouse effect. In a dim auditorium, before a painted backdrop of a pretty blue sky, Lutzenberger railed about the unbridled destruction of the tropical forests. It was a perfect example of how humankind had become a pestilence on the living tissue of planet Earth. "Deforestation is far greater even than I'd been estimating," he said. Quoting Alberto Setzer's studies, he reeled off a frightening list of numbers describing the decimation of the Amazon, ending with: "This is nothing less than a biological holocaust." He spoke of Gaia, the conception of the planet as a single living, breathing organism, saying, "We humans, in the context of Gaia, are cells. And now we are cancerous cells. A cancer can go into remission, but this will only happen if we abandon our present exclusive ethic in favor of a Gaia ethic." In classic Lutzenberger fashion, he concluded with a flourish. "Either we harmonize or we go," he said, pounding the rostrum. "Gaia will throw us out like pus from a wound."

For Chico Mendes, the environmental aspects of the fight to save the Amazon had now become secondary. He saw only the stark human side of the problem as the body count in Xapuri continued to mount. In early September a former rubber tapper, José Ribeiro, got into a fistfight in a bar with Sérgio Pereira, one of the Mineirinhos. While walking home past the cemetery late that night, Ribeiro was shot in the mouth and belly; he fell dead on the road. Typically, no investigation followed; there was still a total lack of justice for the region's disenfranchised poor. Xapuri had no full-time prosecutors, and for a decade the town had had no judge of its own. As a result, the court overflowed with ten years of unfinished cases. No murder case had proceeded to a judgment in more than twenty years.

Mendes was becoming wary of being cast as an environmentalist by the media. Those who lived outside the rain forest, both in Brazil and abroad, seemed interested only in the hummingbirds and the trees. One night, while Mendes watched television at the union hall with some friends and a reporter, a documentary described the greenhouse effect and the carbon dioxide that was spewing from the burning forests of the Amazon. Suddenly, there was Chico

Mendes, the Amazon's own ecologist, depicted as fighting to save the "lungs of the world." In a rare display of frustration, Mendes jumped up and yelled at the television, "I'm not protecting the forest because I'm worried that in twenty years the world will be affected. I'm worried about it because there are thousands of people living here who depend on the forest—and their lives are in danger every day."

The character of Acre was speedily changing for the worse. Rio Branco had swelled from the sleepy outpost of 40,000 it had been in 1960 into a city of 250,000, with most of the population living in slums created as the rubber tappers and squatters were pushed off the land. It now had a grimy industrial district and a growing array of sawmills and ceramic kilns (for brick and roof tiles). The beehive-shape kilns glowed as they were fed timber taken from tall piles harvested from the surrounding forest. The sawmills were messy places where great chunks of wasted tropical hardwood lay warping in the heat of the sun. Where Rio Branco had six sawmills in 1986, by 1988 it had more than forty. (In Rondônia, the number of sawmills was already dropping because the accessible stands of trees there had all been cut.) The lumber trucks rolled constantly down BR-317 into town, hauling massive sections of tree trunk to be skinned and sliced. The sawmill owners saw no need to avoid buying Brazil nut logs, despite the ban. They were a dangerous lot, quick to use intimidation and violence against any opponent, including the few government officials who tried to enforce the forestry laws.

In August, João Branco, the head of the UDR in Acre, and two other powerful right-wing landowners had bought one of Acre's daily papers, *O Rio Branco*. Branco's two partners were extremely conservative brothers, Narciso and Naildo Mendes; Narciso was a federal congressman who consistently supported the UDR position on all legislation. Initially, the paper's staff continued to report the news from a relatively liberal standpoint. Antonio Alves, a reporter there, later recalled that they ran a headline one day that read: "Two Thousand Hectares Murdered" (a hectare is 2.47 acres). Naildo Mendes came storming into the newsroom, screaming and shaking a copy of the paper. It was his property they were describing. "From now on, this paper writes what I want it to write," he said. And then the owners proceeded to "clean" the staff, just as they would a newly purchased tract of forest. Almost everyone was fired.

When the paper resumed publication a month later, it was unrecognizable. The new staff was under strict orders to attack the PT, Chico Mendes, and the church whenever possible. As Branco later said to the filmmaker Miranda Smith, "We got Chico Mendes out of circulation when we bought the newspaper. Also the local bishop. Their politics were of no interest to our business interests. They preach socialism while we preach free initiative. I'm not going to give them space or get these gentlemen in the news." Shortly thereafter, Branco and his partners bought one of Acre's television stations, and it too became a platform for the UDR's gospel of tradition, family, and property—and pasture.

Even as Chico Mendes was losing support in the local press— which had for so long been a valued support—his dangerous duel with the Alves family escalated dramatically. Mendes was outraged that months were passing without any progress on the police investigations of the shooting at the forestry office and the killing of Higino. In fact, there were no investigations to speak of. Part of the problem was the Alves family's close friendship with the sheriff of Xapuri. Darci could often be seen lounging outside the police station, just yards from Mendes's front door. He would sit on the wooden bench beneath the shade tree, listening to the chirping of the caged bird that was hung on a branch each day, and joke around with the officers—who were never busy. Mendes was still unwilling to resort to violence, but he longed for some weapon with which to attack the Alves family and their private army.

He found his weapon in an unlikely place. Around the time of José Ribeiro's death, Mendes flew south to a national meeting of union organizers and then on to Curitiba, the capital of Paraná and the home base of Mary Allegretti. There he participated in the first large conference on extractive reserves: Allegretti's Institute for Amazonian Studies had invited scientists and policymakers from around Brazil and overseas to help refine the legal and scientific questions surrounding this new conservation strategy. Genesio Natividade, the young lawyer who was working for the tappers, also attended the meeting, along with another lawyer. Mendes mentioned to them that his main opponents, the Alveses, had come from Paraná, and that there were persistent rumors that Alvarino, Darly, and their father, Sebastião, might be wanted on past crimes. As the meeting got under way, Natividade and his partner volunteered to drive downtown to the Justice Department archives, where they could look for any cases involving the family.

Not surprisingly, they found a reference to an old but active case against Alvarino. There was a mention of an order of imprisonment issued in 1973 because Alvarino had resisted arrest and wounded a police officer. The complete file was said to be at the Justice Department in Umuarama, the town 250 miles northwest of Curitiba where the Alveses had lived before moving to the Amazon. By coincidence, a law school classmate of Natividade's was now a prosecutor there. Natividade telephoned his friend, who quickly reported that there was indeed a voluminous file on the case.

When the lawyer returned to the meeting and excitedly told Mendes and Allegretti the news, Mendes was delighted. Allegretti gave Natividade money for his trip to Umuarama to dig up what he could. That same day, Natividade flew west, knowing only that there was an imprisonment order for Alvarino—nothing more. But when he sat down the next day with the four-hundred-page legal file, it quickly became apparent that here was a massive amount of damaging information on the family's violent past. Most important was the case in which the Alveses were said to have killed a neighbor of Sebastião's after a land dispute. The judge had found sufficient evidence to justify holding Alvarino and Darly for trial, and imprisonment orders had been issued for both men. The orders had never been served, however, because the two had fled the state.

Late one afternoon a few days later, Natividade and his old friend, the prosecutor, met with Judge Abel Antônio Rebello in his paneled office and went over the case. The judge, along with many veterans of the legal system in the town, remembered the Alveses's exploits. Still eager to see justice served, he issued two imprisonment orders and two letters requesting that Xapuri's officials take the ranchers into custody. Turning over the documents to the visiting lawyer, the judge said this called for a celebratory round of *chimarrão*, a green tea—and potent stimulant—that is the favorite drink in the south of Brazil, and bid Natividade good luck. After the lawyer finished drinking his tea through the silver straw customarily used for *chimarrão*, he told the judge, "If only everything I now have to do goes this easily, all will be well."

Natividade returned to Curitiba with the fate of Chico Mendes in his briefcase. There, in a tense meeting, he and Mendes, Gomercindo Rodrigues, Mary Allegretti, and a few others from the core of the movement discussed their next move. Mendes was elated because now he had the information he needed to justify his going after the Alveses. But at the same time, everyone acknowledged that if the information leaked, the Alveses might go after *him*. The decision was left up to Mendes. Without hesitating, he insisted that the documents had to be taken to the police in Acre. Despite any personal risk, he said, he was tired of the unanswered killings of his *companheiros*. From this moment, Mendes's fight with Darly Alves and his family became less a fight between a rubber tapper and a rancher and more a battle between two strong-willed men. When Allegretti urged caution, Mendes responded, "I'm going to show them that they can't push this *nordestino* around."

When Mendes returned to Acre, he seemed revitalized. There was new energy in his step, energy that people had not seen for months. In Xapuri, he told Sister Zelia that he had finally gotten the goods on Darly. As he put it, "Now I am touching the snake in his own hole." In late September, Natividade flew up to Rio Branco to meet with Mendes and the bishop, Moacyr Grechi, to decide how to proceed. The conventional approach was not feasible because Darly was so friendly with the Xapuri police. So Mendes and the others decided to take the documents directly to the chief of the Federal Police in Rio Branco. Of all the police services in Brazil, the Federal Police, the equivalent of the Federal Bureau of

Investigation in the United States, had lately developed a reputation for honesty.

The chief, Mauro Spósito, was the same man who, during the dark days of military rule eight years earlier, had interrogated Mendes time and again. Since then, the two men had not had much to do with each other. Now, when Natividade presented the papers to Spósito, he appeared genuinely pleased to have something on the Alves family. Afterward, as Mendes and his friends walked down the street, the tapper spotted Darly himself sitting in a car in front of a restaurant just a few blocks from the police station. Going quickly to Mary Allegretti's hotel, they called Spósito. Mendes implored him to arrest Darly on the spot, but Spósito hesitated and in the end did nothing.

In fact, nothing was done for weeks. The judicial letters sat on Spósito's desk while his enthusiasm for capturing the Alveses dried up. He demanded that Natividade provide more documentation to substantiate the letters, which had come in an unsealed envelope. Spósito later claimed that he could not have done anything regardless. Such judicial requests only have force if they are first brought to a local judge, who then issues a fresh warrant; technically, Spósito said, his hands were tied. Later, Mendes discovered that Spósito was a friend of Alvarino Alves's. Finally, on October 19, after the papers from Umuarama were indeed given to a judge assigned to Xapuri, new arrest warrants were issued for Darly and Alvarino. The Military Police were sent to the Paraná ranch and to Alvarino's small spread, but by that time the brothers had heard about the warrants and disappeared. The police issued a nationwide alert.

The unwitting source of the leak was Malu Maranhão, the reporter from Paraná who had spent part of the previous dry season writing about Mendes and who had also attended the September meeting in Curitiba. When she decided to write an article about the arrest warrant—against the wishes of Allegretti—she never anticipated that it might be read by one of Darly's friends or relatives still in Paraná. But that is exactly what happened. As Darly later recalled in an interview, "My brother-in-law Djair Gomes . . .

called me and said, 'Friend, there is an article here in the *Folha de Londrina* which says that you are going to be arrested, that you committed many crimes here.'" Darly was worried, but at first he did nothing. Then, just before the police finally executed the warrants, he went to the courthouse in Xapuri and asked a stenographer he knew whether there was some kind of warrant against him. He was told that Mendes had brought it from Paraná and that it was already in the hands of the Federal Police. Darly was enraged; according to later testimony by the stenographer, he shouted, "I'm going to show Chico Mendes that he will never bother me and my wife again."

Darly and Alvarino at first hid near the Bolivian border. They sent word back to town that they would only reappear after Mendes was in his grave. There was evidence that Alvarino eventually headed south and fled to a ranch he owned in Paraguay; he had retreated there before when he was in trouble with the law. In November, Darly was able to sneak back to his ranch, where one of his sons dropped him off at a worker's shack in a remote corner of the property. The police stationed guards at the ranch and conducted cursory searches but lacked adequate manpower to cover the entire spread.

Even for a wanted man, hiding out in the Amazon is not especially difficult. Darly's younger sons took food to their father each day and filled him in on the news. Occasionally, he hiked back to the central compound at night to visit his women. He put Oloci in charge of the ranch's operations. While Darly hid, he planned his revenge. As one resident of the ranch later testified, Darly said, "Chico won't live out the year. No one has ever bested me. And Chico wants to do that."

By the end of October, it was obvious that Mendes was in deep trouble. Little was being done to pursue the Alveses; little could be done. The Military Police in Xapuri had few functioning vehicles and hardly any ammunition. The Federal Police had only a token force in Rio Branco. And the sheriff in Xapuri was not apt to conduct an intensive search for his friend.

The tension was broken briefly that month when the rubber tappers of Cachoeira staged a rally to mark the official announcement of the disappropriation of the *seringal* before it was designated an extractive reserve. Hundreds of tappers gathered at the central clearing. There was singing and dancing and soccer games and speeches. And there was drinking, with *cachaça* and cola the beverage of the day. Mendes joined the tappers for a few rounds. Adrian Cowell was in town, and his camera captured the essence of the day —a mixture of joy and sadness and foreboding. Looking more than a little drunk, Mendes squinted into the late afternoon sun, smiled his wide, walrus smile, lifted his cup of *cachaça*, and told the camera, "We're commemorating the victory of the rubber tappers of Cachoeira and the first extractive reserve in Xapuri. But it's just the first step. We need many more reserves. This is just one percent of what is needed." Behind his smile, you could see the tension. And Mendes was starting to show his years: gray had steadily infiltrated what had been a tousled mop of shining black hair.

Later that day, the tappers gathered in front of a table that had been set up beneath a tree for a mass. Children gathered in the front. Luis Ceppi, Xapuri's priest, spoke eloquently of the events of the last few months. A pair of *sapatos de seringueiro* was placed on the table—the homemade rubber shoes of the tappers. "No one likes to die," Ceppi said. "But if it has to happen, then it should be to create more life. The blood spilled in these recent days must be the seed of a new liberty, a new life." Mendes stood toward the back and stared pensively at his feet, and then out to the forest canopy, which surrounded the clearing like a delicate tapestry. Finally, the service concluded with the communion wafer and wine. As the sun set behind the treetops, Mendes and Ilzamar, with Sandino and Elenira, walked across the pasture to Cecília's house. They gave their aunt a hug, then walked up the slope toward the ravine and the path back to Xapuri.

Soon the fires of the burning season began to hiss and die under the first heavy downpours of the rainy season. In the Amazon's

unchanging rhythm, the tappers switched from collecting latex to
harvesting Brazil nuts. Out on the *estradas,* the steady *whack, whack,
whack* of machetes lopping open the nut casings could be heard.
And in Xapuri, as October came to an end, Chico Mendes seemed
to know that he was running out of time.

Few of his friends understood why he chose to stay in Xapuri.
Some speculated that he had become overconfident because of the
growing international attention; Mendes had often said that it
prolonged his life. Others said there was just enough of the *macho*
Brazilian in Mendes to push him to stand and fight even if the odds
were against him. Sister Zelia disagreed. By this time, she felt he
had totally abnegated his personal life to the fight for the rubber
tappers. As she later recalled, "Every day we were waiting for Chico's death. Sometimes he'd sleep at a friend's house or at the *seringal.* But there was always someone watching, following. So we
were always afraid. It became almost routine." She asked Mendes
many times why he did not leave Xapuri for a while, until things
cooled off. One night he gave her an answer: "I would be a coward
to do this. My blood is the same blood as that of these people
suffering here. I can't run. There's something inside me that cannot
leave here. This is the place where I will finish my mission."

While Mendes spoke his mind to Sister Zelia, to others he
continually repeated his refrain about the relative values of a living
person and a corpse. And he was not ready to give up without a
fight. At the end of October, he sent a letter to Governor Melo and
the Acre secretary for public safety; it was an eloquent plea for
help: "My main objective is to communicate my concern with the
present situation. . . . At certain times I've been misinterpreted, at
other times I've been censored by the authorities of our state. I've
been accused of being an agitator and a generator of violence. I'd
like to be allowed to prove to all the authorities that never has a
drop of blood been drawn on my own responsibility. I intend to
continue with the same attitude until the end. And I'd like to get
support in my struggle. Are you interested in helping me, sir?"

He went on to list the people who were plotting to kill him and
Osmarino Rodrigues. He said that a closely placed source had in-

formed him of two meetings in Brasiléia in late October at which Darly, Darci, and their friends worked out the details. He claimed that they had the support of the judge and police in Brasiléia. Then he complained about the inaction of Mauro Spósito. Mendes concluded, "I cannot be quiet looking at what is happening. People can't keep suffering this way. Through being humble, I have gained the support of very powerful people. If you really want to help, I'm going to wait."

He gave a copy of the letter to Fatima Mastub, his next-door neighbor and confidante, for safekeeping and told her to show it to no one. That day, he displayed a bit of the triumphant spark he had felt when he had learned of the warrants. "Now these guys are going to be arrested," he told her confidently. But when he came by a few days later, he seemed broken, Mastub recalled. As she watched television, Mendes came into her cottage, just ten feet from his own, and sat on her sagging couch. His eyes were full of tears, and he would start to say something, then stop. When she asked him what was wrong, he said, "Nothing." Eventually he told her that he had gotten no response to his letter.

The days passed, and still nothing was done. The authorities' one concession was to give Mendes bodyguards from the Military Police—but there was no new effort to round up the people who made the guards necessary. Mendes granted long, patient interviews now to any reporter who came through town. He wanted to make sure that his story, and the story of the century-long struggle of the *seringueiros*, was told.

The tension reached a new peak on election day, November 15. The town was full of soldiers; troops with heavy machine guns stood on street corners. Mendes went through his daily routine—drinking coffee at the stand of his good friend Dona Maria, urging people to vote—but he looked uncomfortable and wary as he was trailed everywhere by two Military Police officers toting submachine guns. Not surprisingly, the PT candidate for mayor, a former priest, lost to the PMDB candidate. But elsewhere in Brazil PT had its first major victories, winning mayoral seats in thirty-one cities, including São Paulo. And Lula, the durable leader of the party, was

considered a strong prospect for the presidential race of 1989. Ironically, the PT victories may have added to the danger for Mendes;
after the election, the ruling class of Acre considered him even more
of a threat.

Mendes had further cause to be tense on election day: an uncle
of his had had a chilling conversation with Sebastião Alves, the
father of Darly and Alvarino. Mendes's uncle, José Amaro da Silva, lived outside town and came in only occasionally to shop. On
November 14, while walking to Xapuri, he was flagged down by
Sebastião, who was sitting on the veranda of his house. Sebastião
did not recognize Amaro as one of Mendes's relatives; he saw only
a potential vote for the PMDB. Sebastião had once been the local
head of PMDB, and he still liked to play an active role in town
politics.

"*Oi, chefe*, come here," Sebastião said, and the men chatted for
a while. "Who are you going to vote for?" Sebastião asked. They
debated politics a bit before the talk turned to Chico Mendes.
Sebastião scoffed at the attention being paid to Mendes and at his
bodyguards. The old man thumped his chest with his fist and said
that after the elections Mendes would die. "Chico may be in the
company of policemen," he said, "but we have professional *companheiros* who can take Chico's life from a distance of a hundred
meters even if he's with three policemen."

Amaro was horrified. He immediately passed the news to Mendes's brother Zuza, and Zuza told Mendes. But Mendes seemed
unperturbed: he took his uncle aside and told him not to worry.
"I'm receiving many threats," he said. "But uncle, I really believe
in God, and I'm going to take hold of God and drive these bad
people away."

Returning from a brief trip to Rio de Janeiro in late November,
Mendes went out to Cachoeira to try to relax a little. He recounted
his latest adventures to his aunt Cecília: he had jogged along the
beach at Ipanema with celebrities, Indians, and local Green party
politicians, demonstrating in defense of the Amazon in the shadow of luxury apartments and the looming slums that crept up the

mountainsides of that troubled city. He had made more speeches and received more accolades and had even been given the key to the city by Rio's mayor.

But his aunt knew that life in Xapuri was altogether different. Here, Mendes walked quickly once darkness fell and always feared for his life. The two lives of Chico Mendes now seemed entirely split: there was the Mendes who was the darling of the Green party and Brazil's labor organizations and the foreign press, and the Mendes who was an isolated local activist with a price on his head. Most dangerous for Mendes, while his enemies in Xapuri were aware of his broader fame, they did not begin to appreciate its significance.

One evening, Mendes, his aunt, and Fatima Mastub shared dinner on Cecília's veranda. Earlier, Mendes had sent a tapper out to hunt some game; he still preferred the meat from the forest. And he had picked some oranges from one of the trees the tappers had planted in the clearing. They all ate from the same plate, then sat silently, looking at the spot where the forest met the manioc fields and pasture, watching the changing light and the scudding clouds. At one point, Mendes looked at the two women and said, "I'm going to cut rubber again. I need to do it." His aunt said, "No, you don't need to do that anymore." But Mendes insisted: "Yes, yes, I need it. I need it because I enjoy it. It makes me feel good. I want to spend a month in the forest. I miss the forest."

On the first of December, Mendes abandoned all caution and took his fight to the *Gazeta do Acre,* the only newspaper not controlled by the ranchers. He gave the editor, his old friend Silvio Martinello, a copy of a letter he had just sent to Mauro Spósito a few days earlier. In it he charged that Spósito, the UDR, and a secret *esquadrão da morte*—death squad—in Acre had all entered into a compact to murder him and other leaders of the rural workers' movement. The paper published the letter the next day under a large headline: "Chico Mendes Charges That the PF [Federal Police] Is Helping Pistoleiros Hide." By taking on the Federal Police, Mendes began playing a very rough game. And any mention of a death squad made people nervous in Brazil. Especially during the military dictatorship, police departments had often been linked to death squads—a melodramatic term for moonlighting officers who would gladly kill for a price.

Spósito was incensed. He saw himself as an honest, professional policeman, and believed that Mendes was jeopardizing his career. Rather than trade accusations, Spósito decided to attack using documents. He went into his files on Mendes and dropped off some material at the office of *O Rio Branco,* the ranchers' newspaper. The next day, the paper published the material as well as a letter from Spósito. The police chief said that Mendes's charges were absurd and that, in fact, Mendes had previously collaborated with the Federal Police—a terrible embarrassment for the tapper, who vociferously denied the assertion. (Spósito said that Mendes regularly briefed the police on the situation of tappers who had been pushed into Bolivia as the ranchers invaded Acre; no one had evidence to the contrary.) Spósito had also dredged up a copy of a letter to Mendes from the banned Revolutionary Communist party, a splinter group that saw him as a traitor because he stayed in PT. Spósito claimed that Mendes had sent him the letter because he felt just as threatened from the far left as the far right. Finally, Spósito announced that he had canceled Mendes's permit for his revolver, citing as a flimsy rationale a lawsuit that Darly and the owners of Seringal Equador had filed against the tappers.

Through early December, charges and countercharges flew. Mendes sent off telegrams and telexes to everyone from President Sarney down through the federal and state justice systems. But no one seemed to be listening. He got only one response, a polite note from Romeu Tuma, the national head of the Federal Police. Then came a different sort of reply: two anonymous *noticiazinhas*—little articles—in the December 6 edition of *O Rio Branco.* It was classic journalism, Amazon style. Said the first: "Chico Mendes is a really courageous man to try to dirty the image of the superintendent of Federal Police and now, cautiously, to want to apologize. The truth: a man who has a tail of thatch shouldn't get too close to a fire." The second notice read: "Soon, a 200-megaton bomb will explode and there will be nationwide repercussions. Important people may be harmed when this is done. Wait and see, because the source of this information is trustworthy."

On December 7, Mendes flew south to take part in a debate at the agricultural campus of the University of São Paulo, in the satellite city of Piracicaba. He noticed a couple of ranchers on the same flight and was startled to see them again on the bus from the São Paulo airport to the university. He made a quick telephone call, and the police agreed to meet him at the bus station and provide an escort to the lecture hall.

While in the south, he got a call from Mary Allegretti. She was passing through the United States on her way home from a forestry conference in Japan and had gotten word that Mendes was in increasing danger. She tried to convince him to stay away from Xapuri, but he refused, saying, "I'm a *nordestino*. Don't expect me to act as you would."

Ilzamar and Mendes's friends put together a forty-fourth birthday party for him on December 15. Through the night they danced and sang and tried to be merry. Ilzamar had been very sick, much of it ascribed to tension. Someone gave Mendes a blue towel decorated with a rainbow and musical notes. But the celebration screeched to a halt when Darci Alves appeared briefly in the crowd. He left without causing any trouble, but the partygoers were spooked. Later that night, as Mendes sat talking with Fatima Mastub, he said, "I don't think I'm going to live until Christmas." She pushed at him and laughed, hiding her fear. "What a bad joke," she said. "Come on, Chico, we're still going to do a lot of things, we're still going to be around a long time."

Mendes continued to tell friends that he would not live past December, yet would then hasten to say that he would never stop fighting. His latest plan was to found a local branch of the Green party. Although earlier in the year he had become impatient with the environmentalists, he now resolved to focus on that aspect of the movement to save the forest. He had lately realized that virtually all of his support had come from those concerned with the environment. The Ford Foundation grants, the truck from Canada, the prospect of a new grant for a large truck and several boats—all had been the result of his work on the environment. Through this issue, therefore, he could deliver the most for his people.

But his enemies had little concern about the environment, and their efforts to stop him were unrelenting. Plans were well under way to "end the confusion in Acre," as Darci Alves told friends at the Paraná ranch. The office of the secretary for public safety, which oversees local police departments, had quietly issued Darci a license for a handgun on December 5, despite his violent behavior and his father's troubles. Darci and several other *pistoleiros* from the ranch had begun staking out Mendes's neighborhood. For most of December, someone camped in the brush by the river behind Mendes's house. A sportswriter named Albertino Chaves later wrote a note to Silvio Martinello, saying that there had been a meeting at a real estate office in Rio Branco at which the ranchers raised a pot of money—some estimates ranged as high as $10,000—to reward the killers of Chico Mendes.

Although it was never proved, João Branco of the UDR was later accused by the tappers of being one of the *mandantes,* masterminds, of the money-raising effort. Others speculated that he and the other power brokers of Acre simply told Darly that, given the lack of response to the previous killings, he could probably kill Mendes with impunity. But Branco just laughed at his accusers. Later, he said that in Acre, it had become "fashionable to call a loud fart a death threat."

On December 17, at a weekly card game in Rio Branco, Efraim Mendoza, an aging doctor from Bolivia who juggled three practices in the city, overheard a conversation that suggested just how concrete plans for Mendes's killing had become. The game was held in a back room of the Rio Branco Soccer Club, a dance hall and social club next door to the dank, rundown movie house. The players sat at several octagonal card tables covered with green felt. That evening, Mendoza noted that they included Adalberto Aragão, the former mayor of Rio Branco and a political foe of Mendes, and a few ranchers. Nearby sat two of Aragão's bodyguards; many of the ranching elite always had someone nearby to protect them from possible assaults by rubber tappers.

During the game, Gaston Mota arrived. A heavyset, dark man with small but penetrating eyes, he had once been the rubber boss of the estate where Raimundo de Barros had grown up; now he was a close associate of Xapuri's ranchers. Mota, who liked to show off a bullet scar he had received when an enemy shot him through a window, was suspected by the police of more than one murder, and he was loathed by the tappers. Mota chatted with Aragão's bodyguards for a few minutes, then left. Soon one of the bodyguards came over to the card table and said quietly, in what was becoming an eerie refrain in Acre, "Chico Mendes will be dead before Christmas."

Meanwhile, Mendes kept his promise to continue fighting for the rubber tappers. On December 20, he flew to Sena Madureira, in the center of Acre, to try and recruit new members for the National Council of Rubber Tappers. He was escorted to the airport by his police guards, and they met him on his return. In Rio Branco, he triumphantly took possession of a heavy-duty Mercedes flatbed truck that the tappers' cooperative had purchased with a grant from a bank that encouraged community development projects. With one of his police guards at the wheel—Mendes himself was famous for his bad driving—they took the truck to Xapuri. Mendes was greeted warmly. Ironically, now that he had forsaken politics, his political stock was rising.

The only thing remarkable about December 22 was that it did not rain. Mendes's routine was unbroken. He got his coffee from Dona Maria's little blue shack. He worked at the union hall and the cooperative office. That afternoon, he told his two guards that he wanted to take the new truck for a spin. One of the guards, Roldão Lucas da Cruz, later recalled that Mendes was the happiest he had been in weeks. He simply wanted to circle the town and visit friends —as if he were saying good-bye. Mendes sat in the front with his two children and the driver. Sandino was now a miniature of his father, with the same dimple and curls; Elenira was approaching school age. Mendes paid a few bills and shopped for groceries. They picked up a refrigerator for a neighbor and dropped it off for her.

Then, at around four-thirty in the afternoon, they stopped at the hospital to pick up drugs and medical supplies for the health posts on the *seringais*. Mendes talked for a while with Sister Zelia. Among other bits of news, she told him that Wanderley Viana, the mayor and a malicious enemy of Mendes's, had come to the hospital early that morning in the throes of an anxiety attack, requesting a sedative. She thought it unusual and had no idea what had caused the breakdown. Later, a friend at the mayor's office told Sister Zelia that she had overheard Viana on the telephone that morning, saying, "Everything is going to be fine."

Chico only wanted to talk about the truck. It had been one of his dreams; with their own transportation, the tappers were freer than ever. He said, "Now we have this truck, and soon we'll have a boat. Now we can ship the rubber ourselves, with no more middlemen. We can now do effective work." Finally, Mendes did talk again of the Alves family and the fear that lurked constantly in his mind. "If I don't end up in the cemetery, I'm going to put these guys in jail," he said as he left.

At 5:00 P.M., Mendes went home to relax with Ilzamar and the children. It had been a gray day, and the light was already fading. His unofficial bodyguard, Gomercindo Rodrigues, was there, and they played dominoes, watched a little television, and talked a bit. At six o'clock, Rodrigues told Mendes that he was going to check things out around the town. He stopped by the cooperative office, then climbed on his motorcycle and drove by the bars where the *pistoleiros* did their drinking. It was quiet—too quiet, he thought. Everyone seemed to have cleared out of town. In the Amazon, this was a bad sign. The same thing had happened in Brasiléia when Wilson Pinheiro was killed.

The six-thirty bell for the special mass for Xapuri's school-children rang. The clacking of the dominoes on Mendes's kitchen table halted so that Ilzamar could set out dinner. Mendes, grumbling about the heat, grabbed his bright new towel to take a shower and lamented the lack of light in the back yard. He picked up the flashlight that Mary Allegretti had given to him long before. And he opened his back door.

That night, Allegretti was far away, attending the opera in New York City, where she was visiting her brother. Adrian Cowell was in London, working feverishly on his film. Stephan Schwartzman was at home in Washington, putting his five-month-old son to bed.

And in Rio Branco, Bishop Grechi was walking to the radio station to broadcast the Christmas novena; three hundred groups of worshipers were gathered by their tinny radios on the *seringais* around Acre. Just before he reached the building, a church worker ran up and said that Rodrigues had phoned from Xapuri in tears. Controlling his emotions, Grechi entered the station. After making a quick call to confirm the awful news, he spoke into the microphone.

As his steady voice echoed throughout the rain forest, hundreds of rubber tappers began to pray for Chico Mendes.

Epilogue

HALFWAY BETWEEN the blue and pink cottage of Chico Mendes and the Xapuri cemetery sits a yellow, two-story house. Just about every other building has only one story, giving this one a top-heavy feel, like the cabin of an old riverboat. On most afternoons, its owner, Sebastião Alves da Silva, can be found on the veranda, chatting with passersby and the children, grandchildren, and great-grandchildren who are always coming and going. At the age of eighty-six, Sebastião has finally been slowed down a step or two by prostate surgery. Because he can no longer ride a horse, he sold his two ranches, Good Find and Edge of the Forest, and moved into town.

The placement of the house seems fitting, for it is Sebastião's son Darly and grandson Darci, along with a hired hand, who stand accused of sending Mendes to that cemetery. And few people in town doubt that the old man approved heartily of the killing.

Late one day eight months after Mendes died, Sebastião sat with two visitors and reflected on all the turmoil that had enveloped the town and the Alves family. The sky was filled with roiling thunderheads that glowed like burnished pewter in the fading light of dusk. A violent windstorm had swept the area the day before, and most of Xapuri still lacked electricity because the power lines from the town's diesel generators had been toppled. The wind had peeled back the tin roofs on the church and dozens of homes as if they were the tops of sardine cans. Sebastião was joined by one of his youngest sons, who at sixteen could easily have been his great-grandson. The boy, shirtless and wearing a beret, curled his lithe brown body on a windowsill like a ferret and enfolded his two-year-old daughter in his long arms.

Sebastião ignored the swarm of mosquitoes that danced above his head; at sunset in that part of the Amazon, anyone who does not keep moving acquires such a halo. His thin body was stooped, but his sinewy arms and hands were still strong. His head had a dusting of white hair that crept far down his tanned neck, and his face was covered by silver stubble. The wisps softened all of his features except his eyes, which had the hard, black glint of obsidian. These were sharp eyes that stabbed and probed, conducting exploratory surgery, missing little.

He still found it hard to believe that the murder of Mendes had created such a stir. "Even when Jesus Christ died, there wasn't as much publicity," he said. Sebastião and the other ranchers had marveled at the extent of the reaction. No one understood how this uneducated rubber tapper could have had so many connections overseas and in the south. Ever since, journalists had been coming around, trying to get Sebastião's picture. "One American reporter came and was incredibly impolite. He asked me, 'How many gunmen do you have inside your house?' I got very angry. I said, 'If I had some *pistoleiros* here, I'd tell them to shoot you right now.'"

As the clouds darkened above him, Sebastião denied his family's involvement in the murder. "We are not violent people," he said, "but if someone starts to treat you badly, to push you, to beat you, you have two choices: you can go look for justice or you can find a gun and kill the man." In Brazil, it is not likely that you will find justice through the courts or police, he said. "You show me a sheriff or soldier who obeys the law, then I won't kill anyone."

He spoke of the time he had killed someone in Minas Gerais, then confessed after having a vision from God. He had spent most of his jail term reading the Bible, and his philosophy was clear. "It's impossible for a man to kill," Sebastião said. "You can point your gun and you can pull the trigger. But only God decides who lives or dies."

His family had always had a tough time with the authorities and so had moved around a lot. "Like Jesus said, 'If you have some pressure in one land, you should move to another land.'" But they had a clean record, he insisted. "You go to the court or the sheriff and check the Alves name. You won't find any crimes." He jabbed at the air with a finger. "All of this is gossip. My kid has his ranch because he worked for it. That is not stolen land."

Now it was getting too dark to see. The mayor strolled past and elicited from Sebastião a friendly "*Oi, chefe.*" The old man stood up, stretched his stiff limbs, and prepared to finish his daily audience. His son took the baby inside. Sebastião said that the rubber tapper leader had brought his fate on himself. "Chico always used to say that if his death would be a solution for Amazonia, he'd be happy to die. In speeches he used to say 'Kill me, come here and kill me. My chest is open.'" The cicadas started their nightly trill. The electricity finally came back on, and moths began to dance around the dim streetlights.

Through thin purple lips, in a voice that crackled, the elder Alves said, "Chico Mendes spent too much time alive." Then he spoke in a conspiratorial whisper: "Darly is in jail now, but he'll be free. There's nothing that proves that he killed Chico."

He pointed down the road; he smiled and his voice grew quieter: "If you really want to know who killed Chico, go to the cemetery. Take up one of his bones. Draw it across your throat. The bone will tell you who the killer was."

Sebastião Alves, like most of the ranchers in Acre, had expected that the repercussions from Mendes's death would fade quickly, just as they always did when someone was killed. And, like everyone else, he had expected that the murderers would never be caught. But this time the situation was different. Faced with an unprecedented media blitz, the Brazilian government did something it had never done before—conduct a thorough investigation of a murder in the Amazon. The chief of the Federal Police, Romeu Tuma, flew up with the secretary-general of the Ministry of Justice to oversee the investigation. Within days, Tuma had transferred the head of the Federal Police in Acre, Mauro Spósito, to São Paulo, where he was given a desk job overseeing passport control.

For the first few days, roadblocks, house-to-house searches, and a sweep of the forests by one hundred and fifty police officers—including dozens of federal agents flown in for the operation—failed to find the prime suspects: Darly, his sons, his brother Alvarino, and the Mineirinhos. The police had a terrible time of it. They were hampered by the return of the rains and the demise within a few days of all but three of their twenty-one vehicles.

Even when they came upon some of their quarry, they were frustrated. On Christmas Day, a squad of Military Police passed the Paraná ranch and noticed some people gathered behind one of the houses. Stopping to investigate, they found that Darly's son Oloci had slaughtered a steer, and he, the Mineirinhos, and many members of the extended Alves clan were having a holiday *churrascada*. The Mineirinhos and Oloci ran toward the forest, pulling handguns from their belts. One of them dropped to the ground and began firing at the approaching officers, who had nothing more than revolvers themselves. As the police ducked for cover, everyone escaped into the trees.

The police camped out at the Alves ranch and neighboring spreads, and on December 26 the pressure paid off. Darci came out of hiding and surrendered at the army barracks in Rio Branco. He then gave a confession in which he described every detail of the crime scene, from the beam of Mendes's flashlight to the piece of wood that made it necessary to duck before entering the back yard. He swore he was alone and that he committed the crime because Mendes would not stop harassing his father.

The next day, the actress Lucélia Santos, who had flown to Acre for the funeral, was riding in the union truck when the driver spotted Darci's brother Oloci and another of Darly's sons as they sped toward Rio Branco in a pickup. Oloci held his hand as if it were a pistol, pointed it at Santos, and pulled the trigger. When she arrived in Rio Branco, she immediately told the police, who tracked down and cornered Oloci. In a shootout, Oloci was hit in the right arm and captured.

On December 28, a team of forensic scientists from the University of Campinas flew to Acre to exhume Mendes's body and perform a detailed autopsy. The group was led by Nelson Massini, a pathologist who had built quite a career out of examining corpses; his most famous accomplishment was confirming that a skeleton found in Argentina was that of the Nazi war criminal Josef Mengele. But there was little mystery in Mendes's death. The specialists quickly confirmed the location of the shooter; within a week of Darci's capture, they found that a hair recovered from a black raincoat left in the woods behind Mendes's house was identical to Darci's. On January 2, Darci participated in a reconstruction of the crime. Wearing a bulletproof vest and escorted by heavily armed soldiers, he walked to Mendes's house and was videotaped as he showed police how he had entered the yard, where he had waited, and how he had shot. Every piece of evidence fit with his description of that night.

Meanwhile, the police arrested or questioned anyone remotely connected with the family, and they soon found that Darci's story did not exactly match the facts. More than half a dozen neighbors had seen two men leaving Mendes's yard, not one. Under intensive questioning—said by those interviewed to have included painful sessions on the *pau de arara*—several Alves relatives and employees alleged that the person who actually pulled the trigger was Jardeir Pereira, one of the Mineirinhos, and that Darci was his partner. The most significant accounts were those of the teenager Genézio Barbosa da Silva, Oloci's brother-in-law. In the past he had acted as a spy for Darly, who, after the old arrest warrant had been issued, paid for Genézio to stay for weeks at a time at the Hotel Veneza in Xapuri and report on the situation in town. Now the boy turned police informer, alleging that Darly had ordered the murder of Mendes and describing other gruesome killings as well. After someone tried to break into the local jail where Genézio was being held in protective custody, he was flown to Rio de Janeiro.

Other witnesses confirmed what Genézio had said. Maria Gorete da Sena, the wife of Amadeus Pereira, one of the Mineirinhos, alleged that around 11:00 P.M. on the night Mendes was killed, Darci and Jardeir came to the gate behind her house and said, "Now the confusion in Xapuri is ended because we have killed Chico Mendes." She said they had camped out in the woods near Mendes's house for two nights before the killing, returning to the ranch each day to work with the cattle. A cowboy from the ranch confirmed that Darly had ordered the killing. And one of Darly's women, Francisca, told police that on December 21 she had overheard Darly say that Mendes had to die.

The pressure on Darly was intense. He was assumed to be hiding in the forest, where there was little food available. The police kept his family under lock and key so that no one could help him or tip him off. Darly's women, who normally lived in separate buildings, were locked up together in one house.

Finally, on January 7, 1989, after a lawyer negotiated terms of surrender, Darly came out of hiding. After dark, so that no one could see what was happening, he was met by his lawyer at a ranch not far from his own and driven to the police. He was haggard and lame after more than two weeks on the run. He handed over a revolver and joined his sons in prison. There was much speculation in the media and around Xapuri that by surrendering, the father and son were acting as the *boi de piranha,* the ailing steer that is sent across a river ahead of a herd: it gets eaten by the piranhas, allowing the rest of the cattle—in this case, any of the powerful ranchers of Acre who might have helped plan or pay for the murder—to pass unscathed. (Jardeir Pereira and his brothers were thought to have fled with Alvarino Alves. According to Sebastião, Alvarino had chosen not to hide like Darly.)

Fourteen hours after Darly was arrested, his mistress Francisca cut her throat with a kitchen knife. Margarete da Sena claimed that the police had frightened her into thinking that "North American ecologists were going to drop an atomic bomb on Fazenda Paraná." But there was speculation in the local papers that she feared Darly would be angry because she had talked to the police.

Once Darly was in custody, lawyers quickly convinced his son

Darci to retract his confession—they said it had been given under duress, that Darci had been tortured repeatedly. The lawyers blamed "friends of Chico" for the killing. One said that only the CIA could have planned such a careful assassination. "Xapuri is full of foreign agents now," he wrote in a document presented in his clients' defense. Who has benefited? the lawyer asked. Outside interests and those who oppose the development of the Amazon.

Pretrial hearings began on February 10, and a parade of witnesses entered the Xapuri courthouse, which was packed with Mendes's supporters and the press. The alleged murder weapon, which had been found leaning against a tree at a ranch next to Darly's property, was admitted as evidence. The forensic evidence was presented. Finally, the judge, Adair Longhini, found that there was sufficient reason to try Darci and Darly for the murder. Everyone in a position of authority—from Longhini to Governor Melo—concluded that the murder was a personal matter, a crime of Darly Alves and his family and no one else. On February 28, 1989, the Federal Police withdrew from the Chico Mendes case. Romeu Tuma declared that the evidence against Darci and Darly was clear-cut. Now it was time for the prosecutor to take over.

But many in Acre felt that the investigation had not gone nearly far enough. The Chico Mendes Committee, representing PT, the Pastoral Land Commission, and other activists, charged that more people were involved in the murder and continued to publicize gaps in the case. No one had questioned the doctor, Efraim Mendoza, even though he had confirmed to Bishop Grechi what he had heard at the card game in the back room of the Rio Branco Soccer Club. Both the bishop and Eva Evangelista, the president of Acre's Tribunal of Justice, received death threats in the days after the Mendes killing. Evangelista's daughter, Gilcely, had received two phone calls within twenty minutes in which a man speaking cultivated Portuguese said, "Tell Doctor Eva that I am well paid to make this phone call and she shouldn't work on the Chico Mendes case or her head will roll just like the head of Chico rolled."

Another lead that was never pursued concerned *O Rio Branco,* the newspaper of João Branco, the UDR president, and his right-wing partners. The same paper that had warned Acreanos about a pending 200-megaton explosion had had two reporters and a photographer at Mendes's house ninety minutes after the murder, even though the rutted road between its office in Rio Branco and Xapuri makes anything less than a three-hour trip a miracle. That same night, it had taken the chief investigator on the case, Nilson Alves de Oliveira, six hours to make the trip.

When the reporters pulled up in front of the Mendes house, they boasted about their speedy arrival. A soldier from the Military Police found their story incredible and felt the hood of the car. It was hardly warm, and the front of the car showed no sign of mud or damage. The next day, the paper had a carefully crafted front-page package on the Mendes killing, complete with a photograph of the corpse laid out in Xapuri's hospital, its right side riddled with holes. There was also a first-person account of the enterprising reporters' race to Xapuri, in which they changed a tire, sipped a beer, struck a cow—and still got the *furo,* the scoop. It seemed clear that the reporters had been tipped off in advance.

The twenty-seven-year-old editor of the paper, Júlio César Fialho —one of the reporters who sped to Xapuri—fled from Acre on February 13 in a car rented to *O Rio Branco.* When he turned up in Brasília in May, he said he feared that his bosses, João Branco and his partners, were going to kill him because he knew too much; Branco in turn charged that Fialho stole the car and sold the newspaper's exclusive photographs of Mendes's corpse to a photo agency for $3,000. Fialho was also never questioned by the police.

Despite these lapses, compared to most murder cases in the Amazon, the Mendes case was proceeding at a blistering pace and was remarkably successful; after all, the principal suspects had surrendered and damning evidence and testimony had been compiled. Even so, most citizens of Xapuri still assumed, like Sebastião Alves, that Darly and Darci would never come to trial. And although Oloci and Darci were also charged with the shootings at the forestry office in May 1988, it was doubtful that that case would be heard either. Even with all the pressure from outside forces, the cases seemed to be falling into the familiar tropical rhythm of Amazon justice: they were slowly disintegrating, like a tree trunk rotting on the forest floor.

The date of the trial was pushed farther into 1989 and then 1990 as the defense lawyers sought a change of venue to Rio Branco and filed one appeal after another to try to get the charges dropped. They had an easy time controlling the pace of the proceedings. Xapuri still had only a part-time prosecutor, and three different people filled the position in 1989. The last one, Eliseu de Oliveira, knew almost nothing of the Mendes case and seemed disinclined to open new lines of inquiry. Indeed, he never understood what all the fuss had been about. As he told one visitor, "The fact is, everybody knew Chico Mendes was going to be killed sooner or later."

At the same time, potential witnesses began to die. One of Darly's *pistoleiros,* nicknamed Zezão—who may have helped plan the killing—was shot dead in January 1989. The Alveses claimed that Zezão was shot by Mendes's brother Assis (who is an officer in the Military Police), but Mendes's allies said it was the Alves family performing the old Brazilian custom of "burning the files." Both of the bodyguards who had been at the card game in Rio Branco turned up dead the following year in separate incidents. Early in the morning after Xapuri's São Sebastião festival in January 1990, José Britto was gunned down by someone on a passing motorcycle. Britto was the former rubber tapper who had sold his *colocação* at Seringal Cachoeira to Darly. Investigators said his murder was probably related to testimony he gave which confirmed that Oloci Alves had a pistol at the time of the forestry office shooting.

Media interest in the Mendes case quickly faded after the first few months, as did the energy of the police investigators. Nilson Alves de Oliveira, a highly trained former paratrooper and judo instructor, at first had diligently tried to check new leads. But by the end of 1989—just as he claimed to be closing in on links between Gaston Mota and the murder—he left Xapuri for a new, unrelated job in Rio Branco. "I have to think of my family," he said.

To top it all off, the Rio Branco penitentiary in which Darly,

Darci, and Oloci were being held was hardly secure. Only ten guards oversaw two hundred and forty prisoners, with a single guard on duty at night. The budget was so meager that the warden often had to use his own car to pick up bread from the bakery. One guard told a visitor that the going price for an escape in 1989 was $800. In August of 1989, a nephew of Darly's who was serving eight years on a murder conviction escaped with twenty other prisoners while the guards watched Brazil play Chile in a soccer match on television.

One week later, Darly walked into a holding room at the penitentiary to meet with two visitors. The window was wide open, yet had no bars. A breeze filled the room with smoke from the trash fires at a nearby sawmill. A guard, wearing civilian clothes and carrying a revolver, stood in the hall outside the door. Darly looked older than his fifty-nine years. His shirt, open to the waist, hung loosely on his thin shoulders, and his sockless feet rattled in ankle-high boots. He scoffed at charges that he had ordered the Mendes killing. "I had nothing to do with it. Two or three times, I saw Chico on the street—before he had any bodyguards. If I wanted to, I could have killed him right then. Instead, I put my hand on his shoulder and said, 'Chico, you can sleep in the middle of the street. I don't have anything against you. What's done is done.'"

He said that a man would be crazy to send a son to do such a job. "Do you really think that with three or four bodyguards around someone I'd tell my son to just go and kill him? Darci could easily have been killed himself." And Jardeir had just moved north from Paraná a few weeks earlier to join his brothers. What would he have to do with such a crime?

"I'm in jail now because I decided to be here," Darly said. "I could have run like my brother. I have places to stay in Espírito Santo, Mato Grosso, Paraná. I didn't surrender because I was afraid; I did it to save my family and friends from all this persecution by the police. The Military Police took all my wives and put them in the same house and two of them don't like each other. They took all the food from the ranch and left nothing for my wives to eat." Another reason he gave up was that one of his lawyers, Rubens Torres, told him that it would be difficult for the prosecution to convict him. "My lawyer said, 'Darly, keep your head cool, put up your hammock, and rock. In a little while you can buy a fancy pickup, relax, and run your life easier.'"

Before he returned to his cell, Darly said, "Look, if you ask me who killed Chico, I think it's people from PT. The people who gained from this are Chico's friends, the ones who were close to him. These people knew his value. I didn't know it. I don't think anybody really knew."

On December 30, 1989, what Chico Mendes's friends feared the most nearly happened. Someone had smuggled two revolvers to the Alveses. When the police received an anonymous tip about the weapons, the warden called the Alveses into his office and had their belongings searched while he met with them. On the way back to their cells, Darci and Oloci overpowered a guard, took his pistol, and the three ran out the front gate. They were only recaptured because Darly, now chronically ill, could barely walk, and had to be half carried along by his sons. The Alveses were moved to a common cell, their punishment thirty days' confinement.

As this book goes to press, no trial date has been set. The case against Darly is thought by lawyers to be very weak, based entirely on hearsay. And, despite continuing doubts—such as a cool hood on a speeding car—the prosecutors clearly have no interest in discovering if anyone else in Acre was linked to the murder of Mendes. Darly's health has deteriorated and he has been moved to a hospital in Rio Branco, where nothing but a lone police guard stands between him and freedom.

Although the murder of Chico Mendes did little to change the way justice is administered in the Amazon, it did much to improve prospects that large tracts of the rain forest might be saved for the people living there. In a way, Mendes contradicted his prime directive: in death, he accomplished even more than he had while alive.

The improvements did not come immediately. In fact, the situation got worse before it got better. On January 3, 1989, Senator Robert Kasten gave a well-intentioned floor speech in which he lamented the loss of Mendes. But one line backfired when it was reported in Brazil. In describing the rain forests, Kasten said, "The fact is, we need them and we use them—so they're our rain forests, too." Brazilian officials thundered that the United States and Europe wanted to make the Amazon into a "green Persian Gulf." Said the foreign minister, "Brazil will not see itself turned into a botanical garden for the rest of humanity."

U.S. Senators Albert Gore, Jr., John Heinz, and Timothy E. Wirth headed a delegation that flew to Acre to talk with rubber tapper leaders and Governor Melo. Melo told them about his dream to complete BR-364 all the way to the Peruvian border and then across the Andes to the Pacific. A mistake by the senators' interpreter caused them to leave thinking that a deal had been cut with Japan to complete the road (in fact, Melo had used the conditional tense, saying said he would welcome such a move). Back in Washington, the senators lashed out against Brazil's damaging development policies. Their trip focused added attention on the rain forest, but it also fomented latent Brazilian nationalism.

The attention of the media drifted away from the murder of Mendes and the goals for which he had been fighting and turned to more trivial pursuits—such as the battle over which studio would made a movie of Mendes's life and which widow would reap the benefits. Ilzamar battled privately with the leadership of the rubber tappers' council and unions, and battled in the courts with Mendes's first wife, Eunice, over who would profit from such a film.

The tappers' movement seemed to flounder—and if the goal of Mendes's killers was to reverse the momentum of the peoples of the forest, they temporarily succeeded. Environmental groups in the United States were quick to appeal for contributions to help the tappers, but slow to send the money to Brazil. There was a lingering feeling that as soon as international attention disappeared entirely and shifted to some new cause, the chain saws would start up again. Indeed, in some parts of the Amazon, the saws had never stopped buzzing. In the huge state of Amazonas, which contains the greatest remaining undisturbed stretches of rain forest, the governor, Amazonino Mendes, was keeping a campaign promise by giving away six thousand chain saws to groups of peasant families. "Bringing agricultural technology to the small farmer" is how he described it.

Despite the initial confusion and squabbling, serious support for the tappers and their Indian allies began to grow again. Heightened interest in the plight of the Amazon produced a large audience in February 1989, when Indians from thirty-seven tribes gathered at the Transamazon highway town of Altamira. There, wearing war paint and wielding machetes and clubs, they confronted government officials to protest the pending construction of the Altamira-Xingu dam, which would flood almost 25,000 square miles of Indian land. A month later—in a meeting that Chico Mendes had planned—two hundred rubber tappers and Indians convened in Rio Branco to celebrate formally the Alliance of the Peoples of the Forest.

In Acre, a fledgling state agricultural technology agency was given a million-dollar annual budget to help the tappers boost their rubber and nut production and devise ways for enriching the bounty on a rubber trail by planting carefully selected commercial crops, such as pepper, coffee, and cocoa, in the existing forest. The need to develop alternative sources of income was crucial; the subsidy propping up the price for Amazon rubber was bound to be cut as Brazil entered a new era of fiscal austerity to combat inflation and reduce its debt. A university in Goiás received funding to establish a research center for the study of Indian cultivation techniques and uses of plants.

The rubber tappers of Acre also received a commitment for more funding from the Netherlands Embassy, more support from the Ford Foundation, and a chance for a five-year, $5 million grant from Canada. Entrepreneurs with a conscience were lured to the Amazon, hoping to develop everything from body oils to pharmaceuticals based on products taken from the rain forest in ecologically sound ways. Ben & Jerry's Homemade, Inc., introduced Rainforest Crunch, an ice cream containing Brazil nuts harvested by Acre's rubber tappers.

With his unpopular term coming to an end, President José

Sarney was eager to leave behind some sort of positive legacy, so he enacted a series of long-delayed environmental programs. The main effort, called Our Nature, fused many government offices into an overarching environmental protection agency. He pledged to create more extractive reserves and national parks and unveiled an ecological zoning plan for Amazonia. Brazil leased eight helicopters to patrol for illegal cutting and burning. In the first month of that operation, fines totaling $10 million were handed out. The Brazilian space agency devised a system for using the fire-spotting ability of American satellites to alert the forestry patrols. Despite the commitment of technology, the program was uneven; as helicopters flew over accessible parts of the Amazon basin, in a remote western corner of Acre, one forestry official did not have $40 he needed to charter a dugout canoe to head up the Juruá River to check on a report of illegal tree cutting.

Another positive development was a dramatic drop in the number of killings of rural union leaders. Mendes had been one of forty-eight rural workers and activists murdered in the Amazon in 1988; in 1989, less than half that number were killed. Human rights groups were cautiously optimistic, but the possibility remained that the right-wing ranchers were merely biding their time.

The most dramatic changes of all occurred in March of 1990. Brazil's entire environmentalist and human rights community had held its breath to see what kind of cabinet would be chosen by President-elect Fernando Collor de Mello. Collor was a wealthy, conservative businessman from the northeast who had long been sympathetic to the cause of the Amazon's ranchers and gold miners. But, on March 2, in a move that stunned environmentalists from Rio to Washington, Collor announced that the new position of secretary of the environment would be filled by José Lutzenberger, perhaps the most outspoken environmentalist in Brazil.

It was an improbable alliance: between an adherent of free-wheeling, free-market capitalism and a leading voice of the Gaia movement, which posits that the earth is a single organism whose parts are in delicate balance. In several meetings before the selection, Lutzenberger had insisted, as a condition of accepting the position, that Collor cancel plans to complete BR-364 across Acre to the Pacific. The announcement coincided with the World Bank's approval of a $117 million loan to Brazil—this time to help pay for environmental research, education, and conservation programs.

Finally, perhaps, a Brazilian president was recognizing the folly of Brazil's old *asfaltamento* policy toward the Amazon. On a world tour before his inauguration, Collor heard familiar criticisms of Brazil from environmentalists in Europe, including Prince Charles. The prince chided Brazil for allowing thousands of gold miners to invade the territory of the imperiled Yanomami tribe of Roraima —the largest unassimilated culture in South America. But Collor gave a surprising response: he agreed and promised him that the Yanomami's land rights would be respected. And he urged world leaders to come to Brasília in 1992 for the United Nations Conference on Environment and Development. Environmentalists were heartened but still wary. There was always the possibility that Collor was *jogando para a torcida*, playing to the crowd.

The appointment of Chico Mendes's old ally as environmental czar might have seemed a fitting legacy of Mendes's battle, but more surprises were in store. On March 12, 1990, three days before Sarney's term expired, his environmental chief, Fernando César Mesquita, convinced him to sign decrees creating three extractive reserves encompassing 6,553 square miles of forest in Acre, Rondônia, and the eastern Amazon state of Amapá. (In January, Mesquita had created a 2,000-square-mile reserve on the Juruá.) An act of Congress was required to nullify the decrees. Moreover, if a rancher claimed to hold the title to the land, he had to prove the validity of his document; tappers no longer had to undertake the difficult process of proving that they had squatter's rights. Mary Allegretti and Osmarino Rodrigues, secretary of the National Council of Rubber Tappers, had spent weeks in Brasília trying to convince military officials to approve Mesquita's plan. Their hope was that the reserves were large enough that the Acreano tappers who had fled to Bolivia could now come home.

No one expected that extractive reserves alone could save the Amazon; the problems, like the region itself, were enormous and variegated. A mosaic of solutions would be required rather than a simplistic grid. After all, there were already more miners in the Amazon—perhaps a million—than rubber tappers and Indians combined. And there were twenty times as many cattle as people. But the reserves were a giant step in the right direction.

The new Acre reserve alone made eighteen *seringais* federal property, with deforestation banned and the right of sustainable use granted to the tappers. It stretched from the forests where Chico Mendes had grown up north to Rio Branco and west to Sena Madureira. Its name was Reserva Extrativista Chico Mendes. When Rodrigues sent word back to Acre that even the generals had agreed to the plan, there was dancing in the forest.

On Seringal Cachoeira, people remarked about how accurate a tapper named José had been when he composed a song a few months after the murder of Mendes. The lyrics went, "Last Christmas tasted like bile. But next Christmas will taste like honey, because Chico Mendes is going to send many gifts through Santa Claus." The gifts now were pouring down like a tropical cloudburst.

Even so, the tappers' joy was muted. Acre's ranchers were not expected to give up without a fight. Indeed, after the decrees were signed, a tapper heard some ranchers in the Rio Branco airport plotting to burn down every union hall. Everyone waited nervously for the arrival of the next burning season.

Perhaps most remarkable, though, at least initially, the matchup of Collor and Lutzenberger seemed to be working. On March 24, Collor made his first trip as president—a helicopter tour with Lutzenberger of the devastation wrought by Roraima's miners. After he looked down at the dozens of airstrips that had been carved into the forest, Collor told Romeu Tuma, the Federal Police chief, "Dynamite them, and be quick about it."

Not all of the developments of significance occurred in Brasília. Back in the forest, two events had the rubber tappers saying that Chico Mendes was looking down and smiling. In Xapuri, late in 1989, the rubber tappers' cooperative moved from a cramped, di-

lapidated warehouse to its new home along the riverfront, a grand
old building that formerly belonged to one of Acre's biggest rub-
ber-trading families, Hadad. The building had a green art deco
façade and great swinging doors, just like the warehouse down the
way that belonged to Cachoeira's old boss, Guilherme Zaire. Huge
storerooms in the back were soon piled high with balls and slabs of
good-quality rubber waiting to be trucked to the factories of the
south. The cooperative's flatbed truck, the one that Mendes had
driven around town the day he was gunned down, sat out front, its
chrome gleaming.

The front room of the warehouse was stacked with bags of beans
and rice and boxes of textbooks, medicine, pads, and pencils, bound
for the schoolhouses out on the *seringais*. At a desk in the rear of
the room, the members of the cooperative made their entries in a
big ledger—just like the books the estate bosses once used to keep
track of the tappers' debts. Space was cleared for a $20,000 Brazil
nut processing and packing machine that had been bought with
profits from the sale of Rainforest Crunch. If all went well, Brazil
nuts hulled with the machine would soon make their way directly
to the ice cream maker, bypassing the middlemen who had cheated
the tappers for so long.

And on August 12, 1989, on the upper reaches of the Juruá River
in western Acre, rubber tappers in an isolated village cheered the
arrival of an aging riverboat with a nameplate that still read *Al-
essandra* but soon was to be changed to *Chico Mendes*. On board
was a delegation of rubber tappers, Indians, and advisers who had
come to a meeting to recruit members for the region's new cooperative. More than one hundred tappers were there, having been
notified by a local radio station, Radio Green Forests. They had
come by canoe or on foot, eager to find a way out of the grip of the
bosses. On the Juruá, the issue was not yet deforestation and land
grabbing, as it was in eastern Acre; it was still *aviamento*.

The delegation was headed by Antonio Macedo, a leader of the
local movement who was living proof that the grass-roots work
Mendes had done in eastern Acre was continuing. Macedo was
proof, too, that the dangers that Mendes had faced persisted. On

March 7, 1989, when a *jagunço* came at Macedo with a revolver, the attacker's hand was blown off by Macedo's shotgun-toting body-guard.

The four-day trip upriver had been slow and hazardous. The 55-foot boat, a recent gift of the Netherlands Embassy, frequently got hung up on sunken tree trunks or sandbars, requiring eight or ten men to jump into the water and heave it free. After it had hit yet another sandbar and lay canted on its side, one passenger, a São Paulo artist named Rubens Matuck, lowered his binoculars. He was illustrating a children's book on the rain forest and had been scanning the trees for flowers and birds. Idly watched the swirling current pass the immobilized hull, Matuck said with a smile, "This boat is a bit like Brazil. It's leaking. It keeps stopping and starting. Sometimes it goes in circles. But slowly, somehow, it keeps moving upstream."

When the boat finally arrived at the village of Marechal Tau-maturgo—named after a hero of the uprising that gave Acre to Brazil—the tappers set off fireworks in celebration. Here was the movement as it had been in Xapuri when Chico Mendes started to build a union.

Everyone gathered that night on the steps in front of the town hall. The electricity had come on at 4:00 P.M., as it did most days. This was one of those odd Amazon towns that still lacked running water and plumbing but had electricity and a few color televisions that became beacons each evening, attracting dozens of villagers with their glow, just as the street lights attracted thousands of moths. Macedo acted as the master of ceremonies and, using a crackly public address system, told the assembled tappers about the union, the National Council of Rubber Tappers.

"I came from this forest," said Macedo, a small, muscular man with warped gold-framed glasses that always threatened to topple from his nose. He had a mop of tightly curled gold-brown hair and the heavy shoulders and thick arms of a stevedore—acquired from years of hauling slabs of rubber. "I'm not from Cuba, as some bosses say. I am a worker like you are." The audience roared its apprecia-tion as he spoke of better health care, schools, and—most of all—

freedom from the tyranny of debt. He was followed by the local monitor for the union, an earnest young rubber tapper named Francisco Xavier de Ramos. "All these people here are fighting for the environment. If you don't know what the environment is, it is the place where man and the animals live together."

Late into the night, the tappers and their families and these visitors from the outside world drank beer and *cachaça,* talked about the future and the past, and danced the sinuous, sensual *forró* (pronounced fo-*haw*), the rough, upcountry version of the *lambada,* which was about to sweep Europe as the latest sexy dance craze. The music was simple and happy. It had the beat of Louisiana Cajun and was played with the same instrumentation: fiddle, triangle, and accordion. Some inebriated voices strayed on the high notes, but everyone was smiling and not one song was played in a minor key.

Three tappers sat in a row on a cement curb near the square, watching the *forró* band and the dancers, whose hips were locked together and swiveling in impossible synchrony. One of the tappers, João Gonzaga, had traveled by canoe for two days. It was less than a year since he had first met with tappers from other parts of the river to talk about the union and cooperatives. It had been a revelation that so many others shared his problems and sought a solution. He was sitting with his brother Sebastião and a friend, Antonio, whose growth was stunted and body misshapen. João said that before the National Council of Rubber Tappers had come up the river, they had had no idea of their rights. Now they had stopped paying rent for their trails and started buying their goods from the cooperative at fair prices. He was also excited that there were plans to build the first school on a *seringal.* "We are like blind people because we cannot read and write," João said. "For me, the National Council of Rubber Tappers is really the national council of liberty."

João and the other tappers talked well past midnight, until the generators were turned off. The air had begun to chill, and condensing mist thickened over the river and flowed into the village. It was nearly a full moon; there was supposed to be an eclipse in a couple of days. João told one last story, about the wonders of the forest that made them want to stay.

At dusk one evening, he was walking home along an *estrada*, surrounded by the buzz of cicadas and whoops of night birds. He did not like to hunt and so was carrying only a small, dull knife. That is why he became nervous when he heard some large animal crashing in the brush up ahead. He crept forward and in the dim half light saw a large jaguar—the biggest he had ever seen. He froze and watched as the jaguar circled and then lay down, completely blocking the trail and oblivious of his presence. The jaguar lazily rolled over, stretched, and twisted from side to side, scratching its back.

João realized that the jaguar had no intention of hurting him, and he had no intention of hurting the jaguar. But it was getting late, and he needed to get home. Finally, he held his dull knife ready, just in case, and spoke to the animal: "Jaguar, I need to pass." The cat leaped from the trail and vanished into the forest.

Just before everyone wandered off to find a place to string a hammock, João's friend Antonio tried to imagine the world that the ranchers wanted to create, the world of open spaces that had already appeared in eastern Acre and was just starting to eat at the jungle along the Juruá. He could not imagine it; his forested world was so complete that any alternative was unthinkable. "If they cut the trees how can anyone live?" Antonio asked. "Can you imagine a country that has only pasture and cattle, without trees and man?" He did not even consider the possibility that there might be men who were able to live outside the forest. "That is no country. Nothing will grow there. There is no game there. The ranchers will die in that kind of country."

For him, and, he hoped, for his children, the forest was home. Here was the fundamental bond between a man and his environment that had been the basis for Chico Mendes's own passionate defense of the Amazon. It was an intimate connection, transcending global considerations and political battles and personal conflicts. "The life of the tapper is very hard," Antonio said. "But it is much better than the life in the towns. It won't be easy, even with the cooperative. We have to start our lives from the beginning. But we need to try. It's hard for me to be outside the forest. When I went down the river to the city once, I started to get a big pain in my head. It only went away when I came back and was on my trail going home."

Afterword

I RETURNED TO Xapuri in December of 1990 to cover the murder trial of Darly Alves and his son Darci for the Brazilian newspaper *O Globo*. Dozens of journalists converged on the town once again, just as they had in the days following the shooting of Chico Mendes two years earlier. Once again, the cheap hotels overflowed. The phone company frantically installed a communications center in the old Bolivian customs house overlooking the river.

Rubber tappers arrived by canoe, bus, and truck to stand vigil outside the stucco courthouse. Behind a cordon of blue-uniformed police, tappers held banners calling for justice and children sold pink tufts of cotton candy. Up and down the brick lanes, merchants sold portraits of Mendes painted on black velvet, silkscreened on shirts, and emblazoned on buttons.

Crammed with several hundred spectators, the courthouse became a hot house. The only air conditioner was in the judge's private chambers, and the ceiling fans did little except redistribute the steamy air. The judges and lawyers wilted under their stiff black robes and tight white collars. In the hard-backed benches sat Mendes's young widow, Ilzamar, his brother Zuza, and many of the rubber tappers who were struggling to run the union and sustain Mendes's vision.

Standing near an open window were Mendes's allies from

outside the rain forest—Mary Allegretti and Stephan Schwartzman. Adrian Cowell's cameras ran once more. Sitting a few rows
ahead of the tappers and their allies was Darly Alves's wife, surrounded by a grim-faced collection of friends and cowboys from
the Alves ranch. Twice a day, the judge allowed a small army of
photographers to invade. They rushed in en masse—a bizarre
kind of multilegged monster, bristling with glass eyes, flash bulbs
flaring.

The trial was remarkable in three ways. First, a jury was not
only assembled, but showed up. The prevailing rumor in Xapuri
was that the jurors would flee rather than sit in judgment of the
Alves family. But there they were: an accountant, a bank teller, a
teacher, and the rest. The middle class of Xapuri seemed determined to put an end to anarchy. Day after day, they sat to the
right of the judge, stiff and resolute, listening to endless hours of
droning testimony.

The second remarkable development was the verdict. Almost
precisely two years after Mendes was felled by a shotgun blast, the
jury found both father and son guilty of murder. Third was the
sentence—nineteen years each. For the first time in the long,
bloody history of the Amazon, both a *pistoleiro* and a *mandante*—
the shooter and the mastermind of a crime—received the same
prison term.

Initially, it appeared as if justice were finally coming to the rain
forest, where violence against man and nature had gone
unchecked for decades. The tappers rejoiced, but their elation was
short-lived. Within months, Darly Alves's conviction was over-
turned on appeal. He only remained in prison to face the old
murder charges dating from his days in the south of Brazil.

Elsewhere in the Amazon—albeit at a reduced pace—the
killings continued. On February 2, 1991, just two months after
the trial in Xapuri, Expedito Ribeiro de Souza, a union leader in
the state of Pará, was shot dead. Shortly afterward, his successor,
Carlos Cabral, was shot in the thigh. On March 8 and 9, two
more union leaders were attacked. José Alves de Souza was shot

three times but survived. Sebastião Ribeiro da Silva died where he fell, on the floor of his home.

The region made headlines again in the summer of 1992, when Brazil hosted the Earth Summit and more than 150 world leaders signed agreements calling for forest protection and efforts to stem global warming. Brazil boasted that the rate of cutting and burning in the Amazon had dropped by more than half from the devastating peak reached before Mendes's death. Critics charged that the change was more a result of Brazil's paralyzed economy than a result of any new environmental policies. And even at the slowed rate, an area of rain forest twice the size of Delaware was being cut and burned every year.

The deep recession had a direct impact on the rubber tappers as well. Prices for rubber and Brazil nuts were too low to produce a profit. The Xapuri cooperative had built a nut-processing plant that, with 140 workers, was the town's biggest employer. Nonetheless, the operation continued to lose money. With some new initiatives, such as a partnership, with Deja Shoe—an American company marketing boots and shoes made with Amazon rubber—the tappers are continuing to test ways to make a living from the living forest. But the challenges are daunting.

Finally, the inevitable happened. In February 1993 plans were under way to transfer Darly Alves from the Amazon prison in southern Brazil. The special treatment he had received in the Acre state penitentiary would be a memory, and the prisons in the south were far more secure. With half a dozen other inmates, Alves and his son cut through the flimsy bars of a window and fled in a waiting truck toward the Bolivian border.

★Alves and his son were recaptured in 1996 and sent to more secure penitentiaries. They were eventually released on probation after serving less than half of their 19-year sentences. Alves moved to a different part of the Amazon. In 2003, officials in Acre reopened the murder investigation to examine the evidence hinting that others knew of, or aided in, the murder plot. No one else has been prosecuted as of this printing.

★A.R. August, 2004

NOTES

APPENDICES

Map of South America, Brazil, and the Amazon

The Murder Scene

A Resource Guide

ACKNOWLEDGMENTS

Notes

Chapter 1. The Burning Season

Details of the murder came from dozens of interviews with Chico Mendes's neighbors, relatives, and bodyguards; testimony given by witnesses during pretrial hearings; transcripts of interviews conducted by the local and federal police; and the autopsy report. Ilzamar Mendes initially claimed to reporters that both bodyguards immediately fled from the murder scene. But all of the neighbors who witnessed the incident confirm the guards' story: Roldão Lucas da Cruz ran to get help; Roldão Roseno de Souza stayed with Chico Mendes.

Chapter 2. Amazonia

This chapter drew in part on the articles gathered in what is perhaps the most comprehensive and lucid book describing the biology, geology, and almost every other aspect of the Amazon basin: *Key Environments: Amazonia* (Oxford: Pergamon Press, 1985), edited by Ghillean T. Prance and Thomas E. Lovejoy.

The book that best conveys the subtle yet spectacular ecology and physiology of the rain forest's biota—from sloths to strangler figs—is *Tropical Nature: Life and Death in the Rain Forests of Central and South America,* by Adrian Forsyth and Kenneth Miyata (New York: Scribners, 1984).

An earlier *Tropical Nature,* by Alfred Russel Wallace (New York: Macmillan, 1878), provides one of the first attempts to comprehend the workings of the rain forest. *The Naturalist on the River Amazons* (London, 1863; New York: Penguin Books, 1989), by Wallace's collecting companion, Henry Walter Bates, is one of the most spellbinding early descriptions of the river and its environs—and it is much easier to find than Wallace's book, having been reissued in paperback.

The Primary Source: Tropical Forests and Our Future, by Norman Myers (New York: Norton, 1985), is an excellent overview, dense with facts, of the wonders of the world's rain forests and their precarious situation. A compelling personal exploration of this ecosystem is contained in *In the Rainforest,* by Catherine Caufield (New York: Knopf, 1985).

Chapter 3. Weeping Wood

The Discovery of the Amazon, edited by José Toribio Medina (New York: Dover, 1988), includes the full translated account of Orellana's voyage by Friar Caspar de Carvajal as well as extensive related references. Rich details of life along the Amazon in the years just before the rubber boom are contained in William H. Edwards's *A Voyage up the River Amazon, Including a Residence at Pará* (London: John Murray, 1847).

The history of the human occupation of the basin is contained in *People of the Tropical Rain Forest* (Berkeley: University of California Press, 1988), an oversize, lushly illustrated survey of rain forest cultures edited by Julie Sloan Denslow and Christine Padoch.

Two American scholars have added great detail to the picture of the rubber boom and subsequent bust. In *The Amazon Rubber Boom, 1850–1920* (Stanford, Calif.: Stanford University Press, 1983), Barbara Weinstein describes the remarkable rush into the rain forest and then the abandonment of the tappers. Warren Dean's *Brazil and the Struggle for Rubber* (Cambridge, England: Cambridge University Press, 1987) has a broader scope, detailing the saga through World War II. *Amazon Frontier: The Defeat of the Brazilian Indians* (Cambridge, Mass.: Harvard University Press, 1987), by John Hemming, provides additional background on the rubber boom, particularly its disastrous effect on the Indians. Finally, a thoroughly researched history of rubber—including the crucial invention of vulcanization—is contained in Austin Coates's *The Commerce in Rubber: The First 250 Years* (New York: Oxford University Press, 1987).

A chronicle of the persistent folly of those who would exploit the Amazon is contained in *The Fate of the Forest: Developers, Destroyers, and Defenders of the Amazon* (London: Verso Books, 1989), by Susanna Hecht and Alexander Cockburn. Jonathan Kandell's *Passage Through El Dorado: Traveling the World's Last Great Wilderness* (New York: Morrow, 1984) describes the perpetual allure of the Amazon and includes a scene in which the author is sitting with the rubber baron Guilherme Zaire and chances to encounter a local tapper leader named Chico.

Chapter 4. Jungle Book

Warren Dean's book (see Chapter 3) describes the situation during World War II in depth. He cites an American document, quoted herein, that sums up the exploitative system of *aviamento* in fewer yet better words than can be found anywhere else. Some material in this chapter is drawn from the work of Malu Maranhão, a reporter for *Folha de Londrina*, who began writing about the rubber tappers in the dry season of 1988 and interviewed some remarkable aging veterans of the war for rubber. The rubber soldier ballads were sung to me by Dona Antonia, who runs the only really good restaurant in Xapuri and who was Chico Mendes's favorite cook. Details on Mendes's childhood and life on the *seringal* were gleaned from days of hiking the same trails he once frequented and interviewing tappers who were relatives or friends.

Details on the design and construction of a rubber tapper's home are contained in Liliane Robacher's *Habitação Amazonica* (Paraná, Brazil: Editora Universitaria Champagnat, 1983).

The threat posed by some forest species was made apparent to me when I slipped on a log catwalk, reached out for the nearest tree, and whipped my hand back in agony; three *Astrocaryum* spines had embedded themselves in my palm, and one had plunged into one side of the fleshy part of a fingertip and come out on the other. Then there was the stingray I trod on while stepping out of a canoe. Luckily its spine missed my foot. Tappers say the pain is so bad that "even a strong man cries out for his mother."

Chapter 5. Coming of Age in the Rain Forest

The reclusiveness of Chico Mendes's mentor, Euclides Távora, resulted in persistent confusion about details of his life. Mendes himself contributed a little to the uncertainty. In the last year of Mendes's life, when his international work started to attract the attention of journalists from around the world, he always said he had been eighteen when he met Távora in 1962. But more than half a dozen people, including Mendes's neighbors, Távora's wife, and his closest friends insist that this man's influence on Mendes dated from a much earlier age. Interviews with Neuza Ramos Pereira and Francisco Siqueira de Aquino helped clear things up.

The lives of important Brazilian figures such as Luís Carlos Prestes, "the Horseman of Hope," and Getúlio Vargas are richly chronicled in a series of excellent volumes by John W. F. Dulles: *Vargas of Brazil: A Political Biography; Anarchists and Communists in Brazil, 1900–1935;* and *Brazilian Communism, 1935–1945* (Austin: University of Texas Press, 1967, 1973, and 1983). Descriptions of the prisoners' life on Fernando de Noronha Island were drawn from the last book. Also recommended is John Gunther's *Inside Latin America*, which has a rich profile of Vargas (New York: Harper & Brothers, 1941).

Chapter 6. Roads to Ruin

Two detailed collections of papers on the occupation of the Amazon have resulted from conferences organized by the Center for Latin American Studies of the University of Florida, Gainesville: *Man in the Amazon,* edited by Charles Wagley, and *Frontier Expansion in Amazonia,* edited by Marianne Schmink and Charles H. Wood (Gainesville: University of Florida Press, 1974 and 1984, respectively). And another indispensable book is *The Last Frontier: Fighting Over Land in the Amazon* (London: Zed Books, 1985). In it, Sue Branford and Oriel Glock provide both a thoroughly reported overview of the human impact of Brazil's development policies and case studies that portray the Amazon's ranchers, businessmen, and colonists. One such account, the sad tale of the São Paulo businessman Carlos Vilela de Andrade, is referred to in this chapter.

I also refer to René Dubos's book-length essay *The Wooing of Earth*

(New York: Scribners, 1980), which in hopeful tones describes how human beings occasionally have shown a capacity to live within nature's laws. The list of American towns that once held the title "Timber Capital of the World" was drawn from *Clearcut: The Deforestation of America* (San Francisco: Sierra Club, 1971), by Nancy Wood. The World Bank pamphlet "Government Policies and Deforestation in Brazil's Amazon Region" (1989), by Dennis J. Mahar, has an excellent overview of the issue described in its title, as does Robert Repetto's report for the World Resources Institute, "The Forest for the Trees? Government Policies and the Misuse of Forest Resources" (1988). Notably, Repetto's paper has a lengthy section on the ongoing misuse of forests by the United States. Other studies have shown that in Hawaii, for example, the pace of the destruction of the rain forest has exceeded that in Brazil. And Hawaii has the highest species extinction rate on the planet.

The demise of Brazil's Indians is described in detail by John Hemming (see Chapter 3). In this chapter, I quote a telling passage from Claude Lévi-Strauss's *Tristes Tropiques* (New York: Washington Square Press, 1977). Gilio Brunelli's report of the last fight of Brazil's Zóro tribe was published in the *Cultural Survival Quarterly* (vol. 10, no. 2, 1986). Almost any issue of this respected journal contains up-to-date accounts of threats to indigenous cultures. In November 1988, Amnesty International published a detailed report called "Brazil: Cases of Killings and Ill-Treatment of Indigenous People."

Chapter 7. The Fight for the Forest

The arrival of liberation theology, the union movement, and *empates* in Acre are documented in *Conflitos Pela Terra no Acre (Land Conflicts in Acre),* a 1987 master's thesis by Élio Garcia Duarte, at the University of Campinas. Information on the tenure of Governor Dantas came from this thesis and from Branford and Glock (see Chapter 6). Dozens of interviews with rubber tappers were required to piece together the history of the *empate*. More background is available in *Fight for the Forest: Chico Mendes in His Own Words* (London: Latin America Bureau, 1989). Most of the book is an extensive interview Mendes gave one month before he was murdered. Helpful annotation is provided by Tony Gross, who now works for CEDI, the Ecumenical Center for Documentation and Information.

Chapter 8. The Wild West

Interviews with Acre ranchers such as João Branco and Orozinho Villas-Boas gave a clear idea of the cattleman's view of this part of Amazonia. As Branco put it, "In the year 2000, Acre will be another Paraná—lots of soy, lots of cattle. The land here is excellent. There's an expression: 'A beautiful woman never misses the wedding.' The fifty percent that can be knocked down, you can be sure it will be knocked down—by me, the ones after me, and after and after." *Conflitos Pela Terra no Acre* (see previous chapter) documents the arrival of organized violence in Acre.

Details of the killing of Wilson Pinheiro were derived from police records, including many interviews with witnesses, and the medical examiners' report. Other information came from interviews with João Antonio Bronzeado and João Maia, as well as interviews with Pinheiro's daughter Iamar. (Maia, incidentally, went on to be elected to Brazil's Congress.) Information about the Alves family's early days was provided by Genesio Felipe de Natividade, a lawyer who looked into their background while working for the rubber tappers.

Chapter 9. Joining Forces

Mary Allegretti and Tony Gross provided detailed accounts of the early years of the movement. Silvio Martinello, editor of *Gazeta do Acre*, kindly let me peruse the paper's extensive morgue. An interview with the sociologist Regina Bruno, at the Federal University of Rio de Janeiro, helped clarify the history and strategy of the UDR. Also useful were articles by Bruno and José Gomes da Silva in the March 1989 issue of *Tempo e Presença*, the magazine of CEDI, the Ecumenical Center for Documentation and Information.

Lively accounts of the winning of the American West are provided in *Land Grab: The Truth about "The Winning of the West"* (New York: Dial Press, 1972), by John Upton Terrell, and *Gun Law: A Study of Violence in the Wild West* (Chicago: Contemporary Books, 1977), by Joseph G. Rosa and Robin May.

Chapter 10. The Greening of Chico Mendes

For an excellent review of the history of the environmentalists' campaign against the multilateral banks, refer to "Environmental Reform and the Multilateral Banks," *World Policy Journal,* Spring 1988, by Pat Aufderheide and Bruce Rich. David Price's *Before the Bulldozer: The Nambiquara Indians and the World Bank* (Cabin John, Md.: Seven Locks Press, 1989) gives an insider's perspective on the way the World Bank ignored consultants' warnings on the Polonoroeste project.

The descriptions of events at the 1985 meeting of rubber tappers came from extensive interviews with participants and the videotape of the meeting taken by Pró Memória. Also helpful was *Fight for the Forest: Chico Mendes in His Own Words* (see Chapter 7). Stephan Schwartzman's report on the meeting, written with support from the World Wildlife Fund and the Threshold Foundation, was an excellent source.

The extractive reserve was only a vague concept after the 1985 meeting. Several years of legal, economic, and sociological analysis were required before it was refined and given a basis in Brazilian law. There remain many questions about the long-term prospects for these forest communities. Several excellent papers explain the promise of this innovative land-use plan: Mary Allegretti and Stephan Schwartzman, "Extractive Production in the Amazon and the Rubber Tappers' Movement" (Washington, D.C.: Environmental Defense Fund, 1987); Philip M. Fearnside, "Extractive Reserves in Brazilian Amazonia: An Opportunity to Maintain Tropical Rain Forest Under Sustainable Use" (Manaus: National Institute of Amazon Research, October 1988). An important, more skeptical view is presented in "Land-use Strategies for Successful Extractive Economies," presented by Anthony B. Anderson at a National Wildlife Federation symposium, "Extractive Economies in Tropical Forests: A Course of Action" (November 30, 1989).

Chapter 11. An Innocent Abroad

The rising violence and the increased effectiveness of *empates* are described in *Conflitos Pela Terra no Acre* and *Fight for the Forest: Chico Mendes in His Own Words* (see Chapter 7). The Amnesty International report "Brazil: Authorized Violence in Rural Areas" (September 1988) provides an excellent discussion of the surge in killings in rural Brazil after 1985.

Chico Mendes's description of the alliance with the Indians was filmed by Miranda Smith, producer and director of *Chico Mendes: Voice of the Amazon* (a coproduction of Miranda Smith Productions and the Better World Society, 1989).

Some descriptions of Mendes's last election campaign were drawn from Adrian Cowell's documentary "Murder in the Amazon" (a coproduction for *Frontline* of Central Independent Television, the Universidade Católico de Goiás, and WGBH-Boston, 1989).

The relative value of ranching versus the extraction of forest products was estimated by Mary Allegretti and Stephan Schwartzman in "Extractive Reserves: A Sustainable Development Alternative for Amazonia" (Washington, D.C.: World Wildlife Fund, 1987). The income of tappers compared to that of urban poor in the Amazon was calculated by Schwartzman in "Extractive Reserves: The Rubber Tappers' Strategy for Sustainable Use of the Amazon Rain Forest," to be published in *Fragile Lands in Latin America: The Search for Sustainable Uses* (Boulder, Colo.: Westview Press, 1989).

Chapter 12. Into the Fire

The history of the use of satellites to monitor deforestation is laid out in several volumes and articles. Among the most useful are: Roberto Pereira da Cunha, "Deforestation Estimates Through Remote Sensing: The State of the Art in the Legal Amazonia" (São José dos Campos: Brazilian Institute for Space Research, 1989); *Tropical Rain Forests and the Atmosphere* (Boulder, Colo.: Westview Press, 1986), edited by Ghillean T. Prance; and Jean-Paul Malingreau and Compton J. Tucker, "Large-scale Deforestation in the Southeastern Amazon Basin of Brazil," *Ambio*, vol. 17, no. 1, 1988. Alberto Setzer's innovative use of weather satellites to spot fires and his dramatic images of the Amazon on fire were first published in "Relatório de Atividades do Projeto IBDF-INPE" (São José dos Campos: Brazilian Institute for Space Research, 1988) by Setzer et al. Interviews with Tucker and Setzer filled in details.

William Denevan's paper "Development and the Imminent Demise of the Amazon Rain Forest" appeared in 1972 in *The Professional Geogra-*

pher, 25 (2):130–135. Goodland and Irwin's book is *Amazon Jungle: Green Hell to Red Desert?* (Amsterdam: Elsevier, 1975).

The description of the confrontation over Seringal Cachoeira grew out of interviews with people on both sides, ranging from Darly Alves da Silva to the rubber tapper who organized the first *empate* there, Manduca Custódio da Silva. Some information was gleaned from the local papers, *O Rio Branco* and *Gazeta do Acre.*

Accounts of the Alves family's violent past came from court records, police interviews with witnesses such as Genézio Barbosa da Silva, and lawyers for the rubber tappers.

The closing account of Mendes's speeches on *seringais* around Xapuri was drawn from interviews with tappers and from scenes in Adrian Cowell's documentary "Murder in the Amazon" (see Chapter 11).

Chapter 13. The Dying Season

George "Pinky" Nelson generously granted an interview in which he described the Amazon from above. An excellent review of the science and politics of the greenhouse effect—and the media frenzy that began in 1988 —is given in Stephen H. Schneider, *Global Warming: Are We Entering the Greenhouse Century?* (San Francisco: Sierra Club Books, 1989). One newspaper article that was influential in amplifying the connection between the Amazon and the atmosphere appeared on page 1 of the *New York Times* on August 12, 1988: "Vast Amazon Fires, Man-made, Linked to Global Warming," by Marlise Simons.

João Branco's statement about the ranchers' effort to get Mendes out of the headlines was filmed by Miranda Smith (see Chapter 12).

The battle between Mendes and Mauro Spósito is contained in the local newspapers, where it can be seen to start on December 2 and finish the day after Mendes was killed. Spósito added some details as he sat in September 1989 in an office in São Paulo, busy at his new position in charge of passport control. The only evidence that this was not a purely bureaucratic job was the enormous chrome-plated revolver jutting from his secretary's belt. Despite the boring work, Spósito was thrilled to be out of the Amazon and back in the south, where he had been raised. "Things became difficult when Chico accused me in the newspapers, saying I was favoring Darly," he said. "This charge that there was a conspiracy was all politics. Even though I had interrogated Chico in the past, we had a very good relationship. The reason Chico and the bishop came to me with the warrant in the first place is that the Federal Police have a lot of respect. We don't fight with accusations, we deal with documents."

Mendes's last hours were reconstructed in a series of interviews with many of the people whom he saw on December 22—including Gomercindo Rodrigues, his bodyguards, and his friend Dona Maria, who concluded her comments by saying, "*Ave Maria,* I miss him a lot. He didn't deserve what they did to him. I don't know why it's like that: Bad people live long lives, and good people always die young."

BRAZIL
and
SOUTH AMERICA

VENEZUELA
GUYANA
SURINAME
FRENCH
GUIANA

COLOMBIA

RORAIMA

AMAPÁ

ECUADOR

Negro
Manaus
Solimões

Amazon

Belém

PARÁ

RIO GRANDE
DO NORTE

AMAZONAS

Juruá

Purus

Fortaleza
CEARÁ

MARANHÃO

PIAUÍ

PARAÍBA

PERNAMBUCO

ALAGOAS

PERU

ACRE
Rio
Branco

RONDÔNIA

MATO
GROSSO

GOIÁS

BAHIA

SERGIPE

BOLIVIA

Brasília

MINAS
GERAIS

MATO
GROSSO
DO SUL

SÃO
PAULO

ESPÍRITO
SANTO

RIO DE JANEIRO

Rio de Janeiro

PARAGUAY

PARANÁ
Curitiba

São Paulo

SANTA
CATARINA

CHILE

PACIFIC
OCEAN

ARGENTINA

RIO GRANDE
DO SUL

URUGUAY

ATLANTIC
OCEAN

Rio Branco
Xapuri

ACRE

Brasiléia

About half the continent of South America is Brazilian territory, and more
than half of Brazil is in the Amazon basin. Most rubber tappers, including
Chico Mendes, trace their ancestry to the Northeast, particularly the state
of Ceará. Acre is drained by two major river systems, the Juruá and the
Purus.

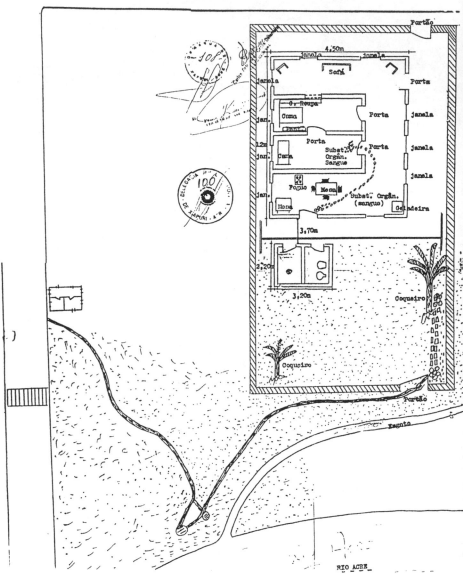

A reconstruction of the murder scene by Brazil's Federal Police shows the trail of bloodstains leading from Chico Mendes's back door into the bedroom. The gunman crouched beside the palm tree in the fenced yard, then escaped through a gate in the fence.

A Resource Guide

Many nonprofit organizations are working to sustain the Amazon rain forest ecosystem and its human inhabitants, including:

Conservation International
1919 M Street, NW Suite 600
Washington, DC 20036
www.conservation.org

Works to conserve Earth's biological diversity and to demonstrate that humans are able to live harmoniously with nature. Focuses on "hot spots," where threats to ecosystems are most severe.

Coordinating Body for Indigenous Organizations of the
    Amazon Basin COICA
Calle Luis Beethoven No. 47-65 y Capitán Rafael Ramos
    Quito, Ecuador
www.coica.org

A network for more than 400 indigenous peoples in Amazonia. Founded in Lima, Peru, in 1982 for native people to fight together to defend their rights and sustain their cultures.

Environmental Defense
257 Park Ave. South
New York, NY 10010
www.environmentaldefense.org

Presses for changes in lending practices by multilateral banks that help make forest preservation part of economic planning. Works with indigenous and rural communities and the government in Brazil to foster sustainable use of the landscape.

Human Rights Watch
350 Fifth Avenue, 34th Floor
New York, NY 10118-3299
www.hrw.org

Has long had an active campaign in Latin America to investigate violations of human rights and challenge governments or other institutions to respect international human rights standards.

National Council of Rubber Tappers
www.cnsnet.org.br

The union, founded by Chico Mendes, that works to sustain the rights and livelihoods of the communities making a living from the living rain forest.

New York Botanical Garden
Institute for Economic Botany
Bronx, NY 10458
www.nybg.org

Sends botanists around the world to study plant species that are a potential source of medicines, foods, or other valuable products and creates partnerships with researchers and local communities in developing countries.

Rainforest Alliance
665 Broadway, Suite 500
New York, NY 10012
www.rainforestalliance.org

Protects rain forest ecosystems and the people and wildlife within them by helping companies adopt business practices that sustain biodiversity. Products generated this way have ranged from bananas and coffee to guitars.

World Wildlife Fund
1250 24th St., NW
Washington, DC 20037
www.wwfus.org

The largest privately supported international conservation organization in the world, has conducted pioneering research on Amazon ecology. Works with Indians and other rain forest communities to improve the ecology and economics of rubber and Brazil nut harvesting.

Acknowledgments

THE BURNING SEASON was written with the aid of dozens of people—
ranging from environmentalists in Washington to rubber tappers along
the Juruá River. I am grateful to all of them.

Most of all, I thank the rubber tappers and Indians who are risking
their lives defending the Amazon. When I presented my proposal to the
leadership of the National Council of Rubber Tappers, they were happy
to give me their full cooperation. Especially helpful were Júlio Barbosa de
Aquino, Osmarino Rodrigues, Raimundo de Barros, Antonio Macedo,
and Gomercindo Rodrigues. Chico Mendes's brothers, Zuza and Assis,
contributed important insights, as did Iamar Pinheiro, the daughter of
Wilson Pinheiro.

Without the linguistic skills, boundless energy, and quick mind of Luiz
Fernando Allegretti, who accompanied me in the Amazon, there would
be no book at all.

I am grateful to Mary Helena Allegretti, president of the Institute for
Amazonian Studies, for many interviews and access to the institute's files.
Sister Michael Mary Nolan, the lawyer conducting a parallel investigation
of the Mendes murder—and of dozens of similar crimes around Brazil
—provided crucial access to a mountain of court and police records.
Adrian Cowell, Mauro Almeida, Tony Gross, João Maia, and Jorge Te-
rena were among many who described the history of the rubber tapper
and Indian movements. Douglas Daly, of the New York Botanical Garden, guided me through the confounding maze of tropical biology. I
crossed paths with Brazil's outgoing environmental chief, Fernando Mes-

quita, and the man who later became Brazil's new secretary of the environment, José Lutzenberger—thanks go to both for their time (and good luck to Secretary Lutzenberger).

Donald D. Pearson provided gracious hospitality during my stay in Brazil. Silvio Martinello, Elson Martins, and Anivaldo Padilha helped round up photographs. In the United States, Veronica Gardiner gamely translated one hundred and twenty hours of tapes. Stephan Schwartzman of the Environmental Defense Fund, Barbara Bramble of the National Wildlife Federation, Daniel Katz of the Rainforest Alliance, and Jason Clay of Cultural Survival gave generously of their time. Linda Rabben and the Brazil Network put me in touch with many helpful people.

My agent, Bob Tabian of ICM, helped conceive the idea for this book. John Sterling, the editor-in-chief of Houghton Mifflin, had the confidence to set me loose in the Amazon; once I returned, his well-placed pencil marks transformed a manuscript into a book. Irene Williams, Audrey Goodman, Luise Erdmann, Rebecca Saikia-Wilson, and the rest of the Houghton Mifflin strike force made the impossible possible.

I thank my parents for tolerating my wandering ways. The constant support of my wife, Linda, prevented me from going around the bend.

My dog, Woody, kept me human.

Finally, there would be no book—and possibly no author—without the able stitchery of Dr. Thomas Gouge, who removed my inflamed appendix twenty-four hours after I returned from Brazil.

A.R.

April 1990